running from the mirror

a memoir

HOWARD SHULMAN

SANDRA JONAS
PUBLISHING HOUSE

BOULDER, CO

Sandra Jonas Publishing House
PO Box 20892
Boulder, CO 80308
www.sandrajonaspublishing.com

Originally self-published in 2013 under the title *Freak.*

Printed in the United States of America
20 19 18 17 16 15   3 4 5 6 7 8

Book and cover design by Sandra Jonas

Publisher's Cataloguing-in-Publication Data

Shulman, Howard.
  Running from the Mirror : A Memoir / Howard Shulman — Boulder, CO : Sandra Jonas Publishing House, c2016.

  pages ; cm

  ISBN: 9780985581534

  1. Shulman, Howard. 2. Face — Abnormalities — Surgery. 3. Abandoned children — United States — Biography.

RD523   617.520592 — dc23

2014948949

To Helena and the girls,
my love, my life, my everything

O N E

THREE DAYS AFTER HIS BIRTH, a perfect baby, the carrier of his young parents' dreams and ambitions, became what some would call a monster. Like ants on honey, a bacterial infection consumed his face—and as quickly as his face disappeared, so did his mother and father. The newborn his parents had been prepared to take home and raise as their beloved son was no longer the child they had the courage to claim.

I was that baby.

Despite their valiant efforts, the doctors, with their arsenal of antibiotics, could not push back the bacteria's devastating aggression. When it finally ran its course, my nose, lower right eyelid, tear ducts, lips, and palate had been eaten away, leaving behind a gaping hole.

Though they lasted so briefly, I can't help but imagine the joyful first days of my life. It's July 17, 1961, and I see my father, filled with youthful optimism, tapping his knuckle against the nursery window. Nodding, the nurse retrieves me from my bassinet and carries me to where he waits, his smile widening at the sight of me.

Reluctantly he turns away and heads down the brightly lit corridor to my mother's room, passing on his way a stream of immaculately starched nurses, who smile at his tell-tale strut of new fatherhood. At his wife's door, he uprights the bouquet of yellow roses he carries and, seeing that she is sleeping, quietly crosses to her bedside. He hesitates, then bends down to press a kiss to her forehead. Her eyes, heavy with sleep, open.

"Hello," he murmurs.

"Have you seen him?" she asks, her words slurred.

"Yes. He's perfect. Get some rest now."

When he stops by the following day, he finds my mother propped up in bed holding the bundle that is me, a look of contentment on her face. Smiling, she hands me to my father, who cradles me in his arms. "Howard. Howard! Hello, my son."

On the third day in my anti-fairy tale, as my dad prepares to leave his office to visit his wife and baby, the phone rings.

"Mr. Shulman, I'm calling about your son." The doctor's voice is grave. "You need to get to the hospital immediately."

"Why? What's wrong?"

"I'll explain when I see you."

"Please tell my wife I'm on my way."

Oblivious to the blare of midday horns or the route he travels, my father maneuvers his car through traffic, his mind on nothing but the chilling tone of the doctor's words. His panic mounts, and he speeds toward the hospital.

Out of breath, he pauses in the doorway of his wife's room, unaware that the fear he sees in her face is mirrored in his own. In two swift strides, he is at her side and reaches for her hand. She begs him to do something, anything, to make whatever is wrong right again.

A faint knock announces the doctor. His jaw is tense, his eyes serious. "Your son has contracted a staph infection in his face," he says. "He's a sick little baby right now, but I want to assure you we're doing everything we can."

In the movie I carry in my head, I'm a healthy, robust baby nursing contentedly, the familiar rhythm of my mother's heart and sound of her voice lulling me to sleep. All is well with my world, and then, in one unmistakable shift—just as I am getting used to lights and startling noises, to alien air and strange materials assaulting my skin—I have a growing sense that something is very wrong.

Suddenly my face is on fire, and I am swallowed up in pain. My shuddering cries, garbled by fluids pouring from my nose and mouth, leave me gasping for breath. Sharp, biting jabs pierce my veins, and tubes ravage my throat. Where is my mother? Where is she? Surely she must know I need her. Why doesn't she come? Doesn't she hear me? Can't she feel my suffering?

I scream and scream and scream until only exhaustion quiets me. My mother is gone and will not return, leaving me adrift on a raft of pain so unbearable that all I can do is shut down.

Even before any capacity for thought has formed, I know my world has shattered.

TWO

ABANDONED BY MY PARENTS, I was made a ward of the state of New Jersey. For the next eighteen years of my life, I was identified as case number XUG-905.

Perhaps my parents assumed or even prayed I would not survive. Or perhaps they believed that without a face, their son had become something less than human, incapable of loving and being loved. Maybe wishful thinking played a part: that someone without their anguish and ego of bloodline would make me theirs and spare them the torment of failure. Whatever the basis of their decision, I know nothing about it.

What I do know of those first years has been reconstructed in the manner of my face—bit by bit, stitch by stitch. I endured scores of operations—ultimately as many as a hundred. Unable to nurse or drink from a bottle, I was fed intravenously, my hands tethered with strips of cloth to my hospital crib to keep me from tearing at my bandages. Through it all, the one person I most wanted to reach out for had long gone.

I have hazy memories of sitting in a cage-like crib, watching anonymous caretakers through the bars as they read me stories that ended too soon, abruptly returning me to the stark loneliness of institutional life in a hospital. Attachments I made never lasted, leaving me confused and unsettled by a parade of new faces. The consistent characters in my life came mostly from the stories read to me, a lifeline I grew to depend on.

One book I remember had a large, pop-up purple dragon, its back jagged and scaled, that both delighted and scared me. How I would hug that dragon, cuddling it as if it were my friend. The story, read to me through a plastic barrier that encased my crib to ward off infection, captivated me with its magical powers. The distant and muted words, filtered as they were through the thick, milky plastic, added to the fairy-tale-like sensation of seeing the dragon as if through a mist, instilling in me the certainty that there is magic in the world.

For me, this life was normal—the staff and hospital were the only family and home I'd ever known. In a strange way I was fortunate because I had never experienced anything different. The hard part was the psychological trauma of abandonment that mere surgery could never fix. Those wounds would take a lifetime to mend.

"Howard, hold still! Just a few more things to check and we'll be done."

Recoiling at the harshness in the doctor's voice, I willed my stubby little legs to stop scissoring the chilly air—not an easy feat, perched on his examination table with paper uncomfortably wadded under me and my anxiety mounting as I sought to avoid the rage of the man I feared.

When I was days old, my medical condition had been so dire that I was transferred from the hospital in New Jersey to Montefiore Medical Center in the Bronx and my care put in the hands of Dr. Richard Gratz. Our relationship could best be described as something akin to that of Dr. Frankenstein and his monster creation—he the demigod and I his diminutive work in progress.

As a ward of the state, and with no caseworker who understood the ramifications of experimental medical procedures or cosmetic surgery, I had no one to oversee or evaluate the merits of Dr. Gratz's ambitious plans for my treatment—and no family to protect my interests. Unrestrained, he was able to proceed with whatever means he deemed necessary to minimize my monstrosity.

Right from the beginning, our relationship was fraught with tension; his unyielding long-term plans to normalize me were pitted against my fear, rebellion, resentment, and, perhaps most damaging, my mistrust. He was the one with whom I associated pain and fear and disruption of those few-and-far-between lulls in my life when I was free of medical tampering or debilitating downtime for recovery.

As the nurses, orderlies, and even janitors who showed me kindness came in and out of my life, only Dr. Gratz remained, although he was certainly no caretaker. Tall and gaunt with gray hair buzzed painfully short, he was the picture of austerity. Accustomed to getting his way, he spoke in a voice meant to intimidate, his Eastern European accent making him all the more frightening to me.

He was perfectly suited for his work. His hands were unusually large, so large they seemed to eclipse the light when he held my head in his viselike grip to examine the state of my face. His manner, every bit as cold as his hands, was predictably mechanical and devoid of expression. I always trembled when he walked into my hospital room, never knowing what he had in store for me. I just knew it wasn't going to be fun.

There was a routine to his examinations. First, he would use his hands to assess my facial structure, his long fingers exploring my features like a blind man reading Braille as he turned my head this way and that. Then he would press cold instruments against my face to map out his plans, taking his time to precisely measure me, all the while sharply reminding me to stop squirming. I learned to sit like a mannequin as he worked to tailor a custom face for me. For him, I imagine, I provided the raw material for an experiment that could catapult his career, and I'd better not get in his way.

All the surgeries of my childhood have melded into one memory, the particulars of which never seem to vary. My only clue that I was slated for an operation was on the evenings when I was forbidden food or drink after an early dinner. In the unsettling darkness of predawn, a hand would shake me awake and roust me from my cage. Groggy with sleep and uncooperative in my disoriented state, I'd resist being helped onto a long gurney, my whimpering, small body a tiny island in a sea of white sheets.

My favorite orderly was a jovial black man who treated me gently, almost motherly. His enormous Afro mightily impressed me, reminding me of Bozo the Clown on TV. "Good morning, little man," he would say in his warm, reassuring voice. "How you doin' today?

Don't you be afraid of nuttin'. Everything is going to be A-okay. I'm right here with you."

Fueled by his cheery talk, we sped along to my "big sleep," as he'd call it. The gurney would follow the yellow directional tape on the gleaming gray linoleum while I watched the rows of fluorescent lights and ceiling tiles stream past overhead.

Zooming down a last hallway and whipping around the corner, I'd arrive at surgery almost breathless after my thrill ride. As we parted ways, the orderly would whisper in my ear, "I'll be here when you get out. Okay, little man?" I nodded solemnly before being rolled through the stainless steel doors and into the operating room.

A burst of cold air would hit me, instantly triggering a ritual shivering that stemmed far more from fear than from the temperature. With my fists clinched to my stomach and my jaw chattering uncontrollably, I tried to avert my eyes from the trays of suspicious shapes hidden under white cloths while the nurse tucked a doubled-over white blanket around my tense body, as if warmth would calm me. The smell of disinfectant ratcheted up my anxiety and dread. I knew what was coming.

Waiting in the room were the usual masked players: two nurses, sometimes three, an anesthesiologist, and Dr. Gratz. I can still hear him barking orders, and his underlings, as intimidated as I, scurrying to obey.

"Good morning, Howard," he would say through his mask. "Are we ready?"

I'm sure he was, but all I wanted was to go back to my warm bed and sleep. I never bothered to answer—what I wanted didn't matter.

On center stage, under the blinding lamp, came the moment to insert the IV. It was the part I hated most and I'd always lose it. "NO, NO, NO—I DON'T WANT TO! NO!" I did everything I could to pull away as one nurse held my arm to the operating table and another wiped it down with an antiseptic sponge. I screamed in terror when I felt the prick of the numbing injection in my hand. Then the familiar warm sensation began to seep into my veins, whereupon the anesthesiologist would lean over me to carefully fit the gas mask over my face.

"Okay, Howard. Count backwards for me." I never counted, but I could hear his voice fade into oblivion as he slowly recited, "Ten, nine, eight, seven . . ." and I was gone.

Pain always woke me. Inevitably I would jerk on the IV in my sleep and jar the needle, triggering a blast of pain in my hand, a signal that the operation was mercifully over and I was in the recovery room. As I drifted in and out of a medicated, dreamless sleep, I gradually became aware of my fellow patients, each of us in varying states of consciousness and lined up in rows.

Back in my bed on the pediatric ward and propped up on a stack of pillows, I watched as families bearing gifts of balloons and stuffed animals crowded into our room during visiting hours. I was always acutely aware of the difference in our visitors. Mine were all in-house: nurses, candy stripers, interns, and the night janitors mopping the floors, each dropping in to cheerfully ask how I was doing or to slip me a treat of ice cream or a picture book.

Pretending to be asleep, I would peer through the slits of my swollen eyes and scrutinize everyone, especially the mothers, who would surreptitiously glance my way. Their looks were mostly of curiosity, though sometimes I saw sympathy or concern. Even so, they never approached my bed or included me in their visits.

A nurse would interrupt. "Howard, here's your juice. Drink up."

Slowly I sipped through the paper straw (trying not to mash it flat) while keeping an eye on every detail of family interaction going on around me: the parents fawning over their kids; the attention the young patients milked from their mothers and fathers; the tenderness, the impatience, the worry—all of it. It was a foreign world to me.

Once I could keep my juice down, the tape securing the IV to my hand would be removed. This was the dreaded moment, but my reward was Jell-O, preferably red, my favorite. It was utter hell when the nurse peeled off the adhesive tape that bound my hand and forearm to the blue Styrofoam board. I would scream and cry, the tears streaming down my cheeks as the nurse calmly went about her business, ignoring my pleas. "Howard, it's okay, it's okay. We're almost done."

When it seemed I could take no more, the needle was out, and the nurse would stroke my brow. "Shhh, honey," she'd say. "Look! It's all over." And sure enough, my consolatory Jell-O would appear on the tray.

When I was quite small, a urinal complemented my IV, but as I grew older, I was allowed to make my way to a closet-sized bathroom accompanied by an IV walker. If I could pee, I'd be given solid food, so I would stand at the sink trying to ignore the pain and hold my finger under a trickle of warm running water, which always did the trick.

Then it was back to my crib, a few stuffed animals, and my five-channel TV mounted high in the corner of my room. Though the nurses controlled the volume, I could control the channel by way of a long brown cord that snaked through the bars into my crib.

I remember *The Jack LaLanne Show* in black and white and, when I was older, *Captain Kangaroo* in color. Utterly captivated by the Treasure House, I'd hold my breath through much of the program. During those early years, when I was confined to the hospital, TV was my most reliable companion.

In 1964, when I was three years old, the state of New Jersey placed me in a foster home. Concerns about the long-term impact of institutional living on such a young boy no doubt led to the state's decision.

The first time I can recall being part of a family, I was sitting on a hardwood staircase, looking down through white banisters at the living room below. This was a real house, in Morristown, New Jersey, and my new mom was tying my shoelaces. Obediently, I held out each foot as I scanned the puzzling scene.

Everything smelled strange too. Rather than the sharp odor of disinfectant, the pleasant scent of something cooking filled the air, and the unfamiliar smell of freshly mowed grass drifted into the house. I also noticed that the sounds were brighter and louder.

I was officially the Mackeys' foster child. Ed (Big Ed), his wife, Shirl, their daughters, Robin and Lisa, and their oldest, Frank, were my new family. I have no memory of meeting them in the hospital or packing my few possessions. Suddenly one day I was living with them.

Their adjustment to having me in their midst must have been daunting: a scarred freak of a child with a stretch of patched-together skin in lieu of a nose, no lower right eyelid or upper lip, a gaping palate—and absolutely no social skills.

In the early '60s, taking in a foster child was not a common occurrence, and though I never learned what prompted their decision, I knew that Shirl and Ed were generous people. They had met during the Korean War in a veterans hospital in Illinois, after Ed suffered a severe concussion that sent him stateside. As he liked to tell it, "I was in Korea, swimming in the ocean with my buddies, when enemy soldiers started chucking grenades at us. I had to keep diving, holding my breath as long as I could." I don't remember much more of his story, but this made him a war hero to me. Anyway, Shirl nursed him back to health and they fell in love—a classic war romance.

Ed was a large, barrel-chested, dark Scot of a man with powerful, hairy forearms and a boisterous laugh—a man you needed to treat cautiously if you wanted to avoid his quick temper. A Jackie Gleason look-alike (jowls and all), he was a domineering husband and the kind of father who made it nearly impossible for his only son to ever win his approval.

Raised in Brooklyn during the Great Depression, Ed jumped the sinking ship of his family at age seventeen to join the navy. His father's decision to leave when Ed was very young had imbued him with the determination to be a responsible family man. That early abandonment also left an indelible mark on his only brother, who tried to escape into alcohol and then likewise disappeared.

His mother moved to upstate New York and became a hoarder and recluse. In reaction to his clutter-filled, unstable childhood, Ed became a neat freak, compulsively cleaning and insisting everything be in its place. Incapable of sitting still, he could be found scrubbing the sink after meals or meticulously organizing his tools on the Peg-Board above his workbench as he dreamed up his next project. The consummate home-improvement guy, he had in Shirl and us kids an obedient 'round-the-clock crew.

As the oldest, Frank was given most of the responsibility for carrying out Ed's plans, which he in turn divvied out to Lisa, Robin, and me. Despite having only six years on me, Frank acted like he was from another generation. He had the advantage of being older, bigger, and stronger, but I always put up the good fight, never hesitating to go head-to-head against him, though I rarely won.

Sharing our basement bedroom that adjoined the kids' den didn't bring us close. It was down there, out of sight and earshot of parents (the linoleum flooring and wood paneling shielding the house above from our racket), that we lived out our power struggles and truces. It mattered little that we had a large bedroom since Frank's half was more like 80 percent. Being not only younger but also the outsider, I accepted the inequity.

The basement den was our private domain. By virtue of his seniority, Frank controlled the TV, so I always had to watch his picks: *Creature Feature*, the late-night horror-movie series, or whatever show suited his mood. If Ed and Shirl were out, the bickering sometimes got so out of hand that even Lisa, the resident peacekeeper, would give up in disgust and retreat with Robin to our parents' bedroom to watch Shirley Temple reruns on an old black-and-white set.

A fragile truce usually coincided with Frank's favorite shows. Our battles put on hold, we would sink into our beanbags chairs and soon become transfixed by the grisly horror unfolding before us. We'd mechanically stuff our faces with popcorn, and Frank, with his massive hands, would make sure to hog the lion's share.

Popular among her peers, Lisa was rarely at home. Smart and pretty with dishwater-blonde hair, she was Daddy's little girl and knew how to get what she wanted. Because she four years older than I, it was natural for me to fall in with Robin, who was only a year older. An exuberant, freckle-faced tomboy, she made the perfect companion. We played together constantly, whether it was Chutes and Ladders, Go Fish, or countless made-up games. Come summer, we cooled off in the backyard by running through the sprinkler, the arcs of water shimmering in the heat. To keep Ed happy, we made sure the brown spots on the lawn got watered.

Our great discovery was the secret world in the acres of undeveloped woods just across the street. We would play our games of survival, climbing rocks, crossing the swampy pond on fallen trees, and building forts with broken branches. The minute Robin rushed in the door from school and dumped her books on the stair landing, we grabbed our snacks and raced for the woods, anxious to see how our lean-tos had fared in our absence. Rusted cans and Budweiser bottles were irrefutable evidence that we were not as hidden as we had supposed, so we'd tear down our camp and venture deeper into the woods to rebuild. It was a perfect place for me: no one to gape in revulsion to remind me of my freakishness.

The Mackeys were probably typical of a thousand other Jersey suburban families, with the exception of my being their foster child. I was treated like one of them and felt loved, but inside I knew I wasn't a "real" Mackey. My legal name was Shulman, and Leonard and Sarah were my biological parents. On top of that, strangers never let me forget how different I was. Whenever I complained to Ed about their stares or shocked glances, he said I was imagining it, but I knew I wasn't.

I felt I was living in limbo, always on the brink of something calamitous. Life seemed precarious, and without hope of adoption, which was never a realistic option because of the astronomical cost of my treatments, I remained a ward of the state. Still, Ed and Shirl went out of their way to reassure me. "Don't you worry, Howard. You're a Mackey now and you always will be."

And it was true. I was part of the family and included in every aspect. But it was another matter with Shirl's parents, my grandpa and grandma. When they arrived for a visit, there were warm greetings and hugs all around except for me, and when crisp dollars were folded into Frank's and my sisters' fists, there was never one pressed into mine. They refused to acknowledge my place in the family, treating me politely enough but as if I were some neighbor kid who'd happened to drop by. I knew better than to expect birthday or Christmas presents from them.

While my siblings were at school, I was Shirl's constant sidekick. She had put her nursing career on hold to be a stay-at-home mom, and although most of my care was routine, she still had a lot to learn. As my liaison with state social workers, she took on the overwhelming task of coordinating my medical scheduling. If she was ever taken aback by my evolving face, I never saw any sign of it. Not only did she feed, monitor, and mother me, she also attended my stitches and swellings, changed my bandages, and waited on me—doing it all with patience.

I was six when I had my most radical operation to date, which was also by far the most excruciating. Dr. Gratz had decided he would use one of my left ribs to reconstruct a nose for me. This was a major procedure and meant I would be hospitalized for weeks.

During my usual presurgery examination, Dr. Gratz attempted for the first time to explain the procedure in terms my six-year-old mind could grasp, although he failed to mention the pain aspect. "Howard, we are going to give you a new nose, and you are going to look wonderful!" Beyond that I understood nothing of what he went on about, but when he plucked at the rib that would do the job, he caught my attention. To a young boy, a rib turning into a nose was no more outlandish than flying purple dragons.

I had no power over my medical destiny and knew it. Shirl would announce upcoming procedures, and predictably, I would run away. I knew it was futile, but I had no other way to protest. "I'm not going! You can't make me! I hate you!" I screamed. No words could express the rage I felt. Viciously I lashed out, kicking chairs, the kitchen cabinets, whatever lay in my path. Slamming the screen door behind me, I'd tear off into the woods, choking on tears.

When I reached the pond, I would launch an aerial attack of sticks and stones into the murky water, and when that failed to quench my fury, I blindly turned on leaves, dirt, cans, and trees, attacking everything around me. Finally spent, I could do nothing more than stare down at my disfigured face floating on the watery surface, my features even more distorted in the reflection. I would lob a rock at my face, sending schools of minnows darting away. With nightfall looming, or when I could no longer bear the cold, I would grudgingly turn homeward in defeat, knowing I had yet again lost the fight that couldn't be won.

Shirl never mentioned my absence but was visibly relieved when I trudged in the door. "You hungry, kiddo?" was all she'd say. I was *not* Ed. Food would not placate me or distract me from my anger and frustration. Hell-bent on unloading my last shred of rage, I turned on her. "You're not my real mother. You can't tell me what to do!"

Never revealing the hurt she must have felt, she would gently reply, "Kid, I'm the only mother you got."

Then I'd slump over the kitchen table and weep. Shirl was right—she was all I had.

After the nose operation, I recall nothing until I woke up in my own room and found I had been promoted to an adult bed with retractable side railings instead of my usual kiddie cage. This was a big deal for me and almost a consolation for the pain I had to endure. Though I took shallow breaths to keep my rib cage still, it felt as if a knife was repeatedly plunged into my side and sadistically turned. I was afraid to move.

I had to stay bedridden for what seemed like weeks, unable to watch TV because my eyes had swelled shut. Eventually I was allowed to shuffle to the bathroom, but the slightest wrong movement set off spasms of pain that careened around my rib cage and left me gasping.

I returned home thin and demoralized. My appearance even shocked Frank, who was actually nice to me. When I could drag myself to the den, feeling and looking like a decrepit old man, Robin did everything she could to keep my spirits up, coming downstairs to watch TV or play board games and bringing me up on all the latest neighborhood news. Even so, it was a very dark time for me.

The day came when hunger returned with a vengeance. Impatiently, I called up the stairs for Shirl to bring me some food. "Mom? Mom? MOM!" It hurt to yell. Where was she? Outside? On the phone? In the bathroom? Ravenous, I was going to get to the kitchen by whatever means I could. From the bottom of the stairs, I looked up to the first landing and wondered how I could possibly make it, but the growling in my stomach spurred me to action.

Gingerly pulling myself up by the handrail, I cried from the pain of it, and my bandage, soggy with tears, soon slid over my nose. After considerable effort, I had managed only a few steps. This wasn't going to work, so I turned around, sat down, and began to negotiate of each step butt first, resting between each to steel myself for the next maneuver.

Just as I was nearing the first landing, Shirl appeared and leaned out over the top banister. "Howard! What on earth are you doing?"

"I'm hungry," I said in a small voice.

I was afraid I had upset her, but that fear vanished when she ran down the stairs and gently picked me up in her arms. I had lost so much weight on my liquid diet that she easily carried me to the kitchen. Despite my swollen eyes, unwieldy bandage, and a rib cage that hurt to move, I savored every morsel of meat loaf. Never had I worked so hard to get food, and never had it tasted so good!

At dinner that evening, Shirl related my stairs adventure as she portioned out the Hamburger Helper. Ed was not one to show his feelings, though his family meant everything to him. He had a soft spot for his girls but was tough on Frank and never cut me any slack either. Convinced I would need to hone some serious survival skills if I was to fend for myself out in the world, he took on the daunting task of teaching me independence. To achieve that and do so with compassion was no small undertaking. Coddling me, he decided, would not be in my best interest.

When Shirl finished her story, Ed turned to me and smiled proudly. "Kid, you and me are the same. We're survivors. You're gonna be okay." Rare praise, but I sensed he believed it. And so did I, somewhere deep within me.

For the most part it was a happy home in the suburbs—a white clapboard, two-story colonial with a large yard, lots of trees, and two cars: Shirl's blue Valiant, along with the family car, a wood-paneled station wagon. Ed commuted every day to Manhattan, where he worked at a bookbindery. He never tired of regaling us with how he had started at the bottom and finally, after years of dedication, was made supervisor. His status secure (signaled by his necktie that set him apart from the assembly-line workers under him), he could survey his little fiefdom of cubicles through the sliding glass doors of his small office.

Ambitious and knowing he wouldn't get any unearned breaks, he often worked evenings and weekends doing construction. Despite his habitual bitching about how rotten his day had been and his quick temper that could flare like a brush fire, all of us admired him.

"Don't be like everyone else, Howard," Ed would tell me. "Work hard. And don't take crap from anybody." That was his philosophy, and he never let me forget it. I already knew I wasn't like anyone else, so he didn't have to remind me about that. I was, however, working on the part about not taking crap from anybody.

Ed always made Shirl nervous when he announced a new project. A perfectionist, he was obsessive about detail. "Make sure the bubble is in the middle of the level," he'd bark at me. "Is it in the middle yet? You sure? Check it again." I carefully eyed the level until it was dead center, and Ed would drill in the screws. Then he'd assign me to sweep up the debris. "Howard, listen to me," he'd say as the two of us stepped back to admire our work. "If you're going to do something, do it once, do it right, or don't do it at all. You got it?"

Though in most regards Ed overshadowed Shirl, he counted on her quiet strength. Slight and fair—evidence of her Dutch forebears—she was strong when it came to matters she was unwilling to compromise on. Refusing to get swallowed up in the density of Ed's shadow, she knew that confrontations weren't the way to handle him. Skillfully and subtly she manipulated him.

In her rare "quiet time," as Shirl called it, which was usually at the kitchen table in the early morning hours while her family slept or during Johnny Carson's *Tonight Show* (Ed's favorite), she escaped to her books. Bella Abzug, Gloria Steinem, and Erica Jong filled her bedroom bookcase, and while never a card-carrying feminist, she did smoke Virginia Slims. Shirl kept her newfound *I'm OK, You're OK* outlook to herself, but through example instilled that attitude in her children.

The summer before I started school, the chore of painting the floor of our enclosed back porch fell to Frank. Ed, under pretense of majority rule, brought home an array of color samples to get everyone's feedback, even though he had already chosen navy blue. To preclude rogue input, he held up the color chip. "The only choice, right?"

"Perfect!" Shirl said, regardless of her preference. After purchasing the paint and instructing Frank, Ed returned home hours later to find his son had literally painted himself into a corner. Big Ed had no humor where Frank was concerned and was "not a happy camper," as Shirl always put it.

Bracing himself for Ed's tirade, Frank suggested he could just climb out through the window. "Jesus Christ, what is wrong with you?" Ed roared. "You're not going to tear off the goddamn screen. I just replaced it. You stay put until the paint dries." He stormed off shaking his head, leaving Frank marooned.

Shirl motioned to him from the doorway. "Hang on, Frank." She ducked around the corner of the house with me close behind, pried off the screen, and freed Frank. If Ed had had his way, Frank would have spent the night squatting in that corner.

Food was Shirl's single greatest weapon in dealing with Ed, and she knew now was the time to deploy it. "Our beautiful new porch! This calls for a celebration."

Before Ed could get himself worked up, we were packed into the station wagon and on our way to his favorite culinary establishment, a Howard Johnson's off the New Jersey Turnpike. Frank knew the routine and needed no reminder to slump, making himself appear younger so he could pass for the cheaper, all-you-can-eat kiddies' menu—usually fried clams. After consuming half of Chesapeake Bay, Ed, satiated and happy, returned to the newly painted porch, his disgust with Frank forgotten.

To prepare me for school, Shirl became my first teacher. She would make use of any spare time—during lunch, in the car or waiting room, at bedtime—to drill me on spelling, reading, and math, using flash cards for my multiplication tables, whether or not I was bandaged. "Okay, Howard, what's three times six?" She always made it fun and understood how well I responded to encouragement. Those moments with Shirl were our private time together that no one else knew about.

One day as I was eating my lunch at the kitchen table and watching Shirl gaze distractedly out the window as she dried her hands, I blurted out, "Does my face bother you?"

She turned toward me, the dish towel forgotten in her hands and the question hanging in the air between us as she studied my face. I suppose I just wanted reassurance, or maybe I was curious about what she thought about me, but her silence was making my question more serious than I had intended.

Slowly she began to speak, her eyes locked on mine. "Howard, how could you think such a thing? You have beautiful brown eyes and lovely hair. Besides, you're my Howie." Her response surprised me; no one had ever used the word "beautiful" in conjunction with me. "Honey, I'm a nurse, and believe me, I've seen much worse."

Worse? How could it be worse?

"When I worked in the hospital, I saw people terribly burned, and I've treated people without arms or legs, and others who were completely blind. Believe me, honey, you're not so bad."

I tried to envision myself without arms or legs, propped up at the table eating my lunch, but the image wouldn't form.

After my ribs healed and the new graft "had taken," as Dr. Gratz would say, it was time to begin my formal education. My social worker and the state of New Jersey decided I'd do best in a school for kids with special needs. Their descriptions of high teacher-to-child ratio and the individual attention I would receive seemed ideal, so Ed and Shirl went along with it.

For weeks my family prepared me. "Howie, you'll be taking the bus to school just like the other kids! Think how many new friends you'll make! You'll have recess and lunch and art and music and games. You're going to love it!"

The night before I started was torturous. I lay in bed too terrified to cry and tried to muffle my moans in my pillow so Frank wouldn't wake up and torment me for being a baby. Why had I wanted this? What was I thinking? I had enough problems with the kids in my neighborhood. I was used to name-calling and teasing, but how would I be treated in school? Had Shirl taught me enough so they wouldn't think I was a dummy? Would I be able to keep up with the class? Would I make any real friends?

In the morning, exhausted and anxious, I climbed the stairs to the kitchen to find Frank, Lisa, and Robin at the breakfast table. "Howie's first day of school!" Shirl announced as she gave me a hug, no doubt sensing the state of my nerves.

Robin, who was cheerful even in the morning, told me not to worry.

"You'll feel weird the first day, Howie, but after you get to know some kids, you'll see how much fun it is."

Ed, his hip jutted against the counter, studied us as he downed his morning coffee. Seeing the time, he grabbed his jacket and rushed out the door, calling out as he did every morning. "Have a good day, gang. Gotta pay the bills!" Never once did I see him smile when he left for work.

Unusually talkative that morning, Shirl tried to distract me. In honor of my first day of school, she walked me down to the bus stop, my hand in hers. The excitement and fear I felt was more than first-day jitters.

When my bus pulled up, my heart sank. I already knew about the "short bus" that came before the regular one so every kid in the neighborhood got to see the freaks being loaded. I was certain that my fellow passengers would not be like the kids boarding Robin's bus that I had watched so often through our front window.

When the doors opened wide, the sounds emitting from the interior almost paralyzed me. I looked back to see Shirl smiling and giving little encouraging flaps with her hands for me to get moving.

I stepped onto the landing and froze. I truly couldn't move—my new Keds might as well have been glued to the rubber flooring. Except for the whooshing hiss of the doors closing behind me, all sound receded, my mind emptying as I tried to comprehend what I was seeing. I stood facing a cargo of writhing kids strapped into their wheelchairs and seats, children yammering unintelligibly and twitching uncontrollably, yelling and drooling and swiveling their eyes. One kid, seated at the back among others who seemed comatose or unnaturally happy, rocked rhythmically to music no one else heard.

Thinking, surely, any second now I would wake up from this nightmare, I somehow got my body to move forward. Spotting a vacant one-person jump seat, I sat down and withdrew as far as I could, pressing my side into the cold steel shell of the bus. In a daze I looked out the window where Shirl stood on the sidewalk. Clutching her red-and-green-plaid JC Penney bathrobe at her throat, she waved her free hand enthusiastically as she mouthed a big, smiling good-bye and then blew a parting kiss.

The situation became more surreal as we bounced along our circuitous route. A half hour later, the bus pulled up to what appeared to be an abandoned warehouse. After we were unloaded and formed into a line reminiscent of a circus sideshow parade, our pitiful little group was escorted snaking and lurching across a bleak playground of packed dirt and then down a ramp to a basement entrance.

When the door opened to our classroom, the screaming and wailing of earlier arrivals assaulted my ears, and the scene before me looked like something out of one of Frank's horror movies. Four teachers, who acted more in the capacity of caretakers, were trying unsuccessfully to establish order. Several kids were armored in football helmets so they wouldn't split their heads open, and everywhere was a tangle of flailing arms and legs.

Tacked on the walls in the art corner were meager attempts at self-expression—little more than a few random lines and blotches of thin color daubed on brown butcher paper. My impression of being in a warehouse had not been an exaggeration. This was an underground holding pen, where kids with terrible challenges were stored eight hours a day. And that's when it hit me: this was the bottom of the bottom, and I was in it.

As if from a great distance I became aware of a woman slowly repeating in a loud voice, "YOU—MUST—BE—HOWARD?" Trying to answer but rendered almost mute by the sights and sounds—and smells—around me, I struggled to refocus. I glanced at the open folder in her hands and saw a black-and-white photo of me clipped to the inside cover.

Not wanting to believe it myself, I managed a meek yes, thinking this must be a horrible mistake—this couldn't be my school. I knew with absolute certainty I didn't belong with these kids. At that point, though, I was so deathly afraid it was my destiny that I could barely speak.

"How—are—you—Howard?" She spoke slowly, as if that would help me understand the question, apparently interpreting my facial deformities as marginal IQ. After leading me to a low table where a square box sat next to wooden blocks of various shapes, she explained even more slowly the object of the game: to see if I could match the blocks to their appropriate openings.

Was she kidding? This wouldn't challenge a toddler!

I was six years old, and Shirl and I had been working on long-division flash cards. Thinking I hadn't understood her directions, the teacher began explaining once again, but I cut her off and completed the task that presumably I was to struggle with all morning, solving it in seconds. "Very good, Howard!" I wondered what she had thought I would do with them.

We moved on to a worksheet that I was to fill in with the numbers one through ten. She seemed impressed by my answers and, after jotting a few notes in my file, left me to draw on a piece of brown paper she tore from a giant roll.

Even at my young age, I knew that we were on lockdown and that this was no school. My impulse was to make a run for it, but a quick assessment of the doors secured with multiple locks nixed that idea. Escape through the windows wasn't an option either—all the glass was embedded with chicken wire. Near panic, I found it difficult to breathe, and the smell of urine made me queasy. The place was demoralizing beyond anything I'd ever imagined: the walls were stained and painted a dreary beige, and the kids, well, I had no words for them. I could see nowhere to turn and knew no one would listen to me. I wanted to scream that this was all wrong and demand that I be sent home *now!* I was trapped! It felt like I was back in my hospital cage, only worse.

I thought I had known misery before, but in that basement I experienced a new low. The kids with multiple sclerosis, Down syndrome, and every degree of mental disability were one thing, but the hollering and moaning and smells were what drove me crazy.

At last, shell-shocked but home again, I tried to make Shirl understand what she'd sent me off to. She had to fix it. *Anything* would be better than that place. I begged her, but Shirl, being Shirl, told me to be patient, that the first day of school was difficult for everyone, and that I would adjust and make friends and everything would be fine. "Give it time, Howie."

My anguish continued much the same for the next few months, bracketed by the dread of each morning and the relief of returning home at the end of the day. I graduated in reading to *See Spot Run*, but at that point I didn't care. Depressed and humiliated by the short bus signaling to the world how deficient I was, I resigned myself to the hellish situation I lived through each and every school day.

Finally, my despondency grew so severe it could no longer be denied, and Shirl realized that something indeed was very wrong. She conferred with my social workers and teachers, who concluded that they had made a mistake. Mercifully, I didn't have to return to that wretched warehouse.

My next placement was just another form of torment, but one I welcomed nonetheless.

I was transferred to Hillcrest Elementary in Morristown, New Jersey, a school in the suburbs that was (I was happy to note) above ground. From my classroom, unobstructed by chicken wire, I had a view of swing sets, merry-go-rounds, and playing fields beyond.

Hillcrest was my first experience in a mainstream public school. My years sequestered in hospitals, and later with my foster family, had never exposed me to hordes of kids, so I was unprepared for the degree of outrage I would trigger in the school bullies. Sure, some of the kids in my neighborhood gave me a hard time, but they all had their own cliques, and I didn't figure prominently in their sights. This was different, and I had no skills to defend myself other than trying to ignore their onslaught.

To help me make friends, Shirl convinced me to join Cub Scouts. That lasted one meeting when I got booted out for punching a mean Scout who picked the wrong person to bully. Only rarely did I participate in group activities, except for occasions like trick-or-treating when everyone was caught up in the excitement of Halloween and had their attentions elsewhere. Masked, I could be forgiven my freakishness, but the irony was that my own face would have been far more frightening. Still, for one short glorious night, I could escape my reality.

At school, though, there would be no reprieve. My joy at being released from the subterranean school did little to sustain me when I met the cruelty awaiting me at Hillcrest. From day one, the vicious verbal assaults slung at me were relentless. Initially, only a couple of kids targeted me, but quickly it escalated to small groups. My very existence seemed to offend them. To those kids I was different in a way that would never be acceptable. For me, there would be no entry into their circles.

Even Robin, who was always ready to defend me and loyally sat next to me on the bus to shield me from the inevitable taunting (which generally worked because she was popular), couldn't protect me once we parted ways. When I headed off alone to my classroom, I had to brace myself for a barrage of jabs. Every name the kids could think up was slung at me—Retard, Pig Boy, Flat Nose, Bug Eyes, Freakoid—none of them original but all accurate in their capacity to wound.

Resorting to my own wits to get through the day however I could, I at first tried to follow Shirl's advice: ignore them and they would eventually get bored and leave me alone. It never worked out that way.

I doubt I could have survived the daily torment if it hadn't been for my wonderful teacher, Mrs. Marriott. Young, blonde, and pretty, she wore colorful mini-skirts like the ones I saw on *The Mod Squad*, making her cool in all our eyes. I adored her. If she caught kids mistreating me, she ended it quickly, sending a clear message that their behavior would not be tolerated. The message she sent to me was that she cared. Somehow, without showing favoritism, she raised my confidence, praising me when I did well, so despite the fierce hostility I constantly struggled with, I blossomed under her tutelage. I earned my share of tiny gold stars and even found the courage to read aloud in class, a huge step for me. Proud that I easily kept up with the class, I never doubted my place was with the mainstream kids.

Their taunts, however, did bother me. I swore I would never let anyone see me cry, so I kept everything inside, grateful just to be there. Almost daily when I returned home, exhausted from defending myself against pure meanness, Shirl repeated her little salvo, which I think she actually believed, "Howard, words never hurt anyone." On that, she couldn't have been more wrong.

On the playground we played games like dodgeball, kickball, and keep-away. For most of the kids, the novelty of my appearance eventually faded, but a few hung on, maniacal in their cruelty. One bully in particular had it in for me: Ricky, a popular, wiry, athletic kid with freckles and a smirky-ass smile pasted on his face.

After lunch one day, as I headed over to a group playing kickball, Ricky and the other cretins cornered me. "Hey, Pig Face. Oink, oink, oink! Wanna play keep-away from the pig?" I continued walking, trying to ignore their howls of delight.

Safely concealed by a crowd of kids, Ricky jumped me from behind and knocked me to the ground. His friends joined in, smashing my face into the grass and pummeling me with their fists, their press of bodies nearly suffocating me. Then, as quickly as they attacked, they evaporated.

Stunned, I slowly got up and brushed the grass off my clothes. Deaf to any sound but the blood surging in my ears and nearly blind with rage, I turned and walked away, my head down. I knew I was in no position to retaliate. My voice quaking, I told Mrs. Marriott what had happened.

Her advice sounded like Ed's. "Howard, you're going to have to learn to take care of yourself. I'll talk to the boys, but I can't be there every second to watch over you."

I knew then I had to stop counting on anyone else's protection. My new strategy, I decided, would be absolute avoidance. I would keep all my activities where the vicious little thugs weren't.

That didn't work long. A few days later, I was enjoying the mounting thrill of pumping myself to ever more daring heights on the swings, intent on touching my toes to the highest cloud, when Ricky grabbed the chain. My upward momentum catapulted me through the air like a rag doll.

I crash-landed on the packed dirt, badly scraping my cheek, palms, and knees. When I dusted myself off and saw the rips in my favorite pants, I tried to swallow my anger. But then Ed's voice filled my head: "Don't take crap from anybody, kid."

That was it. I sprang at the miserable creep. The pleasure of seeing his eyes go wide and his jaw drop goaded me to tackle him to the ground. I straddled him and started smashing at his face. "Pig! You're the pig!" I screamed. Only vaguely do I remember a teacher pulling me off, but I do know that freckled-faced jerk never bothered me again.

Shirl gasped when she saw me. "Howie, what happened?"

When I finished my sorry tale, she shook her head. "Well, don't make a habit of this." It must have been a dilemma for her—she knew not defending myself wasn't the solution.

As for Ed, I understood his silence to be tacit approval.

The Ricky episode didn't elevate my popularity, but some good did come of it. I didn't have to eat lunch alone anymore. Now I ate with the fat kids and the four eyes and felt I was making headway. Gradually I did make some friends and was even invited to a birthday party with kids in my neighborhood, and occasionally a few would come over to play in my backyard.

Challenging as school was, it kept my mind off looming medical procedures. I got through each day the best I could, some better and some worse. On the dreaded picture day, I would try to ignore the barrage of jeering and name-calling while the photographer struggled with the impossible task of making me look normal. Invariably, disappointment followed when I saw the results. The other kids exchanged pictures. I never did.

One afternoon after school as I was getting a snack, Shirl came into the kitchen. "Howie?"

I looked at her. "Yeah?"

"Dr. Gratz thinks it's time for you to have another skin graft for your nose." When she saw my face blanch, she hastily added, "Because you're growing so fast."

I wasn't one of those kids who love to hear about how tall they are getting, proudly stretching themselves to full height against the door frame to measure how much they've grown. This was not one of those charts.

My life was dictated by Dr. Gratz's plans for me, or as he put it, "Howard's progression." In turn, my progression was determined by his surgical success and my physical growth. I doubt any consideration was given to psychological fallout. Function and appearance seemed to be his sole concerns.

The surgery was necessary, Shirl told me, and I would have to be hospitalized for a few days. Crestfallen, I stared at the floor, saying nothing.

By this point, I had learned the difference between procedures and surgeries. For procedures, I was given small amounts of anesthesia that made me feel like I was on a cloud for a few hours, but I was then allowed to go home or, at the most, kept overnight for observation. For surgeries, I'd be knocked out with a general anesthesia and stay in the hospital for an extended period. That meant pain, lots of it. Dr. Gratz's plastic surgery techniques were in accordance with accepted practices at the time, but much later I discovered he had performed procedures that would now seem barbaric.

When the day came, I lost it. "NO, NO, NO! PLEASE, I DON'T WANT TO." I threw a tantrum unlike any I'd ever had. I fell to the floor outside my room, and Shirl had to drag me kicking and screaming, pulling my hands away as I grabbed at the door frame and tried to wriggle out of her grasp. I cried bitterly and begged her not to make me go, and nothing she could do or say comforted me. At the hospital I still tried to bargain with her until the moment she left. The despair I felt at enduring yet another round of pain and recovery was more than I could bear.

A large nine-by-eight-inch patch of skin was excised from my chest and shoulder, and the graft was then rolled up and stitched along the seam to create a headless snake of raw, living flesh. One end was attached under my chin and the other to the tip of my reconstructed nose. This appendage, left to dangle in front of my face for the next six weeks, constantly reminded me of what I had gone through—but gave me no idea where I was going. Dr. Gratz literally held my future in his hands.

Ordered not to bathe or shower and allowed only a careful wash in the sink, I gingerly padded to the small bathroom adjoining my hospital room to dutifully wash up. When I looked up and caught a glimpse of myself in the mirror, I froze. Staring back at me was a creature more gruesome than the late-night horror-movie monsters I watched on TV. That the alien in the reflection was *me*, Howard, was too much.

I slid helplessly down the wall to the cold tile floor. "Why me? Why me?" I sobbed, over and over. "God must hate me. What terrible thing did I do to deserve this?"

Bone weary when I returned home, I dragged myself into the den and collapsed on my beanbag chair to wait for Robin to come home. Stuck to the vinyl with sweat and tears and cradled by thousands of beans molded to the shape of my body, I cried myself to sleep.

Those weeks of recuperation were difficult and lonely. I was out of school nearly ten weeks and imprisoned at home. Forbidden to be in the sun, I couldn't play outside, and going out in public at night was not an option.

"Howie, come on. Let's play!" Robin, unaware of my torment, just wanted to have fun with her little brother. Excited to have her playmate back, she grabbed my hands and pulled me up.

THREE

FOLLOWING THE "SNAKE" SURGERY, I HAD a long period of down-time with no surgeries on the horizon. I was fully mended and bandage-free, so in the late spring of 1971, Shirl announced, "Howie, I have wonderful news! We enrolled you for a month of summer camp. Four weeks of fun! Isn't that great?"

This was not good news. No doubt most kids would have been thrilled by a month of adventures, but I wasn't one of them. Incessant ridicule without escape was not my idea of a summer vacation. I quickly assumed the attitude of any balking ten-year-old and flatly refused.

"What do you mean, you don't want to go?" Shirl asked. "You'll have a terrific time."

"I don't want to" was all I would offer. This wasn't a medical necessity and didn't affect my schooling, so I figured I had the option of declining. There I was dead wrong because it was Shirl who needed a vacation from me.

Ed, silent until now, rose from his easy chair and placed both hands on his hips. "Howard, the state is sponsoring you and you are enrolled. I don't want to hear any more about it."

In Big Ed speak, that meant "it's free and you're going." I would be a happy camper, like it or not.

Weeks later, Shirl and I stood over my bed surveying my camp gear. My welcome package from Camp Fuller had arrived in the mail, full of glowing reviews and the activities offered, all verified with photos of smiling kids wielding tomahawks. On the form for medical disclosure, which didn't allow enough space to list my first week of life, Shirl checked the "No" box on the allergy list and that was that.

Checklist in hand, Shirl waited for each unenthusiastic "got it" from me as she ticked off every item. After she had Frank bring down his old sleeping bag from the attic and he gave me his Boy Scout–camouflaged boonie hat, we were done.

"Mom, this stinks," I said, holding up the funky-smelling bag.

"Nonsense. It'll be fine." She ordered Frank to lay the hat and bag out in the sun to air.

"What's the use?" he muttered under his breath as he brushed past me. "You're going to hate it anyway. Camp sucks."

Reasoning that I didn't need anything new since I'd be gone only four weeks, Shirl went to the army and navy surplus store downtown and bought a used army belt with a camouflaged canteen. Images of Walter Cronkite's coverage of the war in Vietnam that Ed and I watched on the evening news made me feel like I was going off to combat, and in a sense I was.

When Ed drove me to the pickup center where all us sponsored kids would be collected and bused off to the great outdoors, he handed me his big chrome flashlight. "Don't lose it, Howard. Have fun." A quick hug and he was gone.

Relief flooded me when our yellow bus pulled up and I saw it was full-size. We boarded, a motley group of state-sponsored kids from foster homes and New Jersey's inner cities, most of them much happier than I to be treated to a few weeks of camp.

Hours later we reached our destination, the miles of incessant screaming still ringing in my ears when I stepped down and surveyed the gathering crowd of kids. Stretching, I took a deep breath and felt excited by the earthy smell of the surrounding woods. Gear in hand, I followed my fellow campers into the cavernous mess hall, noticing as we filed past the kitchen a great quantity of hanging pots and pans large enough to cook for a platoon of starving troops.

While waiting for the assembly to begin, I gazed up at the high-pitched ceiling and the flags and banners hanging from the open rafters. The walls were covered with plaques and old black-and-white photographs of alumni, interspersed with groupings of vividly painted tomahawks.

At one end of the stage, the counselors stood behind the director, who thumped on the microphone, then cleared his throat and welcomed us. Camp Fuller, he explained, was an all-boys camp steeped in tradition, the third oldest in the United States and situated on prize land overlooking the Atlantic Ocean; it even had its own saltwater inlet. There was something for everyone, he promised—canoeing, sailing, soccer, crafts—more than enough to keep us busy.

After briefing us about the flag-raising during morning reveille, we were duly introduced to the camp staff, some with nicknames like "Bear" or "Stretch" (the latter hunched over as if buckled by his own height). We concluded with the camp song, reading off mimeographed sheets as we awkwardly tried to keep pace with the catchy beating of drums.

Following our indoctrination, we were called up one by one to self-consciously cluster around our respective counselors. I belonged to the Shermans, the youngest of the three groups.

Larry Hockman, better known as Mother Hockman, was head counselor for my cabin. I thought it strange that a man would be called Mother, but I soon came to understand why—he loved kids. Tan, sturdy-legged, young, and overweight, he had an unmanageable mane of brown hair streaked with gold from long days in the sun. Easy to spot in his colorful tie-dye T-shirts and cut-off jeans frayed at the bottom, he wore his sneakers without socks, which was very cool. Shirl always made me wear socks, convinced that my feet would rot without them.

I felt like I was on the *Daniel Boone* show. Coming from New Jersey suburbia, I thought this was roughing it. After unrolling my sleeping bag on the musty mattress on the crude bunk assigned to me and unpacking my toiletries from the footlocker Frank had begrudgingly loaned me, I realized there was no bathroom, only an outhouse fifty yards away. The boy next to me was furtively eyeing me as he unpacked his gear and, as kids do without censoring their thoughts, asked what had happened to my face. Well schooled in recognizing the intent behind people's questions, I knew this boy was curious, not malicious, so I answered ambiguously, as Shirl had taught me. "I had an operation when I was a baby." This usually deflected more questions. The fewer details the better.

"What kind?"

"I had an infection when I was born."

"Does it hurt?"

"No, I'm okay." The room had fallen quiet, all ears tuned in to our exchange. The boy shrugged, apparently satisfied. I was accustomed to these inquisitions but decided that with these particular kids, I wasn't going to be burned at the stake. I'd passed the test, and the chatter resumed.

When the lunch bell rang, we swarmed en masse to the mess hall, where we devoured our first camp meal of hot dogs, burgers, chips, and some syrupy drink called "bug juice" that had an odd red color and tasted like something between Tang and cherry Kool-Aid.

Back in our cabin, Mother Hockman explained to us how we would raise our cabin flag on the flagpole in our sector of the camp and compete against the other cabins in various events. I had never officially participated with a group of kids at play, let alone as a team with goals and incentives, and without thinking was caught up in the camaraderie.

Later that evening, the ten of us ventured a short distance into the woods to gather wood. Before long, we were sitting around a roaring fire and roasting marshmallows on sticks our senior instructor had sharpened. Sticky and satiated, we grew quiet and sat staring at the flames. On that humid June night, I felt my anxiety lift, dissipating like the sparks that rose into the star-studded sky over Rhode Island.

Tired from the day's events, I happily snuggled down into my sleeping bag that smelled of home, the taste of charred marshmallow still on my tongue. For the first time I could remember, I fell into an utterly contented sleep.

The days passed. I played soccer, made handicrafts, and, best of all, played Capture the Flag. Whichever team captured the other's flag and hoisted it up the camp's flagpole would win the coveted Camp Fuller Champions title.

This was war, and I, who had always been excessively competitive and conditioned by a lifetime of struggle, was determined to win. Together with my band of warriors, we planned our strategy, down to hand signals and diversionary tactics to draw our opponents away from our planned assault. Hiding behind rocks and trees and dashing across open spaces, I ran silently, my heart pounding as shrieks erupted from my teammates and the melee began in earnest. In the final push to capture the flag, our valiant efforts weren't enough and we lost the battle. Some of my teammates cried, and I admit I was disappointed, but the fact that games were now my main concern made me realize my customary worries were no longer at the forefront—a novel state for me.

Nonetheless, I was growing increasingly nervous about sailing and swimming. The other kids would see the massive cratered scar on my shoulder and the scarring around my midriff. Shirtless, I'd be vulnerable to the inevitable questions I dreaded: "Skin for your nose?" and "They took your rib out?" All I wanted was to blend in and just be one of the campers.

My first day of sailing was exhilarating. Nearly hypnotized, I watched the dark water streak by as the boat gathered speed. The smell and taste of the ocean and the joy I felt flying over the water so distracted me from my usual preoccupations that it wasn't until we had sailed beyond the bay that I noticed half the kids had taken off their shirts, and no one seemed to wonder why I was still wearing mine.

I'd been lucky thus far: in soccer games between rivaling teams, my cabin had been the "shirts" pitted against the "skins," and in our cabin I'd been able to keep my chest turned to the wall or wait until lights-out before removing my shirt. Mornings I avoided curious glances by wrestling my shirt on while still in my sleeping bag. And the showers, to my relief, were individual stalls where I could dress in privacy behind closed doors.

But swimming was another matter. When I arrived at the shore for my first session, I scanned the open expanse of beach and was dismayed to find nowhere to hide. While the other kids tore off their shirts and ran into the water, shouting with delight as they dove into the waves, I lagged behind trying to figure out a game plan. I wanted nothing more than to follow them in and cool off. Instead, I turned my back and retreated to a small dune.

From my vantage point hidden by tall sea grasses, I peered down on my new friends leaping about in the waves, their shrieks of pleasure reaching me and heightening my misery. My absence wasn't noticed until a head count to verify that we were all above water drew attention to my disappearance.

"Anybody seen Howard?" floated up to my blind of grass and forced me to come out. I stood up and reluctantly obeyed the counselor who waved me down.

Over the crash of the waves, I heard Shirl's advice echoing in my head, "If you don't care, no one else will."

"No, that's okay," I said, turning down my counselor's invitation to join them in the water.

"Howard, can you swim?"

"Yes, but I'm not feeling well," I lied, my stock excuse when I felt trapped.

"Do you want to visit the camp nurse?"

"No, I'm okay."

"Fine. When you feel better, come join in."

I told him I would, so of course he believed me. What kid wouldn't want to go swimming?

The next session I used the same tactic, even though I knew I'd eventually run out of counselors. Fortunately, it was soon Mother Hockman's turn to play lifeguard. "Come on, Howard. The water's great! Take your shirt off and get in!"

"No, I'm okay, really." If three times is a charm, it didn't work for me.

"Howard, what's wrong?" I felt his arm around my shoulders and fought back the tears. Apart from taking off my shirt, crying was the one other thing I wouldn't do.

Because I felt closer to Mother Hockman than to any of the others, I reluctantly confessed. With a heart bigger than his mop of wild hair, he was incapable of allowing anyone to feel left out. His arm still around me, he guided me some distance down the shoreline and led me into shallow water. The coolness of the surf was so tempting, but I still wasn't convinced.

"Do whatever you'd like, Howard, whatever makes you feel more comfortable." He dropped his arm and moved into the water.

Watching him bob neck-high in the surf and be lifted on the swell of waves was finally more than I could resist. Though we were well beyond the range where any kids could see my scars, I strategically threw down my towel and shirt at the water's edge, close enough that they could be quickly retrieved. Mother Hockman challenged me to see how long I could hold my breath, and soon my fears were nearly forgotten.

As an extra precaution, I swam as much as I could underwater until the whistle's blare summoned us back to the beach. I dashed out and, in one graceful, practiced motion, pulled on my shirt. For the remainder of camp, although it took me a while to figure it out, Mother Hockman was always on beach duty when I was scheduled to swim. I would like to boast that I overcame my modesty that summer, but I didn't. Even so, managing to take my shirt off was a big step for me.

When camp ended, I returned to our new home in New Hampshire where my foster family had moved while I was gone. Our new twenty-room Victorian country house was nestled on twenty-two lush acres of rolling hills and apple orchards. The house, in dire need of renovation both inside and out, could not have been a more perfect project to keep Ed's compulsive tendencies steadily engaged. Stately wrap-around porches and vestiges of elaborate trim were all that remained of its previous grandeur. In no time Ed brought in rental income by partitioning off half the house and adding a second kitchen. The dilapidated barn, nearly twice the size of our home in New Jersey, would have to wait. Ed's idea was that we kids could be junior partners, profiting down the road from his "gold mine," as he put it.

One afternoon when Ed took off with Frank to a country auction, he told Shirl he was just going to look. I was dead asleep when Frank rousted us out of bed at one in the morning. "C'mon. Dad needs help."

Bleary-eyed, all of us staggered down the stairs to the front yard in time to see Ed helping some guy unload horses off a trailer. Of course, we kids were thrilled, but Shirl, who didn't share our enthusiasm, muttered that she'd be the one feeding them. "Jesus, Ed. Horses?"

"Yeah, I got a great deal. We got a barn, what the hell!"

The stalls in the barn had no doors, so Ed had us scouring everywhere for spare lumber. We managed to find enough to jerry-rig doors to keep the horses penned. As we nailed boards in the dead of night, the bales of hay delivered with the horses kept them from wandering off. For weeks, until we finished enclosing a few acres with an electric fence, whenever we let the horses out, we had to pry the lumber off their stalls and then nail it back on.

An early riser, Ed was always up by five working on some project and waking us with his infernal banging. Long before breakfast we were up, ripping out wire or pulling down Sheetrock. He had Robin and me soaking old wallpaper with buckets of vinegar so we could scrape it off, one soggy piece at a time. In complete frustration I would give up and throw my scraper down. "Howie, just go slower." Robin knew how to gently encourage me, unlike Ed or Frank who had no patience with me.

At the table one evening, Ed sat staring at the exterior kitchen wall. As we ate, we kept a wary eye on him, all of us knowing something was afoot. In the middle of someone's sentence, he jumped up, grabbed his tape measure, and enlisted Frank's help. Shirl ignored his bad table manners, and dinner continued as if this were normal. Ed then sent Frank off to get a sledgehammer and crowbars, and within minutes had all of us tearing down the wall.

After the dust had settled and the last staple driven in to secure the heavy plastic that marginally separated us from the elements, it was time for dessert. Between mouthfuls of pie, Ed beamed, "Like I always said, your mom's a trooper!" Shirl rolled her eyes.

While I was away at camp, Ed had taken up wearing overalls, I suppose in keeping with his new image of himself as a farmer, and had plotted a large garden alongside the house, ambitious like everything else he did. While he went off to rent a Rototiller, I was to clear out all the rocks so the machine wouldn't jam. Crab-like, I was making my way up and down the furrows, heaving rocks to the side, when it started raining so hard the garden quickly turned into a quagmire of mud. Shivering in my soaked T-shirt and shorts and staggering like a drunk from the ten pounds of mud clinging to my tennis shoes, I suggested we take a break until it cleared.

"C'mon. A little rain never hurt anybody." There was no way in hell he was going to pay a rental fee for a second day. He always acted as if our place was *Little House on the Prairie*, and if we didn't get the crops in on time, we would surely starve come winter.

Harvest time found us all (except Ed) sitting around the kitchen table for hours at a time, snapping green beans, plucking stems off cherry tomatoes, and dicing squash. Shirl, now a canning expert, managed our factory production line in the hot, steaming kitchen.

Every morning during the summer, Ed left me a slew of chores. He had me stacking hay or wielding a crowbar to tear out the old lath-and-plaster walls so he could rewire the house. When that was done, I had to scrape off old paint or do anything else he deemed urgent for the construction zone we lived in.

Sometimes he returned home for lunch to check up on me. I often blew off my chores and instead watched TV on one of our measly three channels. I needed to stay alert, though, because Ed would vary the time he arrived. When I heard his car pull in the driveway, I'd jump up and dash out the back door. Suspicious, he would lay his hand on the TV in the den to test if it was warm, then yell at me for being a lazy son of a bitch. If I was out stacking cords of wood, he would ask in disbelief, "Is that all you've done?" He and I fought constantly.

Ed believed that work—morning, noon, and night—built character. Any objection we might make was summarily dismissed, because under General Big Ed, we were his conscripted renovation soldiers. As Shirl repeatedly put it, "Your father is a wonderful supervisor."

Unfortunately, Dr. Gratz had not disappeared from my life. Since my last visit, he had come up with a way to expand my nostrils. His ingenious idea was to implant plastic tubes that would shape functioning symmetrical nostrils for me, thus creating permanent passageways. The plan, he estimated, would require me to wear them for six months.

Ill-fitting, they kept falling out, a situation not helped by Shirl who applied Vaseline around my nostrils to soothe the chafing and redness, compounding the problem. In a vicious circle, his solution was to give me bigger tubes that fit more tightly but hurt and irritated my skin.

Disgusted with the whole stupid concept, I would take them out and tell Shirl I had lost them. I also quickly "lost" all the backups Dr. Gratz supplied.

By now I was well into adolescence and in the throes of rebellion. After a few rounds of the tube standoff, Shirl had had enough and threw her hands up in frustration. "Fine, do what you wish. It's your nose. I'm tired. I tried."

It was my nose and she did try. I simply didn't care anymore. What would perfect nostrils do for me anyway? It was a bad time for us, so bad that I was sent to a state psychiatrist, who proved to be no help. In perpetual battle with Ed and Shirl, even I recognized that something had to change. had to be done with me.

My Hillcrest teacher sent a letter to Ed, Shirl, and my state social worker:

```
Howard is of normal intelligence, but his work is marginal
at best. He has low self-esteem and is often the subject
of ridicule and abuse regarding his nose. He has little
carryover regarding acceptable social behavior from one day
to the next. He appears sincere, remorseful, apologetic,
and afraid of reprimand, but the pattern continues. Despite
full and complete cooperation from his foster parents, it is
my recommendation that Howard be placed in a private school
where classes are smaller and where adequate supervision,
both academic and social, will be provided for him.
```

"Yes, structure and discipline are what you need," Ed said after reading the letter. If he'd had his way, I would have been shipped off to military school. Instead, it was agreed that I should go to Bement, an exclusive private boarding school in Deerfield, Massachusetts. Rather than doing push-ups and marching drills, I would be skiing and taking scenic bike rides along New England country roads. No way could I have ever passed a physical, so the state of New Jersey hoped I would transform myself into a proper preppie.

When the brochures arrived from the school, I was summoned to the kitchen for a sit-down with Ed and Shirl, and together we pored over the materials. I was struck by the immaculately groomed boys in brown leather Docksiders standing beside shiny-haired girls in school blazers and knee-length plaid skirts, the students looking as if they had just stepped out of one of Lisa's *Town & Country* magazines, all smiles and perfect hair. Geez, I thought, boys wearing ties to school? The only men I knew who wore ties were Ed and Dr. Gratz. And Ed never wore a sports jacket, let alone one with an emblem on the pocket.

So in September of 1972, Ed, Robin, Lisa, and I made the drive from New Hampshire to Massachusetts (Shirl couldn't go because she had just started work at a nursing home to help Ed finance the renovations). When our car wound into the narrow streets of Deerfield, I was impressed by the quaint New England town and the registered national landmarks with polished brass plaques at their entryways. I knew then my new school would be unlike anything I'd experienced before. Of course, I had studied about the thirteen colonies, Paul Revere, and Benjamin Franklin, but it hit me for the first time that I might be attending a school built along the very path they once traveled.

When we arrived at Bement, the four of us piled out and made our way to the school office, located in a red barnlike building. Classes were in session, so I got only a glimpse of a few scattered boys in coats and ties cutting across campus.

Our guide, Mr. Anderson, both a coach and a teacher, he told us, was a short man whose bald head and startlingly yellow teeth would never have made the Bement brochures. He began our tour with the two dining rooms, where we saw rows of long tables that sat eight to ten students on benches or spindle-backed chairs. I half-listened as he described the protocol requiring a teacher to sit at the head of each table. At the other end, an appointed student would distribute the food from the carts and later collect the dishes to be wheeled back to the kitchen.

We followed Mr. Anderson into the larger room, and when he pointed out the head table and explained that the students rotated every few weeks to dine with Mr. Hamilton, the headmaster, I knew that this was exactly where I did *not* want to sit. The headmaster's chair looked like a throne—would I be the court jester? God, I hoped not. I had spent enough time trying to avoid the principal at Hillcrest, and now I was supposed to eat with one?

On our way to the classrooms, we came to a wooden bridge that crossed over a dry ravine, from which we could see the tennis courts and behind us, on the other side, a wooded area. As we passed by the girls' field-hockey lawn, as smooth as a putting green, I lagged behind, trying to envision myself in such a place, playing tennis, chumming with friends. It was a stretch. I shrugged off the thought and ran to catch up with the others as they stepped onto the cement bridge that segregated the upper grades' campus from the elementary side. This place felt more like a resort than a school. There was even a pond with ducks! Bement was definitely no New Jersey public school.

The main building's angular wood-shingled roof rose high above long banks of windows, zigzagging against the crisp autumn sky. We skirted the amphitheater and crossed a brick courtyard to a building where I was shocked to find the hallways clean and carpeted and the walls lined with photographs of staff and students. I couldn't help but compare it to my first school, the one in the basement with reinforced windows and stained walls.

As we passed from one classroom to another, I puzzled over the wooden cubicles in the halls stuffed with books and personal belongings. "No lockers?" I asked Mr. Anderson.

"No, Howard. Here at Bement we operate under the honor system." Ed shot me his don't-say-it-whatever-it-is look, so I held my tongue.

The tilt-top desks got my attention. Their polished lids free of carvings made me take mental note that here at Bement, defacing them might not be such a good idea.

After glancing into an expensive-looking science lab, equipped with white lab coats and stainless steel instruments that reminded me of things I'd rather not think about, we continued on.

The library, like a witch's house hidden in the trees, had a strangely inviting high-pitched roof and weatherworn façade of dark shingles. Greeted by the musty odor of old books, we duly admired the walls of leather-bound editions mixed with faded paperbacks and the ladder that ran along a ceiling track. At one end a stone fireplace faced a cozy reading area made up of armchairs and a few old oriental rugs scattered on the dark wood floors.

Off in one corner, a rickety staircase led down to a well-lit reading room. Ed, bringing up the rear, whacked his head on the low door frame, and Lisa, Robin, and I waited to hear his customary "goddamn it." Instead we watched in amazement as he just rubbed his head, nodding when our guide asked if he was okay. I wished Shirl could have seen him.

"Anyone hungry?" Mr. Anderson asked, clapping his hands. At the mention of food, Ed quickly forgot his throbbing head.

Herded back into the dining room, we were introduced to Mary Ann, the head cook. Round and rosy-cheeked, she was obviously fond of her own cooking. Full of maternal good cheer, with an accent somewhat like Dr. Gratz's, but friendlier, she welcomed us. "So nice to see such beautiful children." Me too? I wondered. Shirl did say I had beautiful hair. "I hope everyone is hungry today, yes?" We nodded and licked our lips like starved dogs as she disappeared back to her kitchen.

"So, Howard, do you see yourself as part of our Bement family?"

"Yes, sir!" I replied quickly, not wanting Mr. Anderson to doubt my enthusiasm. I noticed Ed listening intently, I'm sure to give Shirl a detailed account, although knowing him, I bet his mind was more on Mary Ann's promised feast.

"Well, what do you think so far?" Mr. Anderson asked me when we'd finished the last of our cobbler.

"Umm, it's very nice," I said, though I was thinking that this was a place for rich, privileged kids. The prospect of being bullied didn't worry me so much because by now I was big for my age. My main concern was whether I could do the work. I wanted to move on with my life and not be a problem kid. More than anything, I didn't want to let Ed and Shirl down. Both of them had fought and cared for me. They were all I had.

Each student at Bement I learned, was assigned two dorm masters, who oversaw scheduling, weekly assignments, and house chores like cleaning the kitchen, taking out the garbage, or scrubbing the bathrooms. Compared to Ed's incessant list of jobs, these sounded like a breeze.

Mr. Anderson opened a folder and handed me a daily schedule. Awake at 6:45 a.m. and shower. First room inspection at 7:30 a.m. Beds to be made in proper manner. All personal belongings put away. Uniforms to be inspected, pants and shirts pressed, coat and tie wrinkle-free. Students to quietly file into the dining room and stand behind their assigned seats.

This was unbelievable! Looking as serious as I could, I nodded, knowing better than to dare question anything in print, especially with Big Ed watching.

"On a lighter note, Howard, you will receive a weekly allowance. For your grade, I believe it's three dollars a week. With that you may buy anything you choose in town on weekend trips or spend it on the soda and candy machines here on campus."

When Mr. Anderson paused, I could only marvel. Money for taking out the garbage! Ed always maintained that giving us food was our allowance.

"We also have a wonderful sports program." Ed grinned when he heard that, and I knew he was thinking that it would "toughen me up." Mr. Anderson continued, "Soccer, baseball. In the winter we go skiing nearby at Mt. Mohawk, three days a week and weekends too. And we have an ice rink available to us at Deerfield Academy, right up the street."

"Wow, Howie, skiing and ice skating. You're so lucky!" Shirl probably coached Robin to give me moral support, but I could tell she was genuinely happy for me.

The dorm I would live in was called Wright House, though why anyone would name a house, I didn't ask. The exterior was classic colonial: white clapboard siding, steep shingled roofs, and windows fitted with black shutters. Across the front a tangle of thick vines wove through white trellises.

We crowded into the dorm's spotless kitchen, where Ed nodded his approval, and then passed into the living room. Rustic oak armchairs faced the large fireplace, and a scattering of oval rugs similar to the ones at home covered the wood-planked floors. Except for the antiquated TV sitting on a slightly rusted cart in the corner, the room was very New England, down to the miniature blue minutemen marching across the wallpaper.

In the dorm rooms upstairs I noticed the sheets were as tightly made as the hospital beds I'd slept in so often, and even the pillows were fluffed and precisely placed. The stereos and record collections were more evidence of rich kids, but what did please me was that each boy had his own space, not like at home, where Frank commandeered the entire room for himself.

"Thursday is laundry day," Mr. Anderson told me. "You'll be given a Bement laundry bag and a checklist." At this, I saw Ed's and my sisters' eyebrows shoot up.

I looked around the room, calculating how I could dress without prying eyes ferreting out the scars I was determined to hide. When I found out that the bathroom was right down the hall, I realized dressing would be even easier than at summer camp. I began strategizing; I would simply wear T-shirts to bed.

"Are you ready to meet Headmaster Hamilton?" (Or, as Ed would say, "the Big Cheese.")

Lisa and Robin headed over to the duck pond, and Ed and I took off for the main building. While waiting on the couch where we stiffly sat facing the receptionist, I tried to relax the knots in my stomach. Minutes later we were shown into the headmaster's office.

A distinguished-looking man rose from behind a large desk and elegantly extended his hand. "Welcome, gentlemen." Instantly I was reminded of Sir Charles, the debonair English thief in *The Pink Panther* movie Robin and I had recently seen. Tall and thin and in his late fifties with a pencil-line mustache, he wore a tailored, camel-hair suit jacket, starched blue shirt, and black tie. A blue silk handkerchief was neatly folded in his breast pocket.

"How do you like Bement thus far?" he asked me, gesturing for us to sit. I waited for Ed to speak first.

"It's a beautiful campus. Thank you for having us." He sat up straight, his hands neatly folded in his lap.

I had never heard him speak so politely, and followed his lead. "It's very nice, thank you." Oops! Should I have added "sir"?

"Wonderful! We here at Bement strive to be our best, Howard. I am sure you will too."

"Yes, sir, I'll try my best."

"Good lad. Well, I have gone over your records." I darted a look at my name on a thick manila folder on his desk. "I understand you've had a rough go of it, yes?"

"Uh . . . I'm okay, sir."

"Yes, I'm sure you are. I'm impressed. You're a tenacious young man who has overcome a great many obstacles. Do you think with our help you could excel here at Bement?"

"Yes, sir."

"Good. I have spoken to your caseworker and we all have trust and faith in you, son. After all the necessary paperwork has been completed, you will be joining us, if that's what you decide." I thought better of telling him that Ed had already made his decision before we even left home.

On the return trip, though I was given the rare privilege of sitting up front, I braced myself for the lecture I knew was coming.

For the first leg of the two-and-a-half-hour drive, Ed was in a good mood, but as the miles fell away, he started in on me. "You're goddamn lucky to be going to school with rich kids. You got it all. Sports, small classes, laundry service. Jesus, they even give you an allowance!"

All the way home I nodded, my head bobbing for most of the trip. What could I say? That I wasn't going? "Kid, this is a clean slate for you. There's nothing else we can do for you. This is your ticket."

I *was* lucky. I had never been hidden away as a family secret, and I knew my foster parents loved me. Shirl was forever telling me so, and though Ed was more reticent and rarely expressed emotion except when he was mad, I knew he did too. That he considered me his son didn't need to be said.

Many kids in foster care never have the opportunity or desire to call someone Mom and Dad, but I had both. I loved them and was indebted to them for their faith in me. I could leave home knowing I had their support.

It would take New Jersey months to process my paperwork before I could begin at Bement. In the interim I anxiously waited for word, all the while hoping they realized there was an actual human being with real needs attached to case number XUG-905, and worrying that my application would get lost in the system.

Shirl kept my spirits up by often talking about Bement and describing to me what an incredible turn my life would take once I was there. "Howie, you understand this is a rare opportunity for you—the state paying for a fancy private school?" I did understand, and I realized how afraid she was for my future. "Honey, just do your best, okay?"

My deteriorating attitude at home had made the family situation untenable, and Bement seemed the only solution available. This had to work out.

FOUR

AFTER A LONG BUREAUCRATIC DELAY, the state's money came through on January 3, 1973, and my new life as a Bementer began. On the day I was to be picked up, Ed had to work and Robin, Lisa, and Frank were in school, so it was Shirl who stayed home to give me a proper send-off. The night before, Ed had patiently walked me through the finer points of knotting a tie. When he had finished and I saw my tie hanging below my crotch, I knew from the brochures that that was not the look I was going for. Seeing the alarm on my face, Ed laughed and told me not to worry. "Your ties will be shorter than mine. Just watch the other boys."

At the appointed hour, a social worker from the New Hampshire Division of Youth and Family Services arrived to pick me up. I've forgotten her name or what she looked like, but I remember her old beat-up car with faded New Hampshire state seals on the doors. Shirl had helped me pack my "play clothes," as the Bement handbook referred to them, and I was ready to go. The bulk of what I needed would be purchased later with the help of my new social worker, which Shirl, and especially Ed, thought was great. They were hard-working middle-class people who had always provided for me, but they had three kids of their own to clothe. With all my special needs, the state's financial contribution was essential. Ed was impressed. "Fancy school, free clothes. Not bad, kid!"

Shirl gripped my shoulders. "Howie, honey. Please behave."

"I will, Mom. I promise."

Gently cupping my face in her hands, she tilted my face up to hers. "Howie, you know we love you very much."

I fought back my tears. "I love you, too, Mom."

Already missing her, I wrapped my arms around her and hugged her long and hard, afraid that I would never again find such love and understanding. When Shirl gently released me from her tight embrace, I saw tears in her eyes—not just tears of sadness or worry about my going off to school, but of fear of what would become of me if this didn't work out.

It was time to go. As the social worker and I pulled away from the house, I turned to see Shirl waving and I waved back, my eyes filling with tears as I craned to keep her in view through the dusty rear window. Then we rounded the bend and she was gone.

Hours later, we arrived in Greenfield, Massachusetts, a few miles north of Deerfield, where we pulled up and parked in front of an upscale men's clothing store. Mannequins in the front windows displayed Hudsucker suits, tweed jackets, and racing caps, nothing like the clothes I was used to at K-Mart, where underwear and socks came in packs of six. Intimidated, I followed my social worker into the carpeted showroom and cautiously looked at the oak-paneled walls lined with rows of suits and pants on wood hangers, and at the silver tray of colognes next to the register.

"May I help you?"

Startled, I turned around to see a well-dressed man, his eyes ever so briefly registering shock as he took in my unsettling features. Before I could answer, my social worker appeared. "Yes, please. This young man is with me. He is starting at Bement School, and we need to get him some clothes."

At the mention of Bement, the salesman visibly relaxed. Now we were bona fide. "Of course! Let's see what we can do for this young man." Referring to her list, the social worker followed him to the suit jackets.

Left on my own, I wandered down an aisle. As I rounded a display of stylish mannequins, I stopped short in front of a three-way mirror. Before me was some weirdly skewed version of myself, nothing like how I imagined I looked.

For the first time, the full impact of the way others saw me came crashing down on me. I took in the grotesque reality of my appearance and felt my spirit fall, landing with a dull thud at my feet. Everything went silent—the classical music in the background, conversations—everything receded and faded to darkness, leaving only me and that frightening face in the mirror.

I was already accustomed to seeing myself in bandages or stitches, even bloody and swollen, but I had always regarded my appearance as a work in progress. How I saw myself bore no resemblance to what stared back at me. I now saw how broad and deformed my constructed nose was—flat and lopsided, misshapen, my flaring nostrils bizarrely uneven. The scars that ran the length of my nose on either side made me appear piecemealed together. My lower lip, fleshy and drooping, reminded me of a calf's lip and made me look appallingly stupid. My upper lip barely existed. My eyes were strangely lidded and made me want to turn away. Yet I stood for what seemed like hours in front of that mirror.

Eerily tired, I felt a despair that threatened to drown me. In the mirror I saw the truth: a hideous, repulsive boy. If only I could sink through the plush carpet and die—anything to escape this anguish. I suppose someone must have awakened me from my nightmare and guided me through the motions of trying on clothes, but all I recall is the drizzling rain making tiny runnels on the windshield as we wound our way to Bement.

I rode silently, my chaperone's chatter falling on deaf ears. Now I was scared, really scared. How could I possibly ever be a Bementer? Those perfect rich kids would never accept someone like me. I had absolutely nothing in common with them. Why had I gone along with this? Why?

Loaded down with bags and packages, I was escorted by the social worker to my dormitory where we found my dorm master, Mr. Young, waiting for us. Amazingly tall, he kindly dipped forward to clasp my hand in his. "Howard, I've heard all about you. It's so good to finally meet you."

Nervous and embarrassed that a social worker and not my parents had delivered me, I managed to awkwardly get through the introductions. Luckily, classes were in session, so I was spared anyone else witnessing my lowly arrival.

Mr. Young showed me up to my room, which turned out to be one I had seen on my tour. Preoccupied by far greater concerns, I distantly paid attention to what he was saying. "Howard, relax, unpack. Come downstairs if you like. You have a few hours until the other boys are dismissed. Tonight you will dine at Mr. Hamilton's table. Do you need anything? Any questions?"

"No. No, thank you." All I wanted was to be alone.

"All right, then. If you need me, I'll be downstairs. We're all glad you're here."

He had done everything he could to make me feel welcome, but I couldn't shake my heartsickness. I wanted to bolt, to furiously kick leaves and hurl rocks like I could in the woods back home. Instead, I sunk down on the edge of my bed. What would the rich kids say? How would I react? I'd had faith when I left New Hampshire, but now every shred of it had evaporated. I cried a silent, shuddering sob. Exhausted, I wiped my tears and proceeded to unpack.

Taking my new clothes out of the suitcase, I felt I was seeing them for the first time: khaki pants, a blue blazer, socks, ties, shirts. Though I found no joy in them, they were a distraction I sorely needed.

Thinking it wise to review my Bement handbook, I turned to the page outlining dining etiquette: stand behind your chair until instructed to sit, maintain an upright posture, pray in unison, commence eating once all students have been served. Keep napkin on lap, pass food to the left. After main course, pass dishes to be neatly stacked on cart. Only two students at a time excused for the bathroom, permission asked first. After dessert and the table cleared of dishes, students may ask to be excused. And this wasn't even military school!

After classes ended for the day, Mr. Young appeared with my two roommates. Eric was a good-looking kid with long blond hair tucked behind his ear on one side, the rest falling over his eye on the other. Ralph, a pudgy boy with dark curly hair, wore thick bottle-bottom glasses that magnified his eyes. Both tried to disguise their curiosity as they introduced themselves and were so nonchalant in their reaction to me I had to wonder if they had been forewarned. Were their manners the product of a privileged upbringing that had taught them compassion for the less fortunate, or were they afraid of Mr. Young? He seemed easygoing, but I also sensed he was a no-nonsense kind of guy.

That first interminable afternoon, I played cards and board games with my dorm mates. After trying to answer the usual questions about my face, I realized their attention was more on our games than on me, and my distress began to subside.

At dinner, when Mr. Young escorted me to my seat at Mr. Hamilton's table, I felt like I was going to church back home, though we only went on Easter or Christmas and I never wore a coat or tie. Minutes before, I had sequestered myself in the bathroom to struggle with my tie. After several attempts, I was satisfied that the knot was reasonably straight and the tip reached where it should, just touching my belt. Had it not been for the distraction the tie provided, my anxiety about my face would have undone me when I entered the dining room.

Seated next to the headmaster, I was afraid to eat for fear of spilling food on my new clothes or of making a mistake. My napkin neatly in my lap, I puzzled over how to eat the dinner placed before me on white china. What was up with the three forks? Out of the corner of my eye, I followed the lead of others and managed to get through the utensil dilemma until I finally relaxed. Guided by Mr. Hamilton, we engaged in mostly small talk about school life and sports. As I looked around at our table of fidgeting boys, it was evident I wasn't the only one who wished he were sitting somewhere else.

My first meal at Bement dragged on forever, but it passed without incident. No one gibed me about my looks or stared at me—the only reason I could fathom was that the head table must be a safe zone. When dessert was finally over and Mr. Hamilton excused us, I could hardly keep from racing out the door.

Outside at last, I stood shivering in the dark, my hands stuffed deep in my pockets, and waited until all the boys had passed so I could be alone. The campus at night should have been a cozy view of scattered lit windows glowing in the dark. Instead, it made me think of home. They were probably having dinner now, but without me. It was too painful to think about . . . I shut my mind to such thoughts and found my way back to the dorm, weary but relieved that I had made it through dinner.

Word about a new odd student gets around quickly in a small school, but with the exception of a few kids asking the usual questions, I was left alone. Everyone was polite, civilized actually. That part of my life at Bement had gotten off to a good start.

Classes were another matter. I was behind in all my subjects; my classmates were two or three years more advanced than what my public school had prepared me for. Their talk of careers they'd one day pursue and the colleges they planned to attend unsettled me. College? The idea had never crossed my mind!

Ski season was well underway, another big frustration for me. All my classmates had shiny new skis, stylish gear, the latest in fiberglass equipment. The state, of course, had not budgeted ski equipment for me, so my instructor took me out to the ski barn where old equipment was stashed. Together we scrounged through mounds of discards and found a chipped pair of skis too long for me and a pair of obsolete boots.

I had to spend my first few weeks on the bunny slope struggling to snowplow while the younger kids whizzed past, laughing at my clumsiness. Fed up, I told my instructor that I quit, but somehow he convinced me to stick with it and kindly didn't write me up. My self-confidence grew, and to my great relief, by the end of the season, I was skiing at a higher level.

With spring came long bike rides down winding lanes lined with trees in bud. Our little group banked left and right as we gathered speed around the bends, the wind whipping our hair and stinging our cheeks. On my red, white, and blue Huffy from a few Christmases before, I pumped like a madman as I strained to keep up with the other boys on their twelve-speed Schwinns and only rarely lagged behind on the inclines.

Though I was included in every activity, I still couldn't shake the belief that I was the ugly duckling among swans. Everything conspired to remind me that I wasn't of their ilk. I remember once stopping for ice cream and Mr. Young, seeing I had no money left, discreetly handed me a chocolate cone without anyone noticing. Though I was grateful, I felt humiliated.

I had difficulty grasping algebra, and despite my efforts to keep up, I couldn't make sense of the equations Mr. Young rapidly jotted on the blackboard. He knew I was struggling and often knelt beside my desk to patiently lead me step-by-step through the problems. Resistant, I became increasingly convinced that the other kids were smarter than I.

My low self-esteem spread like a cancer. Was I stupid? Slow? Rudimentary arithmetic at Hillcrest had been no great challenge, but this stuff was beyond me. Was I too far behind to ever catch up? Tired of what didn't come easily, I spent my time daydreaming and gazing out the window, wanting to run away and be done with the whole wretched business. Fixated on the clock, I tried to will its hands to jump ahead and release me, indifferent to all of Mr. Young's prodding to participate. The minutes ticked by one excruciating second at a time.

Certain I was the class idiot, I lost all patience one day and shoved my books off my desk onto the floor. Mr. Young acted swiftly. As he walked toward me, I could tell by the look in his eyes I had gone too far. "Howard, you're interrupting the class. Explain yourself."

"I can't do this!"

"Yes, you can. Just concentrate and make an effort."

"I did and I can't and I won't!"

"Howard, pick up your books now," he said, keeping his voice calm. "All you have to do is ask for help." For the remainder of class, he guided me through one equation after another as I pretended to follow along. When class was dismissed, he called me to his desk.

"Look here, Howard, I won't report your disruptive behavior this time, but rest assured that there will be no next time. Understood?" For a while his reprimand kept me in check, if only in his class.

Before long, I was acting out in all my classes. The other teachers were more tolerant and didn't intimidate me, and I knew they would give me more leeway than they did my peers.

Art class was the worst. We were studying ceramics and using a potter's wheel, an entirely new experience for me, though not for the other kids. The sight of their perfectly round bowls made me feel the way I did in algebra—inferior—only this time instead of numbers it was clay. My bowls always came out as sad, little lopsided messes. Pressed beyond my limited patience, one day I smashed my spinning lump of clay on the wheel and stomped out of the classroom, not caring that my hands were caked with clay.

In my other classes I passed the time by throwing erasers. Years later I came across disciplinary notes in my school records about my eraser wars. I had found a partner in crime in Karen Lidbolt, the pretty, long-haired blonde daughter of Upper East Side Manhattan socialites. A silver-spoon-fed, pearl-wearing princess, she had a decided rebellious streak. We were an unlikely team.

I was doing everything possible to prove to myself I didn't belong there—and was hell-bent on making sure the school agreed with me. Despite knowing that my actions could have severe consequences, I couldn't stop myself. I was grateful to be a student there—no hospitals, no Dr. Gratz—but the contrast between my background and my classmates' made my envy grow and my fragile self-esteem crumble. They all came from elite families, whereas I felt I had none. One classmate, whose father was a Saudi king, had bodyguards posted outside his classroom doors. Other students came from old money and Fortune 500 dads with family crests. My coat of arms was the seal from the state of New Jersey.

I had to listen to descriptions of their latest ski vacations in Vail or summers in the Hamptons or Europe while having nothing to contribute. For my vacation, I would be shoveling horseshit or performing some other equally dreary chore.

I barely made it through my first semester. Then, after a fun-filled summer of tearing down walls and scraping paint, I returned to Bement. My attitude was lousy, but I was glad to be back. The high point of that fall was when I made goalie on the soccer team. Having resurrected my summer camp quick-change technique of facing the wall in the locker room, I could, with the speed of a magician, change into my soccer jersey.

I loved being a goalie; it was perfect for me—I depended on no one but myself. Even the color of my shirt was different. I could aggressively go after my opponents or slide into them to block a shot with no regard for further scarring my face or hurting them. With my bottled-up anger, being a goalie provided a much-needed release. While I fought doggedly to save every point, my teammates took advantage of any time-out to straighten their jerseys or comb their hair. They wanted to look good. I wanted to win.

We played other prep schools in the area, but the match against Eaglebrook was a watershed for me. A bite to the air that day and the pungent smell of a nearby tobacco field heightened my awareness. In the stands, the other kids' parents, bundled against the cold in cashmere sweaters and long scarves, stomped their feet and sipped hot coffee from Scottish plaid thermoses as they cheered on their precious sons.

With just a minute left in the grueling, scoreless game, one of our players stuck out his hand to block a shot to our goal, thereby awarding Eaglebrook a penalty kick. Our only hope was a tie, and it all came down to me.

I positioned myself in front of the net. Mr. Butler, our new headmaster, paced the sidelines with teachers and students, who all called out to me, "Come on, Howard. You can do it!"

Quiet settled over the field. I dug my cleats into the ground and glued my eyes on the ball, my palms sweating in the cold air. The Eaglebrook kicker, a big C on his jersey signaling he was team captain, momentarily posed then ran toward the ball. I dove to my left, crashing onto my shoulder as the sting of hard leather hit my stomach with such force I curled around it.

When I stood up holding the ball in the air, the crowd erupted in a roar. My teammates and supporters swarmed onto the field to hug me. *A tie! I did it!* For the first time in my life, I was the center of good attention and acceptance. Better than anything, though, I was admired.

Basking in the sweet elixir of triumph, I was too elated to care when one Eaglebrook player snidely remarked as he shook my hand, "Lucky stop, Flat Face."

But Billy, my dorm- and teammate, who was standing next to me during after-game handshakes, wasn't going to let it slide. Besides being my friend, he was the first person outside my family ever to defend me. Later I learned he had arranged a fight between this kid and me behind a nearby church the following day.

Word of the fight swept through the school. I wasn't upset about the comments—I had heard worse—but now it was the principle of not running away from a fight, something Ed would never have done.

The next day, everyone chickened out except Billy, my backup. Tall and lanky and wearing a colorful sweatband to hold back his shoulder-length hair, he gave me a pep talk as we waded ankle-deep through the leaves. We didn't have to wait long. My opponent arrived all posture and swagger, his support team of three friends in tow. Making up the rules as he went along, Billy instructed our little group: "No jumping in, no sticks, no rocks. Whoever says 'quit' or 'give' loses. Agreed?" This was not the Friday night fight on TV, just a bunch of testosterone-crazed boys.

For a boxing ring, we designated a patch of dry leaves, the corners marked by century-old hickory trees. I squared off with my Eaglebrook opponent and was preparing myself for the start when, without notice, he swung a roundhouse punch at my jaw that missed me by a foot. Off balance, he toppled to my feet. I exploded. Like a leopard I jumped on him, clinching one arm around his neck in a headlock and pummeling him savagely in the face with my free fist.

That unsuspecting kid was powerless against years of pent-up rage. I went at him mercilessly, smashing his face again and again and again, goaded on by Billy, who yelled, "Get him, get him!"

Adding a few more blows, I yelled, "Do you give?"

"No!" he roared, refusing to capitulate. I started in on him again, whaling on him until I heard a muffled croak: "Give, give!"

"What? I can't hear you!"

"Give! I said, give," he gasped.

Flinging him away from me, I rose to my feet and looked down at his battered face covered with his own blood, his shirt torn and blood-stained. Billy and I turned on our heels and tore off through the woods back to school, my adrenalin surging the whole way.

Back in our dorm, Billy and I couldn't resist some boasting, embellishing the details to make the fight more heroic than it had actually been. "Man, you should have seen him! There was blood everywhere!"

Though we made our friends swear on their mothers not to breathe a word to anyone, we didn't anticipate that the kid I'd battered would lie to one of his teachers, claiming I had assaulted him as he innocently walked down the street.

The next morning I was called into the new headmaster's office. The antithesis of Mr. Hamilton, Mr. Butler looked like a very large man-child with a round face, rosy-red cheeks, and thick, black-framed glasses he constantly pushed back into place. He had a chuckling way of laughing with none of Mr. Hamilton's formality. I knew him to be firm but fair, and it was evident seeing him interact with the kids around campus that he loved his job.

Mr. Butler wasn't chuckling when he greeted me that morning.

Certain I was about to be suspended, I nonetheless explained my version of the events that led up to the fight. A long period of silence followed as Mr. Butler contemplated me over his fingers he held steepled in front of his face. "Well now, Howard," he finally said. "I do understand that boys will be boys, but let me warn you that this is the last time you will engage in this kind of behavior. Under no circumstances will this be tolerated again. Ever. Are we clear on that, Howard?"

My punishment wasn't so bad: two weekends confined to my dorm, which was better than a weekend working at home in New Hampshire.

I was too rebellious to appreciate the break I got. A few weeks later, I foolishly cut class and was grounded with after-school study hall for one week, which kept me imprisoned every evening with a handful of fellow delinquents. They weren't troublemakers from inner-city Jersey, but kids who cared about their school records and future trust funds. Having nothing at stake (or so I believed), I thought myself clever and asked to go to the restroom and simply didn't return. With the stars to keep me company, I wandered campus that night until I could safely return to my dorm.

The next morning, I was back in Mr. Butler's office. It was my second infraction in as many weeks, so he grounded me again for an additional two weeks. "Howard, this is not how we conduct ourselves at Bement."

The punishment seemed excessive, and I said so. I had expected more study hall, but Mr. Butler assured me that the subject was not up for debate. "Howard, the punishment stands."

I stormed out and ran towards the cement bridge. Behind me I heard Mr. Butler calling, "Howard, if you cross over that bridge, you will not be coming back!"

I kept moving, though I knew he meant it. At that moment I realized how being told what to do—whether coming from the state, Dr. Gratz, Ed, or Shirl—made me determined to do just the opposite, even with guidance that was for my own good. Poised in the middle of the bridge, it became instantly clear.

This was my point of no return.

I slid down the cement wall and sat with my back to it, my knees drawn up to my chest when it hit me. Where would I go? Would Ed and Shirl give me back to the state? Was this my last chance at ever having a decent life? Along with the cold from the cement penetrating my thin khaki pants, I felt the bleakness of my prospects and heard Ed's voice in my head: "You really fucked up this time, kid."

Minutes later, two shiny brown penny loafers stepped into view before my downcast eyes. I looked up to see Mr. Young's towering silhouette against the sky. "What's going on, Howard?"

As best I could, I tried to keep the fear out of my voice as I recounted the detention saga. Leaning on the bridge railing, Mr. Young listened. "Another two weeks for that? You're lucky that was all. Had it been my decision, it would have been much worse. Repeatedly you've been given more chances. You *do* realize that? We all understand your circumstances, Howard, but you cannot and will not dictate to the teachers or the administration of this school. You have been given a wonderful opportunity here and a chance to grow. It's up to you to take advantage of it."

"But, but I . . ."

"There are no buts. You will go to Mr. Butler. You will apologize. And you will accept any consequences for your actions. Understood?"

Another year passed. I continued to struggle with my classes, my resolve to self-destruct well entrenched. My resentment toward my classmates grew. They had everything handed to them, while I had nothing. In the dorm I would watch them open care packages containing colorful sweaters from Bergdorf Goodman and boxes of real Swiss chocolates. Once, I snidely remembered, Ed had brought me a packet of generic chocolate bars he'd found on sale.

These kids' lives had been choreographed from birth: prep school, an Ivy League college, and then a home in an exclusive suburb with a perfect mate to breed the next generation of preppies. It made me gnash my teeth.

I didn't know if I would make it through the school year. Would surgery interrupt my schooling regardless? And what then? Placement in another foster home? All the uncertainty weighed heavily on me.

Apart from receiving a B in both writing class and English, and improving my skiing from snowplowing to managing a decent slalom (to the point of making it down the intermediate run without falling), I considered the year remarkable because I somehow managed to get through it.

Home again for summer in New Hampshire and back to the usual routine. It wasn't that I was kept chained in the house as an indentured servant, because Ed would take us to the movies on dollar night or to a nearby lake to go swimming or to a restaurant for fried clams. The problem was that he couldn't accept that I had zero aptitude or interest in banging nails or fixing the lawn mower.

After exposure to finer things, I saw myself in a different light: wearing nicer clothes and even sitting up straight with one hand in my lap to eat my dinner of Hamburger Helper. It made me proud that Shirl noticed my good manners.

I had outgrown the penny loafers I had bought with the state social worker, and now I wanted leather Docksiders like the ones the other boys wore at school.

"How much?" Ed asked.

"Forty dollars."

"Jesus Christ! Forty dollars for a pair of goddamn shoes!"

"Yeah, but all the kids at school have them."

Ed then ranted about how he was raised in the Depression and about the value of a dollar, ending with his favorite line about how money doesn't grow on trees. "I started working when I was eight and so can you." I got the message and began searching the classifieds for a summer job.

There it was in bold type: "Wanted: Dishwasher, $1.25/hr." The job was at the Lamplighter Inn, about five miles away, just over the state line in Brattleboro, Vermont. I asked Ed and Shirl if it would be all right with them if I applied. All right? They were ecstatic! I would be out of the house on weekends, and Ed wouldn't have to hear any more about my preppie shoes.

The inn, named for the tiny lamps that glowed on each table, had a dimly lit interior that disguised the fake-wood paneling, worn red tufted-leather booths, and frayed carpet. Underneath the aroma of food was the smell of stale cigarette smoke.

The owner, Nick, a short, fat, balding Greek with a heavy accent, didn't give much of an interview and hardly glanced at my application. Ed had told me to lie about my age. "Tell him you're sixteen," he said.

"Can you work weekends? Is $1.25 an hour okay?" In forty hours, I figured, I could have my Docksiders. "Oh, and don't eat my food, yes?"

He scheduled me to work Friday and Saturday nights and all day on Sundays, when they served a brunch consisting of the weekend's leftovers. I mopped floors, washed dishes, took out the garbage, cleaned behind the bar, and helped Norman, the cook, if it got too busy (which rarely happened), spooning vegetables onto entree plates.

Norman was a big, fat, gregarious guy who chain-smoked behind the line, the cigarette wagging between his lips as he jovially yelled out to the waitresses, "C'mon, girls, pick up 1." Sometimes when I was washing dishes, he would sneak me a slice of pecan pie. "Keep it covered so Nick doesn't see it," he'd say.

Ed insisted I hitchhike back and forth to work, though if it was raining hard, he would send Shirl for me. By the end of summer, I had saved enough for my new shoes and a bike and had a little left over to take back to school.

"You're being a good kid," Ed told me in a rare demonstrative moment, patting me on the back.

My last year at Bement was not a banner one. My shoes were new, but my attitude hadn't improved, particularly when I was subjected, yet again, to my classmates' tales of their lavish vacations.

That fall I was moved to Stebbins House, situated about half a mile off campus. Though it was a dorm for the older boys, the consensus was that I, who had taken to bullying the younger ones, would be held in check by upperclassmen who wouldn't tolerate my aggression.

On one Saturday outing that winter, our dorm went into Greenfield, one town away. We split into smaller groups, some heading for the local arcade to play Pac-Man or air hockey, others to stock up on candy and comics. Billy and I headed over to the sporting-goods store for some thick ski socks he needed. Left to wait for him, I wandered the aisles, checking out expensive skis and boots priced way beyond anything I could afford. That was when I came across the ski gloves: thick blue ones filled with real down, everything my cheap plastic ones with cotton liners that got soaked and froze my hands weren't. Even though I could have easily bought them with my savings, I chose my own method of acquisition.

Furtively, I looked around. The manager was busy at the register, and a townie appeared to be absorbed in his task of stocking shelves. I tucked my booty inside my winter coat just as Billy came up behind me. "You ready?" he asked.

"Yeah, let's go."

Billy, oblivious of my theft, followed me to the door. With my thoughts on having something nice like the other boys, something besides my Docksiders, consequences never entered my mind. My heart pounding, I picked up the pace.

Within feet of the door, the stock boy stepped in front of me, blocking my getaway as he called for the manager, who grabbed me by the arm and yanked my coat open, exposing the incriminating evidence. Looking grim, he hauled me to the register and ordered Billy, whom he assumed to be my accomplice, to come along. "I know you boys go to Bement. The school has an account with us. I'm calling your headmaster."

It was just my luck that he had Mr. Butler's home number. I would have preferred he call the police.

December 8, 1975
Mr. and Mrs. Milton E. Mackey
Box 162
West Chesterfield, New Hampshire 03466

Dear Mr. and Mrs. Mackey,

I'm sorry to inform you that this Saturday while on a
town trip, Howard was caught shoplifting in one of our local
stores. Fortunately, it was a store with a long association
with Bement, and the owner was willing to accept our
assurance that we would properly punish Howard.

This has been done. Howard will pay for the stolen items
out of his allowance and by working for the school for most of
this weekend. Howard had to return the items to the store and
personally apologize to the manager.

Howard assures me that he has learned his lesson and will
never do such a thing again. We hope this is the case. As far
as we are concerned, the punishment I have just described
is perfectly adequate. We will do our best to see that this
incident does not mar what has been an excellent fall term for
Howard.

Sincerely yours,
John N. Butler
Headmaster

Now that I was known as a thief among future kings, things went
downhill quickly. As for the ski gloves, I honestly hadn't needed them;
I was simply tired of being the outsider. When I returned for spring
semester, I felt as though I were wearing prison stripes on my Bement
blazer.

Every year the school celebrated Spring Fling, a weekend carnival
that gave parents the opportunity to spend time with their kids and
the faculty. Dunk tanks, dart booths, balloon popping, and all the
standard carnival arcade games ended with a grand finale, a tug-of-

war contest over the duck pond that pitted Bement faculty and parents against the students. There was fun for all—or for everyone but me.

It was an event I dreaded. Ed and Shirl could never make the trip for some reason or another, so I would spend the entire weekend wandering around campus alone. The occasional introduction to a dorm mate's family or the greetings from well-meaning friends and acquaintances only increased my feelings of alienation and loneliness. Faking pleasure I didn't feel, I circulated until I could no longer keep up my pretense, then retreated to my room to wait until the last car drove away.

Years later, as an adult, I found an incident report in my school records that reminded me of just how alienated I had become: "Howard has been referred to Mr. Young for his latest outburst in class. Mr. Young said he would deal personally with Howard's punishment."

I remember it vividly. He led me down to the girls' field-hockey lawn and handed me a bent kitchen serving spoon. (I didn't merit a silver spoon reserved for the likes of my blue-blooded classmates). Like a field general providing one of his infantrymen with an instrument for his own humiliation, he ordered me to dig up every dandelion in the lawn. Placing a bucket at my feet, he wasted few words. "I expect this bucket to be completely filled by the end of today. Do we understand each other?"

For the next five hours, as the damp grass soaked my jeans, I scoured the field for dandelions. Digging them up, one by one, I was indifferent to students walking by who snickered at my humiliating task. All my previous punishments had desensitized me.

Though Mr. Young periodically checked on my progress throughout the afternoon, that wasn't the reason I obeyed. I wasn't afraid of him; in fact, I respected him and understood his punishment was the result of my refusal to accept boundaries. Cause and effect. Alone, my head down, I crawled around the open field, each flower I dug up adding to the disappointment I felt in myself for not taking advantage of everything the school had to offer me.

In the end, all I had to show for my rebellion was a bucket of weeds.

The following letter sealed my fate at Bement:

May 28, 1976
N.J. Division of Youth and Family Services
Bureau of Fiscal Services-Review Unit
163 West Hanover Street
Trenton, New Jersey 08611

Gentlemen:

By copy of this letter, I am recommending to our
Headmaster, John Butler, that Howard be dismissed from school
immediately.

We have requested in three separate letters, dated
February 14, April 14, and May 6, that your office approve a
new contract for our services to Howard. The old contract
expired in January, and we are continuing to receive payment
for services based on that contract, and since the old
contract is not adequate, we must terminate our services.
Questions concerning Howard's dismissal should be directed
to John M. Butler, Headmaster.

Yours truly,
Robert A. Scott
Business Manager

Apparently, I wasn't destined to be a Bementer.

F I V E

AFTER MY UNCEREMONIOUS DEPARTURE at the end of the term, I spent a difficult summer subjected to Ed's constant berating. "What the hell is wrong with you, for Christ's sake?"

That fall brought no improvement. After Bement, public school felt like a demotion, and it didn't help that Keene High was an eighteen-mile bus ride away. My freshman year was miserable. I was angry and went out of my way to make sure everyone around me suffered equally. Though I never would have admitted it, I missed Bement's structure and superior curriculum—and even Mr. Young who had held me in check.

By the following summer, Shirl couldn't take it anymore. Both she and Ed decided that I needed to try another foster home. "Howie, you're not happy. Let's just see how it goes for a while." That she had not closed the door on me gave me some hope.

In the ensuing days, a shadow settled over the house. I spent my remaining time with Robin, who cried and pleaded with Ed and Shirl to give me another chance. Seeing her so upset zapped me of any rebellion I had left. Even Frank tried to comfort me. I had lived with them for nearly twelve years, and I was scared, really scared when I realized this was the end of the line with the only family I'd ever known. Shirl assured me that it was best for everyone, and as always, she was right.

On a sad June day, a month before my sixteenth birthday, a state worker picked me up to deliver me to New Jersey, where I was temporarily placed in the home of a German woman, whose feet were so swollen she could barely navigate her way around the house.

Next was a placement with a nice Jewish family, who said blessings in Hebrew before each meal. That lasted a week. Seeing their family photos on the mantle saddened and angered me—sad that I was without a family and angry that I had destroyed being with the one I had. They insisted I go to synagogue, which I adamantly refused. Perhaps they thought conversion would mend my ways.

Oddly enough, it was Dr. Gratz who intervened. During an examination, he determined it was time for another skin graft. Realizing I had better use the state's medical funding while I still could, I didn't fight it.

When the state found a temporary placement for me close to the Albert Einstein Hospital in the Bronx where my operation was slated, I felt I'd come full circle, back to the very borough where all my pain and loneliness had started. With yet another caseworker, I drove to my new foster home where I would stay for the duration of my surgery and recovery.

I became concerned as we passed abandoned warehouses and graffiti-covered walls, the smell of garbage rotting in the summer heat filling our car. My new foster family's neighborhood was somewhat better, though not by much, and not at all what I had expected. It wasn't the ghetto, but it sure as hell wasn't historic Deerfield.

We soon pulled up in front of a block of identical brick row houses. I hadn't finished knocking when the door opened, and Vito and Mary Signorelli stepped out to welcome me. My caseworker hastily departed, anxious to get out of the neighborhood before the sun went down.

First-generation Italians, my interim foster parents greeted me enthusiastically. Vito, gray-haired and unshaven, wore his baggy, black-and-white-checkered kitchen pants loosely cinched below his large belly. Over a stained white V-necked T-shirt hung an impressive collection of gold chains that made faint clanking noises whenever he moved. Mary, short and stout like a tree trunk, had black hair thick with ringlets. On each of her short fingers, she wore several inexpensive gold rings, outdoing Vito with his one pinkie ring.

Feeling awkward and out of place, I made my way into the living room. Everything was covered in plastic: the chairs, lamps, sofa—even the carpet was protected with plastic runners. Plaster statues of the Madonna, Jesus, St. Francis, and St. Christopher cluttered the room and decorated the turquoise walls. In the dining room, a velvet tapestry of the Last Supper hung opposite a giant crucifix.

"Anthony, get-a down here!" Jolted from my culture shock by Vito's bellowing, I turned to see a slovenly dressed, overweight boy appear on the stairs. Scarcely bothering to lift his head of long, stringy hair when we were introduced, Anthony struck me as someone lost in his own home. Moving like a sleepwalker, he showed me to my tiny room with a daybed, over which hung another cross. In the time it took me to throw my bags on the bed, Anthony was gone. I heard the door closing behind him, then rock music pulsating through our common wall.

I returned downstairs to rejoin Vito in the living room. Looking pensive, his head tilted as he studied my face, he asked, "Howard, you-a Jewish?"

"Yes," I said, wanting to give him the satisfaction of thinking he had guessed correctly. In reality, I knew nothing about my background and always tried to avoid that line of questioning. Once, because of my surname, Ed had told me he and Shirl had always assumed my biological family was Jewish.

"That's-a okay. You-a hungry?" I nodded, whiffing the tantalizing aroma that filled the house. "Good, Mary make-a dinner for us. I make-a fresh bread. I still-a help out at the bakery if they-a need me." The bakery, I gathered, was his second home, where even after retirement he dropped in almost daily.

While we waited for dinner, Vito and I went outside. I watched him from the front porch, kneeling to inspect the miniscule patch of lawn he kept hemmed in by a frame of bricked-in flower beds. I especially liked that it was tiny and would be a lot easier to care for than Ed's.

I turned my attention to the street. Beyond the low wrought-iron fence that abutted the sidewalk, two black kids sauntered by, the blaring boom box one of them carried on his shoulder disrupting the peace. Vito yelled, "Hey, shut the fuck up!" The boys never broke stride, so I doubt they heard him, and soon the music faded in the distance.

"These kids, they got no-a respect. This used to be a nice Italian neighborhood. A forty years I been here. When I moved here all Italian, a couple-a Jews, but a nice neighborhood. Now *mulignan, capisce?*" I don't think Vito really hated anyone. He was just a tough old man trying to protect his way of life.

Interrupted by Mary's call to dinner, we returned to the kitchen and sat down to a spread of sausage and grilled pepper, along with Vito's fresh bread, my first meal with my new family.

Every Sunday the extended family gathered for a big midday meal. In the Signorelli clan, there were Vito and Mary's two biological kids, Big Michael, a banker in Manhattan who had escaped the Bronx and had "made it" (even though I heard Mary calling his girlfriend a *"puta"*), and his sister, Maria. Their other kids, Anthony and his brothers, Little Michael and Peter, were all adopted. Maria, who lived a few blocks away, was dating Peter, her brother by adoption. It took me a while to figure out things weren't as kinky as I had feared.

During dinner they argued about everything, the current hot topic being the Son of Sam murders. As the debate heated up and everyone took turns describing how they'd make that son of a bitch pay, Mary silently moved her lips in prayer while repeatedly making the sign of the cross.

Poor Anthony was their whipping boy. "Anthony, be like-a your brothers. Look at you! You-a fat, you-a lazy. Why you no dress like-a Howard?" Anthony would hunch lower over his pasta. Mary, who thought I was such a nice boy with lovely manners, thanks to my training at Bement, held me up as an example, which didn't exactly ingratiate me with Anthony.

After dinner the men would go outside to watch Peter wash his gold Camero while Vito belittled Anthony some more. "You never gonna have a car like-a this," he would tell his son, at which point Anthony would retreat to his room, leaving the rest to argue about the latest Yankee game.

Often late at night I would hear Vito screaming at Anthony in a mixture of English and Italian. As I lay sweltering on my daybed on those long, hot summer nights, trying to fall asleep, I couldn't help thinking I could have been raised here, and then what would have become of me? I really did screw up. I had it all and I blew it, like everyone had told me. Homesick for Ed and Shirl and the rest of my family, I tossed and turned as I stared through the gloom at a print of the Virgin Mary gazing down at me. Soon I reverted to an old habit I'd had as a young child in the hospital: rocking my head back and forth on my pillow for hours, a self-soothing habit to keep the fear and loneliness at bay. Inevitably, when I finally fell into an uneasy sleep, I'd be awakened by Vito or Mary's screaming. "Anthony! Turn off the music!" Again I would resume my cycle of tossing and turning and worrying. In the dark of night, I felt as if I had been abandoned all over again.

Occasionally I joined Vito when he took Mary shopping in his beat-up old car. We went to discount stores and mom-and-pop markets or bought from street vendors who sold their wares out of cardboard boxes. Mary always returned home with a copy of the *National Enquirer*, her escape from the insanity of the house. Several times a week Vito would drive her to church, which was the only time I ever saw her change out of her housecoats. Off to Mass, she would promise to include me in her prayers for my upcoming surgery and, for herself, pray for the strength to be patient with Anthony.

As for Anthony, the only time I ever spent alone with him was when Vito and Mary were out of the house and he brought out his girlie magazines. Sharing his stash with me was the only connection we ever had. God help us if Mary had found out.

Finally, the day for my surgery arrived. I was sixteen now, and though I understood the progression of each stage, I felt I was repeating the same old story but with a different body part. Dr. Gratz's plan was to attach another headless snake of skin to my nose, only this time he'd take a twelve-by-fifteen-inch graft from my left thigh. This would be another serious surgery, and to lower the chance of infection, my stay would be two weeks. Fortunately, since I had no prior association with Albert Einstein Hospital, I was at least spared flashbacks of my grim beginnings at Montefiore.

After the surgery, I was overjoyed when Ed and Shirl, along with Robin, Frank, and Lisa, showed up to visit me. If only for a few hours, I was with my family again and didn't feel quite so alone in the world. They seemed happy to see me, and their news of home helped ease my homesickness. Vito and Mary visited me too, bringing me fresh cannolis when I was able to eat solid food again.

Discharged, I returned to the Signorellis, where everyone was taken aback at the sight of my swelling. It wasn't a coincidence that they spoke more often in Italian than they had before my surgery. Ordered to stay out of the sun, I spent my entire summer indoors watching Yankee ball games or *Bowling for Dollars* while Vito yelled at the TV as though the contestants were with us in the living room.

They both did everything they could to help me. Mary decided that food was what I needed most. "Howard, *manga, manga,* you need-a strength." Between her pastas, sausages, and minestrone, I gained back all the weight I had lost—and then some. But their insistence that I not lift a finger left me with nothing to do. Vito, seeing me depressed and limping around the house with my leg still sore from the graft, tried to cheer me up with Italian ices he bought on the street.

When I saw Dr. Gratz a few weeks later to have my bandages removed, the old anxiety returned as I lay back on the rustling paper.

"Howard, relax. I will take this off, yes?"

I nodded.

In one swift move, he grabbed the tape and ripped it off my leg. My whole body went into shock—and then my mind registered the pain. "FUUUUUUUUUUUUUUCK!" I screamed.

Dr. Gratz's head jerked back like a chicken's, his eyes bulging like headlights. "Howard, Howard, it's fine. It's over."

It wasn't fine. I looked down at the droplets of blood floating above a sticky yellow pebbling where the skin had been removed from my thigh and thought of the yellow fly strips dotted with insects that hung in my old neighborhood's backyards.

I glared at him, seething with contempt at how cavalierly he treated me, as if he had been pulling a Band-Aid off a finger. I wanted to jump up and smash his face. With great effort I resisted the urge, consoling myself with the fact that we would soon part ways.

My stay with the Signorellis was over, and though they had been kind and generous, it was time to move on.

"Howard, you are a wonderful boy!" Mary said as we hugged good-bye. "God bless-a you. I will-a pray for you."

With my bus ticket provided by the state, I returned to New Jersey.

During the month it took for a placement, the state put me up in a cheap motel off some now-forgotten exit of the New Jersey Turnpike. The days monotonously ground by. My only activity was taking my meals at a Chinese all-you-can-eat restaurant down the road. Stressed and in limbo, I wasn't up for much more than going back and forth between the motel room and the buffet. Meals had become more a matter of having something to do than of satisfying an appetite I'd lost. Even so, in case I got hungry in the night, I'd stuff my pockets full of greasy egg rolls wrapped in napkins before stealing back to my room.

The social worker who had driven me to the Signorellis' house now had me in her official caseload, and though I was still a number to her, we at least recognized each other. I even remember her name: Mrs. Brill. Middle-aged and conservative, in her polyester pantsuits and wire-rim glasses, she reminded me of a well-meaning librarian.

When at last the state had figured out what to do with me, Mrs. Brill drove me north to the upscale community of Summit, New Jersey, where arrangements had been made for me to stay in a boardinghouse; the state would provide rent and a monthly stipend. I suppose that for liability purposes, the state figured I would be safer there than living in some inner-city housing project.

As we drove along quiet tree-lined streets, I couldn't help thinking how impressed Vito would be with all the stately homes and manicured lawns we passed. When we pulled up in front of a beautiful, three-story Victorian, we sat quietly in the car, and Mrs. Brill allowed me a few minutes to size up my new home. A feeling of remorse took hold of me as I studied the gray-shingled exterior and oversized bay windows that reminded me of my years in Deerfield.

Together we climbed the broad front steps, and at the leaded-glass door, I paused, fervently hoping that here I would find the stability I longed for. This would be my first time living on my own. All I had to do was stay out of trouble. I was well aware of the scary alternative—a new placement with God knows who.

The large woman who opened the door looked me up and down and, in an accent I couldn't place, said, "I have four rules: no cooking, no overnight guests, no noise, and pay your rent on time." With that, she handed me my key to independence.

My landlady lived on the ground floor with her family, whom I rarely saw. My room was two stories up. As I climbed the creaky hardwood stairs with Mrs. Brill puffing behind, I noted the spotless floorboards and the strong scent of Pine-Sol.

I opened the door to a converted attic the size of two standard bedrooms, wide enough that it took a good eight strides to cross. The ceiling was low and angled, so I decided not to place my bed close to the wall, knowing I would smack my head when I got up in the dark. There was one tiny, musty-smelling closet, and along one side of the room, a row of small windows looked out on green treetops and peaked roofs. Though not a bachelor's pad, it felt cozy and was perfect for my needs. When I checked out the shared bathroom and noticed no shampoo or toothbrushes, it struck me how truly on my own I was.

I returned to the motel until a $300 disbursement came through for me to buy some furniture, and when it did, Mrs. Brill kindly drove me to a discount store a few miles outside of Summit. After searching for anything that was chipped or scratched so we could haggle a few more dollars off the price, I finally settled on a white metal daybed that came with a set of bedding. With the cash left over, I bought a black floor lamp, a round pseudo-colonial coffee table that wasn't too badly dinged, and a chocolate-colored chest of drawers.

Mrs. Brill and I stopped for lunch at a little diner. When we finished our sandwiches, she primly dabbed her napkin to her lips and haltingly broached a more serious subject. "Howard, you do know that when you turn eighteen, you will receive funds that the state has held in escrow for you?"

Ed and Shirl had told me about a small account being held in trust for me, but because they had never wanted me to count on it, I'd never been told the specifics. My head filled with visions of a costly sports car and a big bachelor pad with an actual kitchen—and maybe a girl-friend. "How much is there?" I asked.

"I don't know the exact amount, but I do know it's enough for you to start a new life for yourself. Are you aware, Howard, where the money came from?"

"No." I felt an adrenaline rush.

"When you were born, the hospital had some sort of liability for your medical issues and they agreed to pay some money for damages." Now I was intrigued. It was the hospital's fault for my facial hell? Finally I had someone or something I could blame.

"Howard, have you thought about perhaps going to college? Do you have any idea what you would like to do with your life?"

Frank had just joined the Coast Guard, and Lisa was going to nursing school. Since working at the Lamplighter Inn and helping Norman, I had thought about becoming a cook.

"That would be great, Howard! You don't have a high school diploma, so what do you think about enrolling in a class to get your GED?"

I looked away, reminded of what could have come of my years at Bement. I had always been more concerned with where I would be living, with whom, and my next surgery than planning for my future.

"It would be a wonderful first step for you," she said. "And Howard, instead of becoming a cook, you could be a chef! There's a famous school in upstate New York called the Culinary Institute of America."

This did pique my interest; I could easily envision myself in a chef's hat. Ed had told me about that school when I was working with Norman at the inn. Insecurities about my prospects weighed on me, and a job in a kitchen might just be the solution. Safely out of sight I could deal with. "I'll think about it," I said.

"Good. I'll see if I can get you a small advance from your trust, but no promises, okay?"

Before long I was enrolled in a GED program that met evenings at a local high school. Thrown in with mostly adult immigrants who spoke little English, I felt completely out of place and was bored by the remedial level of the class. It seemed a waste of time, so I stopped attending after the first week. Besides, I figured I would soon have plenty of money.

Shortly afterward, I received a $2,000 advance from my trust, and since I had no identification for opening an account, Mrs. Brill accompanied me to the bank. When she asked me about my GED classes, I lied and told her everything was going well. I had more important things on my mind. My money in hand, I went out and purchased a silver moped to get around town. It would do until my windfall came in and I could buy my sports car.

For the next several weeks, I explored Summit on my new two-wheeler adventure seeker and actually got it up to thirty-five miles an hour, fast enough to take me to a mall in the next town. There I would spend entire days in the multiplex theatre watching three movies for the price of one. I bought some new clothes and joined the YMCA, where I began lifting weights. After my body had been surgically torn down all my life, I couldn't wait to build it up on my own terms.

That fall I repeatedly returned to a small ridge where I sat for hours watching the high school football team practice below while I tried to imagine the direction my life would take. A realist, I wondered if I would ever have a girlfriend or if I would be alone for the rest of my life, shunned by the world. I was scared, but I relished my new freedom.

My emancipation from the state of New Jersey was fast approaching. To take advantage of the free medical care I was entitled to until age eighteen, I made an appointment with Dr. Gratz to have the bulbous tip of my nose taken off. While the removal of protruding tissue left from previous grafts was minor, this was a major turning point for me. It would be the first time I had ever gone to see him without a social worker or guardian in attendance, and best of all, it would be the final act in our protracted medical drama.

As I made my way to his office by train and subway, lulled by mile upon mile of abandoned industrial sites flashing past my window, I sensed a newfound inner strength growing within me. After almost two decades, and despite all the obstacles that life could possibly have put in my way, I was still here. Everything Dr. Gratz had envisioned for me, I had survived.

"Howard, we meet again, yes?"

Without responding, I pondered this austere man who over the years had not softened at all. His strong German accent was as pronounced as ever, but its capability to instill fear in me was gone, and the child who had once been so afraid of the mere sight of him was no more. Before he could hold out his hand that had so often gripped my face, I looked him directly in the eye and initiated a firm handshake. Never again would I cower before him like a scared puppy.

"Howard, you look good. Tell me, what you are doing now?"

"I'm attending culinary school in New York," I lied.

"Wonderful, wonderful! I will come and see you when you are a famous chef. You will make me a delicious dinner!"

I cringed at the thought of ever meeting him on a personal level, but in some strange way felt obliged not to disappoint him. He had been the most constant fixture in my life, and I felt ashamed of the mere cook I aspired to be. Since my birth he had wielded great power with the cold, sterile instruments of his trade, but now I wanted him to know that it was I, not he, who would determine my future.

When the procedure was over, I checked myself out of the hospital after agreeing to return in six weeks to have my stitches removed. Hastily I felt my pockets to double-check that I had my backup supplies of cotton gauze and surgical tape.

On the train back to New Jersey, I thought about Dr. Gratz. Instead of the resentment I'd always felt toward him, I now felt ambivalence. I had been assigned to him as case number XUG-905 some sixteen years before, and now we were done, simple as that.

Weeks later, I found a hospital in Summit to have my stitches removed. Dr. Gratz and I never saw each other again. No words were needed. My body of permanent scars spoke for us both.

In no time I went through my entire advance. I bought a color TV, a stereo, new clothes, and the moped, along with a mini-refrigerator and a hot plate so I could heat up my meals of canned stews and soups.

By keeping my windows open and stuffing a towel under the door, I managed to conceal my clandestine activities from my landlady, with the added bonus of taking my usual delight in breaking the rules.

Now that I had made my place more livable, I needed to get a job. A crisp shirt or new outfit is what most people wear to an interview—for mine, I changed my gauze dressing. I set out from my walk-up determined to find some work, forging past the dread of subjecting myself to more rejection, which almost made me turn back. My nose was still healing, and though I had applied at several restaurants for a dishwasher job, I was summarily turned away before I could fill out an application. One look at my bandaged face was more than enough to elicit one "sorry, no" after another.

If I couldn't even get a job as a dishwasher, how much lower could I descend on the workforce ladder? Gravedigger? Porn house janitor?

About to give up, I walked into the Office, a trendy restaurant decorated in an early 1900s office theme with waitstaff who wore file clerk uniforms. The baby-faced manager, Mike, was built like a football player and seemed a friendly sort.

Bracing myself for another rejection, I politely inquired if there was a position open. Mike considered my bandage a moment. "Are you okay? That must be quite a cut under there."

His question threw me. "Uh, yes. Just a couple of stitches—I fell off my bike." To my relief he seemed to accept my explanation and didn't quiz me about the fading hooked scar on my forehead, another souvenir from one of my numerous grafts.

He scanned my application. "Good, you have experience. We're very busy here, anywhere between two and three hundred diners a night. You'll start at $2.25 an hour. It's the night shift till closing, which is around 12, 12:30, five days a week. How's that sound?"

"It sounds fine." It was better than fine. "I live close by and won't be late."

He chuckled at my eagerness to be a dishwasher. "Can you start tomorrow?"

That night I slept poorly, worrying about how my coworkers would react to me and how I'd deal with it. I simply wanted to stay behind the scenes and be invisible.

The kid who trained me was a tall, skinny redhead about my age, who wore his long hair in a ponytail and planned to move to the "city" to put a band together. He showed me the ropes: putting away the dishes, hosing off the heavy rubber mats, taking the garbage out to the dumpster in the back alley. I'd been so fixated on my coworkers' reaction to me that I had failed to take into account that the heat and steam from the industrial dishwasher would wilt my bandage. Throughout the night I had to keep pressing on the tape, praying it would hold until the end of my shift. They would fire me, I was sure, if they saw my raw suture marks and discovered my potential medical liability.

When my first shift ended around one in the morning, I sneaked out the back door, smelling of sweat and discarded food. Looking around to make sure no one saw me, I tossed my deteriorated bandage into the dumpster and sped away.

Back at my apartment I fell into bed, thankful I had gotten through my shift without having to explain my wounds. The next night I went prepared with extra bandaging for a quick change, which I needed every shift.

It was 1978, and bistros sprang up in the neighborhood serving quiche, fruit plates, and carafes of California wines. The Office was popular, and I was kept busy in the kitchen away from the public. That was okay with me. I knew a bandaged employee was not what diners wanted to see.

My job was going smoothly until Jeff, the assistant manager, set me in his sights. Disco was on the way out, but this guy looked as if he had just stepped out of *Saturday Night Fever*. In his early thirties and average in all regards, he wore an absurd Burt Reynolds mustache, dyed black like his hair. More ludicrous was the mass of gold chains that filled the V of his unbuttoned shirt. Jeff saw himself as the epitome of cool and began to screw with me for no reason, pointing out spots I had missed with the mop or some smudge on the dishwasher. I took it, smoldering inside but biting my tongue.

Mostly I kept to myself, cranking out the dishes until the early morning hours and then going home to sleep. During my free time, besides going to the movies or working out at the Y, I would ride aimlessly around town on my moped. Occasionally I went out for a pizza and sat alone, always careful to keep my head down to repel the on-slaught of curious glances. I ate slowly, pretending to concentrate on reeling in loops of melted mozzarella so I could eavesdrop on tables of shrieking kids chatting about parties and school. Though I was their age, our lives couldn't have been more different. The state of New Jersey was my safety net, but it was no family, and listening to those kids made me yearn for what I didn't have.

At work I was treated well. Out of fear, I continued to wear my bandage for weeks longer than necessary. When I finally summoned the courage to go unmasked, I was met with the predictable curious glances and whispers. A few asked if I was all right, except for Disco Jeff, who thought himself clever. "It's about time I saw you face-to-face." If that was the best he had, he was a lightweight.

One night after six months of scraping and washing dishes, I looked up from the rack I was loading to see Mike's cherubic face studying me. "Howard, how would you like to be a prep cook?" It wasn't a move up the corporate ladder, but it beat going home smelling of grease. So I got moved up in pay and down to the basement.

I worked alone—the radio was my only company. Now on days, I spent my shift pulling off cherry tomato stems by the thousands, slic-ing carrots and celery into long, thin strips until my hands turned orange and green, and cracking cases of eggs for hundreds of omelets and quiches. I got so proficient I could handily crack two at a time without a single shell falling into the vat. In the basement I remained, except for hasty deliveries upstairs—when I always stole a look at lovely Annie the waitress, whose high, rounded breasts and sweet, dimpled smile nearly made me forget my errand.

On my days off, I began taking the train into Manhattan to ex-plore. One late, overcast afternoon, I found myself hanging around Times Square, watching the velvet-coated pimps in platform shoes hustle passers-by. My loneliness and curiosity must have been obvious because a young black man working his turf in front of a tenement waved me over. "Girls inside—check it out."

My horniness trumped caution, and I impulsively stepped into the stairwell, where a balding, overweight Italian guy with forearms cov-ered in tattoos sat on a ridiculously small chair. "Twenty dollars!" he barked. After folding my bills over a fat wad of cash, he jabbed upward with his forefinger. "Third floor."

Slowly I zigzagged my way up the dirty stairs, each step making me almost more nervous than I'd ever been before an operation. This was unknown territory I was entering.

The parlor was dimly lit, and in the gloom I could make out one of "Guido's" associates leaning against a dirty pink wall, smoking a cigar. The women, in varying states of undress, sat eyeing me from worn velvet couches and chairs shoved together along the walls. When I approached, they rose unenthusiastically, making me feel like a visiting dignitary who'd arrived after the pomp was over. This, however, was no stately visit, even though they looked like the United Nations of sexual favors—white, black, Latino, Asian—the whole gamut lined up before me, most with bad skin and too much makeup, a few with bloodshot eyes. They all looked tired and bored, their smiles perfunctory, rehearsed, and as transparent as my reason for being there.

I'm sure I was facing an assemblage of mothers and daughters, addicts and runaways—struggling human beings who had probably been through much worse than I. Wasting no time, I chose the first woman who returned my gaze, a young Puerto Rican with short jet-black hair, pretty despite the acne scars that pocked her face.

I followed her swaying hips down a narrow hall into a closet-sized room painted the same dirty pink and just big enough to hold a sagging twin bed. On the nightstand, the lamp's torn shade cast a ragged shaft of light on the blighted wall. In such tight quarters, it wasn't possible to turn my back to her—like so many other moments in my life.

Would she be horrified and send me away? A knot formed in the pit of my stomach. I was terrified of this young prostitute's reaction to my face and what she would think of my scarred chest. I never got out of my shirt—the thin layer of cotton was my only defense against the fear that nearly made me flee.

After a few words of awkward introduction, she motioned for me to sit on the frayed bedspread, then kneeled down in front of me. Seeing my nervousness, she patted my thigh and tried to reassure me with a wan smile. "Eet's okay." Her voice, practiced and accepting, was the nudge I needed. My adolescent blood now surging and my legs quivering with excitement, I watched as she deftly unbuttoned my jeans. For a fleeting second as she bent over me, I was oddly moved by the brown roots that showed in her part, but forgot everything as her moist lips closed around me.

Feeling physically drained and morally tarnished, I left quickly with my head down and scampered back down the stairs, anxious to breathe fresh air, or as fresh as I would find in New York. On my walk back to the subway, Simon and Garfunkel's song "The Boxer" popped into my head, the part about taking comfort from the whores on 7th Avenue to ease the loneliness. I realized I, too, had taken comfort there, but felt no less lonely for it.

"Two quiche Lorraines, one chef's salad, table sixteen. One bacon blues burger, rare, one steak sandwich, medium, table nine." A year and a half later, I was a line cook, having been promoted to the rank of kitchen staff and now working in tandem with the waiters. I even had the clout to send busboys and dishwashers on gofer errands and had become comfortable with my coworkers, many of whom I had worked with since I first started. Having gained admittance to their inner circle, I had been granted the ultimate gesture of trust: the sharing of an occasional joint in the basement recesses behind the lockers.

After work I was invited to their homes for get-togethers or to all-night diners to unwind over a cup of coffee. Once in a while we would join the "bridge and tunnel" crowd and go as a group into the city, occasionally heading to CBGB's, a punk rock club. I wasn't much of a drinker, whereas stoned I could relax and submerge myself in the pounding music. In a hypnotic trance, I scanned the room, taking in the neon-pink Mohawks and facial piercings, the tattoos, the bizarre makeup, hairstyles, and outlandish outfits.

There on the Lower East Side, I realized I didn't stick out at all. I could have shown up with my snake-head graft dangling in front of my face and still not have been the most outrageous. Would anyone have noticed? Was this where I belonged? Among the outcasts, misfits, and rebels?

On the way back to Jersey one night, we piled into the car we'd left at the train station and dropped off the couples along the way. Back in my room with the effects of the pot wearing off, I felt emptier than ever. Would I ever be loved? What woman would want a disfigured man who lived in an attic?

Miserable, I curled up in a fetal position and fell asleep hugging my pillow. Sometimes it seemed loneliness was the only thing that made me feel alive.

Late one afternoon, Shirl called me at work. "Your father and I are heading down your way. How 'bout making us lunch?"

"Absolutely! I'll make something special."

They both greeted me with warm smiles when they arrived, and it felt wonderful to hug them and to know my love was returned. Though the Office wasn't close to being a multi-star restaurant, I wanted to fix them something that would show off my creativity, so I was disappointed to see what they had ordered. Still, I made sure Shirl's salad and Ed's burger looked as appealing as possible.

I took my break with them afterward for coffee and cheesecake I had topped with extra cherries. While Ed dug into his dessert, Shirl updated me on everyone's life. Robin was seeing a guy in New Hampshire and doing well. "She's become a flower child," Ed interjected between bites,

Lisa was living in Arizona with her husband, Peter (they had gotten married the year before), and both would be attending college at ASU. After a "quick ceremony," as Shirl described it, Frank had married, and he, his wife, and baby girl were living in Washington State.

Then came Shirl's news. "Howie, you're not going to believe it. We're moving to New Mexico!"

I was taken aback and could only repeat, "Mexico?"

"No, honey, *New* Mexico." Knowing Ed, I wouldn't have been surprised if they meant Mexico.

"Why?" Cactuses and cowboys came to mind, but I had never been west of New Jersey.

Ed's eyes lit up. "It's a cheap place to live with great weather, and, well, what the hell, why not?" Now I understood: the operative word was "cheap."

Shirl, always the practical one, added, "We don't need a big house anymore. All you kids are grown now and, like your father said, why not?"

I was stunned, but when I saw how excited they were to be moving on, there was nothing to do but accept it. "Howie, come visit us. You know you're always welcome."

"I know, Mom, I will. I promise." The idea of exploring John Wayne landscapes did have a certain appeal.

When Ed asked for the bill, I refused and proudly signed for their lunch. Though a small gesture, it gave me great satisfaction.

I walked them outside where Shirl and I hugged good-bye on the sidewalk under the awning. We had been through so much and were bound together in ways no one else could understand. I tried not to cry with Ed looking on, but I couldn't hold back my tears. Unable to let go, we held each other in a long embrace, both of us weeping until Shirl broke away. Tenderly she cupped my face in her hands. "We both love you and always will. Never forget that."

Locking my eyes with hers, I silently mouthed, "I love you, Mom."

I turned to Ed and we stood looking at each other with our hands at our sides. We rarely spoke of our love; it was something understood and what Shirl called "being stubborn as mules." Suddenly, Ed opened his arms and drew me into the safe haven of his love that he had given me for so many years. He laid my head on his broad shoulder, his bear-like arms tightening around me as I wept, hugging me so close I could hear him choke back his tears. Patting me on my back, he turned his head to kiss me on the forehead and whispered, "I love you." Then they were gone.

An hour later, down in the stockroom, I was still feeling emotionally drained when it hit me how alone I really was—my family roots were shallow. Shirl and Ed were all I had, and now I was out of their lives. I didn't feel abandoned; it was more like what little identity I had, aside from my state number, left the restaurant with them.

I threw myself into work, and not until weeks later did I rejoin our "bridge and tunnel" group to go partying in Greenwich Village. Everyone was set on barhopping until closing, but Annie (the waitress I had a crush on) and I had had enough, so we headed back to Jersey. At the train station in Summit, she invited me to her apartment for tea and I accepted, not thinking anything of it since she had always been kind to me.

Her apartment exuded the same warmth she did and was nothing like the sparse attic I lived in. She put on a Cat Stevens record and told me to relax, then disappeared into a tiny kitchen. I circled the room filled with stacks of paintings and an easel against one wall, and browsed a shelf of family photographs, pausing at one of Annie as a small child leaning against a man I presumed to be her father. Studying it, I felt the void that no such picture existed for me.

I was swinging comfortably in the hanging rattan chair when she returned with our tea. After serving me, she sank down on a pile of throw pillows and pulled her legs up to her chest.

"You're a painter?" I asked.

Her eyes sparkled. "Yes! Would you like to see them?"

Flinging her red hair behind her shoulders, she told me about her art school as she pulled out a few of her favorites from a stack leaning against the wall. "Well, it's really just a community college, but I paint every day." Between sips of tea she told me about the artist she wanted to be. "Enough about me," she said, smiling. "I hardly know anything about you."

I shied away, feeling uncomfortable and reluctant to spoil things by talking about myself. Sensing my reticence, she didn't press me further. "It's okay, Howard. You don't have to explain anything."

To my great surprise she stood up, took my hand, and led me into the bedroom. Under the cover of darkness, lit only by the streetlight that filtered in from the street below, I stripped and crawled in next to her. The shock of our nakedness, of my skin touching hers, stilled me; my sordid encounter in Times Square was no preparation for the wonder I felt. Free of anxiety, judgment, or expectations, and with all the exuberance of my seventeen years, I lost my virginity.

In the morning I was awakened by the sound of curtains pulled aside and opened my eyes to a cup of hot tea placed on my pillow. Turning to her, I laughed with pleasure, my chest bared as I stroked her pale, luminous skin sprinkled with tiny freckles. I told her she looked like a country girl in a painting.

We saw each other almost daily at work but never spoke of our night together, only smiled at each other with our eyes when she picked up her orders from the line. I never said anything, too afraid to presume that a simple line cook living in an attic apartment had any right to wish there could be more such nights. I don't think she acted out of pity—I think compassion drove her and maybe intrigue. Perhaps we recognized some void in each other we could fill. Whatever it was, I knew instinctively it would never happen again. I also knew my future would not be completely dark.

Now that Ed and Shirl were in New Mexico, I began assessing my life, imagining how it could have been if I had "behaved," as Shirl would say, and had taken advantage of what prep school offered. Instead, I had practically guaranteed myself ever more challenging obstacles, and my self-imposed exile had likely cut off all avenues except that of line cook. I had to face up to my mistakes and take responsibility for the actions that had compromised my future, assuming I had one.

Hell, I should have tried harder.

My poor attitude and the blame I relentlessly heaped on myself made me increasingly ill-tempered. I started blowing little things out of proportion. One waitress was always a bit slow, and we often had to remake her orders. On a day when I had zero patience and her entrées were backing up and getting cold, I flipped her plates onto the floor. She burst into tears, and I realized I was becoming what Dr. Gratz had been with me: intractable and tyrannical. Yet I felt powerless to stop my behavior.

My ego, bolstered by the trust fund I would soon receive from the state when I turned eighteen, made me insufferable. While $60,000 was, for me, a staggering sum (and an amount I assumed would catapult me several rungs up the social ladder), no amount of money would ever compensate for the pain and loss I had suffered. Still, I waited anxiously for my birthday just months away—and for the money that would change my life.

Mike moved on and Disco Jeff became the manager. Nit-picking everything I did, he repeatedly wrote me up, threatening me that every incident would go into my "permanent file," as if he were going to forward it to the state. Tensions between us mounted.

One afternoon, he ordered me to change the oil in the deep-fryer, which I had already done. "Do it now or get a write-up, Howard. You're walking a fine line," he squawked, a poor polyester version of Mr. Butler at Bement.

"Things are going to be my way," he told me, his teeth clenched as he flexed his fists. "I'm the manager of this place. Do we have a problem?"

I stared at him thinking, yes, we have a problem—you are an ass. I realized that with Mike gone, Jeff was going to make my job hell. There was no point in dragging out the inevitable. I quit.

"You'll never work in this town again. I'll personally see to it!" he screamed after me. He was right about that. I wouldn't.

S I X

A FEW DAYS AFTER MY EIGHTEENTH BIRTHDAY, my social worker, Mrs. Brill, appeared at my boardinghouse. She suggested a diner nearby, and as we drove there, I thought of the many times she had ferried me around and of how we had forged a bond of sorts, despite the tenuousness of our relationship. Now all that was coming to an end.

We celebrated with banana splits, and when the waitress set them down before us, Mrs. Brill held up her finger and insisted I wait. A broad smile on her face, she pulled an envelope out of her purse and handed it to me.

Holding my breath, I ripped it open and pulled out the check. Slowly I exhaled. This was it, the moment I had been waiting for. But it was also the moment I had feared: no more state to fall back on, no more foster families, no free medical care, and no more caseworkers. It was a bittersweet moment, but a freeing one. And I knew the first thing I would do with my money.

I flew out to Albuquerque to visit Ed and Shirl for a week, the first time I was not only on a plane but also away from the East Coast. They seemed content with their new life and were nicely settled in a small home they had purchased in the foothills of the Sandia Mountains. The evening I arrived, we sat in their small xeric-scaped backyard of native plants and drank iced tea as the mountain turned watermelon pink at sunset. "This is how you do it out here," Ed told me. "Put some tea bags in a large glass jug, fill it with water, and let the sun do the rest! It's cheaper than that crap you get at the store."

He had definitely mellowed in his later years, but a lifetime of smoking and terrible eating habits had caught up with him. Despite being overweight, diabetic, and arthritic, he had opened a custom wheelchair business with the idea of revolutionizing the industry, though how he meant to achieve that I never understood.

They had done well with the sale of their house in New Hampshire but still didn't have enough to retire. Ed's small company was struggling, and Shirl, loyal as ever, was working as a nursing-home supervisor. I asked if they needed anything, even though I knew they were too proud to accept help. "No, we're fine," Ed said. "Once this thing takes off we'll be set, and your mother's got a great job, just in case."

Shirl rolled her eyes. Later in the kitchen, she confided that she would be working long after my father was in the grave. I offered money, wanting to do something to ease their lives and compensate in some small way for all they had done for me, but she hushed me and told me not to worry myself—everything was fine.

We celebrated that night. Shirl and Ed treated me to my first taste of local Mexican food at a little place that served authentic red and green chile. Ed had taken up wearing Western shirts and bolo ties, and Shirl was wearing cowboy boots. It was disturbing to see how easily they seemed to have left their old life behind.

The following day they took me on a tour of the area. Everything intrigued me—the vistas, the searing blue sky, the Native Americans waiting at bus stops, and even the tumbleweeds that bounced across the road. The spaciousness of the high desert was a world away from anything I'd known.

At night, sitting out on Ed and Shirl's patio and gazing up at the clear sky scattered with stars, I felt a deep sense of peace and security. Being with them made me realize how much I missed my family, especially Ed's no-nonsense reality checks and Shirl's unconditional love.

I couldn't tell them about my impulsive departure from my cooking job, considering they had both encouraged me to go to culinary school. They deserved to enjoy themselves at this stage in their lives, and I didn't want to worry them with my lack of direction.

———

Back in New Jersey again, I realized I had two options: stay in Jersey and find another restaurant job (and ignore Disco Jeff's promise that I'd never get hired in Summit again), or leave and see what else life had to offer. New Mexico excited me, and living close to Ed and Shirl would help ease my loneliness.

"Mom, it's Howard."

"Hi, honey, is everything okay?"

"Yes, fine, I'm all right. I just, uh . . ." Nervous and fearing the worst, I blurted into the phone, "Well, actually, I was wondering if you and Dad wouldn't mind if, uh . . ."

"You want to come out here?"

"Uh, yes."

"Are you in trouble?"

"No, no, I just quit my job, that's all."

"Of course you can. You're always welcome, Howie."

How good that was to hear. Years ago they had welcomed me into their home as an abandoned child, and now, as a young man, I was welcomed again. I wasn't surprised—she was my mom.

Anxious not to intrude on Ed and Shirl any longer than necessary and impatient to start my new adult life, I stayed only briefly. It was enough to know they were nearby. Within days I found an apartment in a vast complex called the Pines, aptly named because there were so many, though they seemed incongruous with the desert landscape. It was in a nice neighborhood and had all the amenities: a pool and clubhouse with a wet bar and pool table.

From my second-story apartment, I could look down on the picnic area and see neatly mowed lawns and pine trees among clusters of adobe-colored stucco buildings identical to mine. It was small with just the basics, but I was thrilled with my new place, despite the ugly stained carpet that emitted odors of cleaning fluids that hadn't done their job. For the first time I had two rooms to myself. I wouldn't have to put towels under the door to hide the evidence of cooking or walk down a hall to a shared bathroom. Best of all, I could wander around shirtless.

In the shower under a spray of hot water, I worried about how I was going to live surrounded by people I didn't know. Was I capable of interacting with strangers who weren't bound to me by school or work? Though I wasn't keen on setting myself up for rejection, I did want to meet people. Somehow I had to work up the nerve to do it.

I dipped further into my trust fund to buy a new stereo and color TV as well as a real bed with an actual headboard. I also bought a pair of rubber sandals like the ones I'd seen others wearing around the complex.

In 1979, Albuquerque was on the cusp between small-town mentality and big-town growth, its new skyline hinting at the city to come. Sprawling from the banks of the Rio Grande up into the foothills, it was bound on the east by the Sandia Mountains and to the west by mesas and the volcanoes beyond. With everything so spread out, I had no choice but to get some transportation.

No longer satisfied with a lowly moped, I raised my sights to a motorcycle, a shiny new silver Yamaha I taught myself to ride in the parking lots at the Pines. Not long afterward, when I picked up my driver's license (my first photo ID unrelated to my case number), I pondered my name, Shulman, and peered at my photo. It was then that I saw myself in a new light—a young man on his own, smiling for what lay ahead. The boy who had stood in front of a three-way mirror in Greenfield nearly a decade earlier was a distant memory.

Getting a job was far from my mind. I was enjoying the dazzling azure skies and fair weather that were nothing like the cloudy days and sweltering nights back east. In this new, beautiful place, I felt anything was possible. I explored the town and beyond, impulsively veering my motorcycle off on dirt roads that led to secluded ranches, wooded areas, and mountain trails. At roadside stands, I'd stop for a quick taco or burger and push on once more, never tiring of the scenery and the novel sight of riders on horseback, worn boots, oversized belt buckles, cowboy hats, and leather chaps.

Back at the Pines, I became a southwestern fashion neophyte: T-shirt, shorts, new sandals, and designer sunglasses. No more heavy winter coats, snow boots, or winter gloves! Now it was bright sunshine, swimming pool, and Coppertone suntan lotion. I sat alone by the pool with my shirt on and within days had become as dark as the Mexican gardeners working around the complex.

From my chair on the sidelines, I watched the girls in their skimpy bikinis bask in the sun while the men, fit and equally tan, lounged beside them for most of each day. No one seemed to have anywhere they needed to be. They all drank, smoked, and talked nonstop, interrupting one another.

When groups of two or three would disappear and return a few minutes later wiping their noses, it wasn't difficult to figure out what they were up to. I had to laugh at their attempts to be discreet. One guy's cocaine-induced paranoia had him constantly scanning the pool area, his head bobbing in all directions like a rooster's. Periodically, he would nod at me and raise an eyebrow, then turn his attention back to the rapid-fire conversation that streamed together in one continuous sentence.

I kept to myself. Dr. Gratz's reconstructions, designed more for function than cosmetic enhancement, had left my lips asymmetrical and the tip of my nose still protruding like a mini Ping-Pong ball, a look guaranteed to attract frequent glances. But after a while, everyone got used to my appearance.

"Hey you! Wanna beer?" I looked up to see a middle-aged guy greased up like a pig at a state fair holding up a can and beckoning me to join him, his East Coast accent sticking out as much as the tip of my nose. I accepted and was introduced to a few of his pool mates who came and went throughout the afternoon. They were an assorted cast: a bounty hunter, strippers, bartenders, and a few "semi-retireds," though retired from what I never found out.

I quickly adopted the Pines' mañana creed, the complete opposite of Ed's or Dr. Gratz's philosophy. After so many years of having to cater to everyone else's rules, I enthusiastically embraced the new lifestyle of sleeping late, hanging out at the pool, and partying till all hours. The smell of pot was as constant as the sunny sky, and before long I was indulging on a daily basis, even snorting a little coke, though neither drug was enough to liberate me from my inhibitions about shedding my shirt. I easily sidestepped the "Aren't you hot?" questions with excuses of sunburn.

About once a week I joined Ed and Shirl for dinner, after which we caught the occasional movie. They always wanted to know my plans.

"I don't know yet," I would say. "I'm getting adjusted."

"Getting adjusted! Hell, get a job." Ed was disappointed with my lack of motivation, but he would catch himself and raise his hands. "I know—it's your life. Do what you want."

Shirl was more understanding. "It's okay. Have some fun," she'd tell me. "Just be careful."

For months I drifted, doing nothing constructive. I was almost twenty and had learned how to survive—but what could I do to make something of myself?

It was then that I got to know Tom.

A clean-cut, athletic type from Kansas City, Tom was an exceptionally good-looking guy with thick, prematurely gray hair. Flashing a Hollywood smile and charming everyone with his easygoing personality, he was popular with the pool crowd. A couple of years older than I, he had moved to Albuquerque to go to business school, but dropped out for a career in pot dealing—nothing major, just enough to provide him with a classic Corvette convertible and sushi a few times a week. Basically, a life of leisure.

Tom never told me what he was doing. Seeing people in his apartment passing a bong around and occasionally disappearing into his bedroom and leaving with a shopping bag or backpack in hand didn't require an explanation.

My new, well-mannered friend came from a private-school upbringing and was a genuinely good guy. He shared my enthusiasm for fitness and never asked me personal questions unless something arose in the natural course of conversation.

One evening Tom invited me out for sushi. "Raw fish?" I grimaced. "You've got to be kidding. No way!"

"C'mon, man, you'll love it."

I cautiously sniffed at the bright red tuna fillet (I do have a good sense of smell) and detected no odor. Unconvinced that eating sushi in the New Mexico desert was wise, I pretended to take a bite.

"It's okay." Tom grinned as he helped himself to another piece. "It's an acquired taste."

We became good friends, working out together, visiting bars at night, and lounging around the pool. Tom was a heavy pot smoker, and in his company, so was I.

My six-month-long vacation had dramatically depleted my funds, and I had no alternative but to find a job. I applied for a line cook position at a hotel restaurant. Although paying just a few dollars over minimum wage, it was a start. A three-hundred-pound black man came lumbering out of the kitchen to interview me, wiping his huge hands on a towel slung over his shoulder, his eyebrows comically lifting when he saw me. Chester introduced himself and then asked the same question Mike had asked me at the restaurant in New Jersey. "You been in an accident?"

"Yeah, a long time ago."

"Oh. Can you cook eggs?"

"I was a cook for two years. Eggs aren't a problem."

Bright and early the next morning, Chester had me cracking flats of eggs. I hadn't lost my touch and caught my new boss observing me and nodding, looking impressed that I knew a thing or two about eggs.

For the next few months, I tolerated mind-numbing quantities of pancakes and eggs, before I gave up out of boredom and returned to lounging by the pool at the Pines.

As I was settling back into my indolent lifestyle, disaster struck. I remember the accident in slow-motion detail: the light switching from yellow to red, my motorcycle surging forward into the intersection, the peripheral view of two cars bearing down on me, and the ensuing spasm of fear seizing my body—all of it void of sound and taking only seconds.

As if in a bad dream, I lifted my head from the pavement and looked down in confusion at my shredded, blood-soaked jeans and my leg that lay strangely askew. Shock quickly turned to horror, and I screamed in pain, my panic rising when I saw the alarming amount of blood pooling under my leg.

Immobilized in the middle of the street and barely aware of the chaos around me, I willed the ambulance to hurry while I lay moaning between howls of pain. How bad was it? *Please, please, let my leg be okay.* Relief was short-lived when the paramedics arrived and I saw the tightness in their faces.

"Calm down, calm down. We know it's your leg. Where else does it hurt? Your back? Neck?"

"No, just my fuckin' leg! Give me morphine!"

"Calm down. What happened to your face?"

My mind registered the question but it made no sense to me. "My leg!" I screamed.

"We need to know!" Bewildered by my battered face, they didn't know what to diagnose.

"Screw my face—I need morphine!" I had spent enough time in hospitals and had seen enough episodes of *M*A*S*H* to know that morphine was my friend. Mercifully, one of them kneeled beside me and pushed up my sleeve. In no time I was floating above myself, oblivious to the pain.

Miraculously, an orthopedic surgeon was on duty when I arrived. Drugged, but determined to make sure there was no mix-up, I somehow managed with great difficulty to move my lips. "Leg . . . bad . . . face . . . okay."

Distantly I heard, "Understood—relax. Put him under." That was all I wanted to hear.

Hours later, I half-opened my eyes to blinding sunlight streaming through the window. Afloat in a realm somewhere between sleep and consciousness, I distantly registered the bed guardrails, then took in the room before my eyes came to rest on my leg and the plaster cast extending its entire length.

I fell back into a dreamless sleep, and when I finally awoke, it was to throbbing pain. I reflexively reached out for the nurse's buzzer, my old friend. By the time a nurse responded, I was deeply scared and begged her to give me more pain medication. Mercifully, she gave me the highest dosage I was allowed.

"Howard, Howard?" I struggled to understand the words. "Howard, I'm Dr. Trumbell. You have had a motorcycle accident. Howard, can you hear me?"

I tried to nod.

"Howard?" He raised his voice, attempting to penetrate my morphine haze.

I turned my head toward someone in white. "Your leg has sustained a lot of damage." Even in my sedated state, I knew this wasn't good news. "Howard, you've broken many bones. You will be laid up for quite a while."

Now comprehending, I was terrified. Losing my leg would threaten my survival, my independence. I stared at him in disbelief.

"Howard, you have a broken femur, ankle, and compound fractures in your tibia."

"M-y w-h-a-t?"

"That means your shin."

Too overwhelmed to absorb what he was saying, I continued to stare at him.

"Howard, are you on any medication?" I shook my head slowly, already knowing his next question. "How did you get those scars? A fire? Accident? Howard, I need to know so I can treat you."

The insistence in his voice rallied me. "B-i-r-t-h d-e-f-e-c-t-s, s-k-i-n g-r-a-f-t-s," I slurred, hoping I had put his mind at rest that I wasn't a psych ward patient who'd set himself on fire. Evidently my answer satisfied him because he vanished, and I slipped back into sleep, the only place I wanted to go.

It was a full week later before I was discharged. As always, Ed and Shirl were there for me when I needed them, both insisting that I come home with them while I convalesced. To be dependent on them again felt humiliating, but I was grateful for their help.

When I was finally able to return to my apartment, Shirl stocked me up with groceries, and Ed wanted to know if I could sue anyone. "No," I said. "It was my fault."

He shook his head. "You'll be okay, son." They were right. I did survive, not by my wits, but by the grace of God, Buddha, light, energy, or whatever power looked out for me.

Back at my apartment, I hobbled around, took my pain pills, and smoked pot as a kicker. For the next twelve weeks, with Tom's help, I managed to take care of myself. Self-medicating got me through each day, along with watching daytime TV, reading, and shoving a coat hanger down my cast in a futile attempt to relieve the itching.

Meanwhile, as my bank account shrank, my fear grew. How would I survive? What could I do? A salesman? Kinda tough—I wasn't the good-looking, glad-handing type. Manual labor? Working with Ed in New Hampshire was never something I excelled at and my leg couldn't handle it. Worries about employment dominated my thoughts, but my greatest concern was my leg: if, and to what degree, it was going to heal.

When the cast came off, I didn't recognize my leg. My once muscular thigh was puny and my calf the size of my forearm. A deep indentation that looked like a small ravine meandered down to my swollen foot. I fell into a deep depression.

I began to work out obsessively, first regaining flexibility in my knee and then progressing from leg lifts to weights until I finally added twenty-five-pound extensions. Years before, when my shoulder graft had been taken, I couldn't lift my arm for months, and later, when my left rib was removed, I could barely breathe. I fully recovered both times, so I knew I could do it again. As if possessed, I did leg presses and hamstring curls until I could do no more, and for hours, I'd limp alone around the university track, persisting until my foot had ballooned to the size of a football.

Eventually, I graduated to hobbling up the stairs of the nearby high school football stadium and then doing hundreds of push-ups and sit-ups out on the field. At the end of six months, I had regained almost complete use of my leg. I had to laugh—more body art! The new scar, a mere addition to my tapestry, didn't really matter. I was never going to be one of the Pines' most eligible bachelors anyway.

As my leg returned to normal, my cash finally ran out. Having few options, I ended up couch surfing at friends' homes and scraping together $4.99 every day for the nearby all-you-can-eat Chinese buffet—a small step above hospital food.

One afternoon when I was at Tom's place recounting my financial woes and homeless state, he said off-handedly, "I think I may have a solution to your problems."

"Yeah, what?" I had a good idea what he was about to propose, and it wouldn't be a nine-to-five gig.

"I have a small pot farm twenty miles south of here. Do you want to sit on it and water the plants? Most of the work has already been done."

"How long and how much?"

Tom smirked and fixed his eyes on mine. "A couple of months. We should get, say, between thirty and forty pounds, $1,500 a pound. Your share would be a third." He looked away briefly, most likely calculating in his head, as was I. "For you, around twenty grand, I'd say."

When I didn't answer, he prodded. "Well, what do you think?"

"I don't want to go to jail."

Tom gave a knowing laugh. "You have no priors, right?"

"Nope."

"You'll get probation the first time."

Probation, like at Bement, only doing roadwork instead of digging up dandelions.

"Look," Tom said, "meet my partner, Roy. He's the one who knows all about growing. You can think about it and let us know."

"Is he cool?"

"Don't worry, this is my third year with him. I sat on a farm once. It worked out."

Tom went on to tell me that Roy was originally from Baltimore and had done time for robbing a liquor store.

"A liquor store! What is he, an idiot?"

"No, an ex-heroin addict. His partner fell asleep at the wheel. He was strung out but now he's okay. Roy's like a pot doctor."

An ex-junkie, an all-American guy, and me. Some trio.

Leaning back on the couch, Tom lit up a joint for me to sample his harvest. "It's simple," he said, pausing for a long toke he then slowly exhaled. "All you have to do is connect some hoses to the trailer spigot and hang out so we don't get ripped off."

Despite the high-grade pot beginning to take effect, I still had the presence of mind to ask, "Ripped off? By who?"

"Anyone wandering by. If someone's there they won't pry. Pull the hose out early in the morning, water each plant, and add chemicals and nutrients as we go along. Help manicure and that's it. You get busted, I pay your lawyer and you get five grand. Deal?"

By now I was totally stoned, which was probably not the best time to embark on a new career. But where else could I make that kind of money that fast?

"Deal," I said, shaking his hand. I was about to become a farmer of cash crops.

A few days later I met Roy when he came by to pick me up. A tall, rail-thin guy with scraggly shoulder-length hair, he wore oil-stained jeans and battered work boots. His slightly amused air and gentle manners immediately won me over.

His old pickup was full of holes and had a badly dented rear bumper. I threw my small bag in the back and jumped into the cab, anxious to see what I had gotten myself into.

Roy drove hunched over the steering wheel, his eyes glued to the road, happily reminiscing about the cars he'd found and rebuilt, including the Corvette he had sold to Tom. A Marlboro Light wagged between his lips the entire way. No, I wasn't looking for a fancy car out of this deal, I told him, just some money to get back on my feet.

Miles later we left the highway and angled off down a rutted, dusty road, the desert stretching out on in all directions. There was no air-conditioner, so we had to keep the windows rolled down, and when clouds of sand billowed into the cab, we both fell silent. Humbled by the stark landscape that spread out before us, I kept thinking, *Jesus, what have I done?*

At the end of the road, a dilapidated tan trailer stood desolate against the desert backdrop. "Here we are!" Roy grinned. "This is it!" Before his feet hit the ground, he had a joint in his mouth.

"You've got to be joking!"

"What did you expect, the Hilton? You've got to blend in." This blended in all right, like a shit box in the middle of fuckin' nowhere.

When we opened the door at the top of three makeshift steps, a blast of scorching air nearly knocked us over. "I stayed here on and off in the beginning," Roy said. "It's not so bad."

I glanced at the shabby furniture and cheap linoleum floor and knew that this wasn't one of those luxury models featured in *Mobile Home Living.*

"Home sweet home," Roy said, laughing. "You've got a TV, radio, couch, and double bed."

Next on the grand tour was the operation itself. About twenty-five yards from the trailer stood a new two-car garage. When Roy opened the side door, I was surprised to step into a miniature jungle in the desert, underneath an open expanse of clear blue sky.

For the next ten weeks, my day started at 5 a.m. I'd haul out garden hoses, connect them, and then feed the end through a hole in the side of the structure. After each plant got a thorough soaking (the parched earth sucked up the water like Roy did his joints), I stashed the hoses and spent my free time, which was about twenty-three hours a day, working out with weights, watching TV, or fighting off boredom by reading bits and pieces from a partial set of *Encyclopedia Britannica* I'd found in the bedroom closet.

In the beginning my paranoia almost got the best of me, isolated as I was in this remote alien landscape. Blue-tailed lizards slithered around my trailer, keeping me company by day, and at night the howl of coyotes floated across the open desert, unsettling me and disturbing my dreams. My imagination ran wild. Hearing the rustle of sagebrush blowing in the wind, I was convinced cops had surrounded my trailer and were only waiting for the signal to bust me. Every sound made me jump, and I'd have to calm myself with one of Roy's joints to get back to sleep. Somehow I got through it.

Roy, meanwhile, taught me the entire process: how to start the seedlings, dig the holes, and add the nutrients—everything to do for optimal yield. When the plants reached maturity, he taught me how to manicure (trim and cure) the crops. Finally, when my part of the enterprise was done, Tom sold my cut of the harvest to his established clientele.

I spent that winter at the Pines trying to figure out my next move. I kept thinking about the pot farm. Why couldn't I do the same thing but on a larger scale? Tom now lived in California, and before leaving, he had introduced me to his Mexican connection, Carlos, and had given me his Pines customers who bought small quantities of inexpensive pot.

I arranged to meet Roy and pitched him my idea, inviting him to be my partner.

"No way," he said. "I've been busted a couple of times. It's too big."

So we cut a deal: To minimize his risk, he would be my consultant and give me good seeds, though he'd get a smaller percentage. I would find a place and put up the money. All he had to do was help me set up our operation.

I had become an entrepreneur before I even knew what the word meant.

I got busy perusing the rental ads in small-town newspapers, hoping to find something remote yet within a fifty-mile radius of Albuquerque. Most of the properties advertised were more suitable for horse owners, survivalists, or hermits, but I checked out a few that sounded promising, telling the owners I was a writer and needed solitude. The place I settled on was an old, isolated frame house about forty miles out of town. It had the bare bones of a stove, a dilapidated refrigerator, and plenty of room for manicuring the harvest.

Then I met with Carlos. Not much more than five feet tall in his ostrich-skin cowboy boots, and maybe a hundred ten pounds, he proudly flashed his gold Rolex. He was a decent sort and, better yet, had had a good relationship with Tom, who vouched for me. Luckily, Carlos spoke a little English.

"I need someone to sit on a small *mota* farm," I told him. "I'll give you two thousand dollars to find me someone. But you must trust him."

"Two thousand for me? *Bueno, no hay problema.* My cousin Hector."

"He lives here, *aquí?*"

"*Sí, Sí.* He go right away for you."

Wow! That was fast.

"Carlos, Hector can't leave for *tres meses*." I held up three fingers. "Three months. No car."

"*Entiendo*. I understand. ¿*Cuanto*? How much for him?"

"*Sí, mucho*. Tell him $10,000. I need to know *pronto*. Understand?"

"*Sí, no hay problema*."

A couple of weeks later, Carlos showed up with Hector, who, to my surprise, had brought along his wife, Marta. Like me, they were in their early twenties, probably trying to get a head start. I was concerned that he didn't speak any English, but Marta spoke a little, and I could tell she was the one in charge.

On the way to my mountain property, I picked up a Spanish-English dictionary and then spent the summer learning some Spanish while I worked with Hector, a man of few words. He came from a family of farmers in northern Mexico and taught Roy and me better irrigation techniques. In no time our little operation was shaping up nicely.

Plump and giggly, Marta was easy to have around. Once a week she gave me her shopping list of groceries and laughed when I'd tell her not to work so hard.

"*No problema*, Mr. Howard. Is okay."

In the *barrio bodegas* in Albuquerque's South Valley, I picked up the corn meal, tortillas, fresh hot chiles, and pork on her list. And, man, could she cook! On my return trips to the farm, I always looked forward to when we would all sit together and enjoy her enchiladas and tamales. How Hector remained skinny was beyond me.

Thank God everything went as planned. I paid them generously, and when Marta and I hugged good-bye, I sighed with relief that our summer adventure was safely over. In parting, Marta said a prayer for me. I didn't tell those good people I prayed they would never again have to do my kind of farming.

It turned out that one of my customers at the Pines, Bob, had a friend in Boston who could sell my entire crop. To find a sole buyer was ideal, and that he was in Boston was especially attractive since the East Coast commanded higher prices than New Mexico.

"You sure this guy's okay?" I asked Bob.

"He's all right. I grew up with him. Tom sent him product and we never had a problem."

I flew out to meet my prospective partner, an Italian named Jimmy. Supposedly he was trustworthy and not someone who would waste my time. It sounded like he met my criteria perfectly.

Jimmy picked me up at Logan Airport in a late-model Mercedes. Forty or so, he extended his hand with a smile. He looked like any suburban middle-aged man, a bit pudgy but muscled, the typical preppie businessman in his khaki pants, polo shirt, and Adidas.

"You're from New Mexico?" he asked as we drove.

I knew he was sizing me up. But then, I was doing the same. "No, I'm from Jersey and went to school out here."

"Really? All right, that's good."

When we arrived at the airport hotel, he circled it a few times to see if we were being followed. I told him to go around again to ease his mind. "Just making sure, pal," he said.

Jimmy already had the key to the room, and the minute we were inside, he turned to me. "Strip," he said.

"What?"

"You heard me. Strip. I don't know you. I want to check you out."

I couldn't let him take complete control, but I needed to assure him I wasn't a cop. I also realized that stripping would give me the advantage of shock value. So I quickly removed my shirt and pants and watched his mouth drop at the sight of my scarred, muscular body.

"What happened to you?"

"I fell. Who the fuck cares. You happy?"

"Yeah . . . yeah . . . you're okay."

"Yeah, I'm okay, so now what?" I asked, zipping up my jeans.

Jimmy wasn't the usual Boston *guido* pot dealer. College educated and no dummy, he was a good guy who wanted to make some extra cash.

"Here's the deal, Jimmy. I have a lot of high-grade product, not that Mexican commercial weed." I handed him a sample.

He raised it to his nose for the "stink test," then nodded, satisfied with the pungent odor that attested to its quality, and the lack of seeds and stems. "You're right, this is good shit."

We discussed price, delivery, and schedule of payment.

"Can you get me some good Mexican stuff in quantity?" he asked.

"Not a problem. I have a contact in Mexico who's a friend of mine."

His eyebrows shot up. I knew I had his attention. "Okay," he said. "Arrange it and come back in two weeks."

"No, no, I need some cash up front."

"Tell you what. I'll pay you half up front and give you the other half in two weeks. Then we'll move on, all right?"

At the agreed-upon price, it was worth it. "Done," I said, shaking his hand.

Working with Carlos would be the key to my transition from growing to shipping. I was tired of sitting alone for months on acres of crops.

"Hey, kid," Jimmy said. "This is no joke. You know what you're getting involved in?"

"Yeah, I get it."

"You understand, anything happens on your end, the trail stops there. You get what I'm saying?"

"Yeah, what's your point?" I took his insinuation seriously but was not about to let him intimidate me.

"Hey, you get busted wherever you are, we can reach out and touch you." His voice had turned steely.

"What are you? A fucking AT&T commercial? I heard you the first time."

That got a small chuckle, and again we shook hands. "Good, we understand each other," he said.

Within a few weeks we were on our way to a mutually profitable partnership. Jimmy came through with my harvest payment, and Carlos made good on his word. "Sí, sí, my friend, forever you want," which meant whatever I needed.

In the beginning we shipped Jimmy as much as he could move by way of Tom's time-tested method: the US mail. I would pack three or four boxes of product, each shipment packed with one carton inside another, and each bundle inside wrapped in six inches of plastic. As an added precaution to disguise the odor, I generously sprinkled baby powder and coffee grounds between each layer before shipping the boxes to Jimmy's associate who owned a retail store.

After nearly six months of using this method, we decided it would be wise to switch delivery tactics. And to keep up with Jimmy's demands, it seemed logical for me to make a quick run myself. So I packed a small trunk and a large hard-shell Samsonite suitcase and booked a private cabin on Amtrak. I didn't want to risk driving across the country and couldn't trust anyone else to do it. Besides, what could be simpler or more comfortable than traveling by train? In my private cabin, I'd be protected from inquisitive passengers and as relaxed as I could be, under the circumstances.

I squeezed my oversized luggage into my tiny cabin and kept to myself, leaving only to go to the dining car for meals. As far as my fellow passengers knew, I was just another traveler. The lulling metallic clack of wheels on rails and the ever-changing scenery both soothed and distracted me. I arrived as planned.

Things went so well I repeated the routine another four or five times. On what would be my final trip, as we pulled into Chicago, where I had a layover before heading on to Boston, the train slowed to a crawl on its approach to the platform. Looking out the window, I saw five men running alongside the train, badges in hand. I had to blink several times to make sure I wasn't having a bad dream.

How could the Drug Enforcement Agency be on to me? My heart began racing wildly, almost beating out of my chest. Telling myself not to panic, I struggled to compose myself.

I hurriedly gathered my luggage, thinking I could exit from the other end of the train—no, that was too obvious and might raise suspicion. I heard voices outside my door and froze. One of the agents was asking a porter about a passenger in a private cabin. *Fuck!* Then the agent mentioned someone else's name, and my legs nearly buckled with relief. I had to get out of this metal trap fast, without getting tangled in other people's problems. But how?

Screw it! I would walk right through them. Who'd be that stupid? Me, but what else could I do?

Stepping off the train, I waved down a porter with an empty cart. Quickly I helped him load my precious cargo. "Let's go!" I said.

"But sir, I need to fill up my cart."

"Look, I'm really late. How's twenty?"

"Sir, yes sir!" And off we went.

In the relative safety of the waiting room, I was still rattled and knew I had to stay on high alert. I settled uncomfortably into a seat among a dozen other passengers, who were distractedly watching soaps and game shows on miniature, coin-operated TVs they steadily fed with quarters. Wedged in a seat near mine, an overweight woman stuffed her face with snacks as she kept her eyes glued to a life-and-death scene on *As the World Turns*, while I grappled with my own drama, one unrelieved by commercial interruptions. Staring at the 1970s decor of color bands circling the walls of the sizable room, I felt as if I were back in a hospital emergency room, but this time with baggage.

With an hour to kill before my train departed, I slumped forward, my head in my hands. *Shit, shit, SHIT! Okay, I'll leave, get a hotel. No. Put my luggage in a station locker. No, that won't work, too damn big. Am I being watched? No, they would have grabbed me. Maybe they want to see who I'm meeting. Okay, to hell with it. I'll just get up and walk away. No, I can't—I'll owe Carlos. Then what? I'll be wiped out, that's what.*

From the doorway I heard a commanding voice. "Ladies and gentlemen, DEA. No one move! We will be conducting a baggage search."

I looked up to see my suited greeting party standing shoulder-to-shoulder, badges in hand, and exhaled in defeat. *This is it. I'm done for. Illinois Department of Corrections, here I come.* Dread seized my body as visions of me in an orange jumpsuit locked up with hard-core criminals crowded out all other thought. *Well, at least I'm not pretty, so the inmates should leave me alone.*

The agents systematically spread out to conduct their search, the largest guy positioning himself to block the exit. With all the willpower I could muster, I concentrated on breathing normally and staying calm. Resigned to my impending arrest, I lowered my head, then picked up the paper on the seat next to me and pretended to read. The print swam meaninglessly before my eyes. The paper could have been upside down and I wouldn't have noticed.

Two shiny black shoes appeared on the patch of dingy blue carpet in front of my downcast eyes.

"Hello, son, where are you headed?"

Jail, was my sinking thought. I looked up and tried to come across as meek as possible. "Boston, for Thanksgiving, sir." I had deliberately worn a University of New Mexico *Lobo* sweatshirt to pass as a college student, the gray wolf displayed prominently on my chest.

"Going to see family?"

"Yes, sir."

"That's nice. Would you mind if we check your bags?"

My heart lurched. "No, sir." I quickly complied, willing my hands to steady as I reached for the shiny locks on my Samsonite case, readying myself to launch into a lost-key routine.

Just as my fingertips touched the locks, I felt a light double tap on my shoulder. "That's okay, son, you're good to go. Have a nice holiday."

I looked up at him, praying my shock didn't show. "Thank you, sir. You too."

I watched the agent walk away, then glanced up at the monitors. Twenty minutes to go before departure. Forcing myself to go slow, I picked up my bags and casually walked out of the waiting room where I hailed a porter pulling a large dolly. As we leisurely made our way across the crowded center of the station, I again spotted my DEA buddies not twenty feet away, a knot of them gathered under the large ornate clock. The same agent who had let me go made eye contact with me and raised the hand that moments before had tapped me on the shoulder. My heart pounding, I could barely breathe until I realized he wasn't motioning me to him but giving me a friendly wave and wishing me a good trip. Smiling, I waved back and kept walking.

Settled safely in my private cabin, my bags stowed and the door locked, I sat to watch the crowd outside and wait for my DEA savior to realize his mistake. "God," I whispered, "if you get me out of this, I will never do it again, I swear." I had never asked him for anything before any of my surgeries, so this time I figured perhaps he owed me one.

On a small pullout shelf sat a hospitality basket containing fruit and snacks and, most conveniently, two mini-bottles of wine. If there was ever a time for me to take up drinking, this was it. Before the train pulled away, I had already torn open one bottle and guzzled it down, a good amount of it spilling on my *Lobo* sweatshirt.

When the train lurched forward, I cracked the second bottle open and downed it at a more civilized pace, but found it had little effect on my nerves that shook more than the passenger car as we pulled out. Watching the Chicago skyline recede in the distance, I strained to order my thoughts and considered my options—from tossing my bags out the window to getting off at the next stop.

Once we had entered the countryside, I headed to the dining car for more wine. Several glasses later, and on legs most unsteady (the motion of the train not helping), I staggered back to my cabin. In my tiny box of a room, I paced back and forth until from sheer exhaustion, I lay down and fell asleep.

Thinking it wise to alter my route, I got off three stops before Boston and took an expensive cab ride into the city. My peace of mind was worth it.

"You're kidding, right?" Jimmy's eyes widened when I told him about my harrowing near-arrest after we met up at a hotel in Cambridge.

"Do I look like I'm joking?"

"No, no. Jesus, you're a lucky son of a bitch!"

After hearing my tale, Jimmy was paranoid that I was being followed. We transferred my cargo into his car and headed into Boston, darting through a maze of side streets while I kept my eyes on the side-view mirror. By the time we reached our stash house, we had agreed it was time to revise our method of transport.

We decided to hit it hard for the next year or so, move as much by car as we could, and get out. Jimmy recruited a few "associate" drivers, one of whom was a widow from the South Shore. Who was going to stop a grandmother? Carlos supplied a few couriers as well.

I had to impress upon Carlos that we needed to get a lot more product and at a better price, so I proposed a new arrangement.

"I'd like you to take me to Mexico, to your *amigos, porque* no more small shit, no. I won't cut you out. You know that I need you."

"*Sí, sí,* Eduardo. (I was Eduardo to him because he couldn't pronounce Howard.) *No hay problema.* I know the big *hombres.*"

"Really?"

"*Sí,* my cousin's husband is the uncle of . . ."

I didn't even try to make sense of Carlos's family tree of pot connections, and I knew enough to present Jimmy as my *tío* (uncle), knowing that Carlos trusted family more than outsiders.

"They go to the Chicago, *Nuevo York*," he said, flourishing his hand, as if they were in the business of delivering milk or newspapers. "Forever you want."

In size Carlos might have been a bantam rooster, but when it came to loyalty, he was a giant. Like Jimmy, I wanted to have a nice stash of money when we walked away from all this, and with Carlos's help, I could pull it off. Judging by the amount of business we'd done together, I figured Carlos had to have done well, and with a wife and kids, he wasn't about to get careless. Besides, I trusted him implicitly. It was time to take advantage of his connections while I could.

"*Bueno*, Carlos. Let's do it."

Within days Carlos and I set off for Juárez, Mexico, making good time in his Chevy pickup. Four hours later we crossed the border and were soon bouncing along a poorly maintained road that wound through cactus and desert for another ten miles. Abruptly he slowed and turned into a long driveway that led to a large concrete-walled compound.

I climbed down and stretched, taking my time while I tucked in my shirt to check out the half-dozen other late-model American trucks, each freshly detailed and fitted with expensive hubcaps. I glanced up at the primitive yet effective security of jagged broken bottles imbedded along the top of the high wall and the heavy grilles on all the windows. Large but unassuming, the place was a veritable fortress.

After nodding to Carlos that I was ready, he turned and led me through a dusty courtyard into the sprawling hacienda, the cool, shaded interior a welcome relief from the glaring midday sun. At the far end of an expanse of gleaming terra-cotta floors, five men gathered around an open bar and the biggest TV screen I had ever seen.

The men, all wearing cowboy hats and exotic-skin boots and holding Coronas, turned to greet us. Calling out Carlos's name, they slapped him on the back and heartily shook our hands. Relaxed yet focused, I had no reservations about being there. I didn't owe anyone money and so had no reason to worry. Hell, I was probably the one who had paid for one or two of the trucks parked outside.

I pegged the man in charge, the one everyone addressed as *El Jefe*, "the boss." His hat was bigger, his spit-shined boots more exotic, and he wore a massive, saucer-size silver belt buckle displaying a longhorn inscribed with "Juárez." While the others bantered in Spanish, I sipped my icy Corona and watched *El Jefe*, each of us sizing up the other. Even if my Spanish were better, they spoke so rapidly it would have been impossible for me to follow them, but I caught a few words—"*dinero . . . gringo.*" After observing the dynamics of the group for a few minutes, I asked Carlos who was in charge.

He jerked his head toward *El Jefe*, whom I greeted in my *gringo* Spanish. "*Señor, mucho gusto. Gracias a estar en su casa. Mucho respecto, señor. Lo siento mi español es más o menos.*" I could tell *El Jefe* appreciated my respect and effort to speak his language, limited as it was.

"Carlos, he knows who I am? All the money I have paid you?"

"*Sí, sí,* Eduardo."

"Okay, tell him I have given you a lot of money for a long time with *no problema*. My uncle in Boston needs *mucho mota*. We no longer want to do small shipments."

With a nod, *El Jefe* let us know he understood but fired back his decision. Carlos translated for me: "No. Everything stays the same. Not bigger shipments."

I hadn't come this far not to make my point and knew it was my only chance. What were they going to do, kill me? Screw it!

I slammed my palm down on his massive coffee table and glared at *El Jefe*, my face contorted in a way that made most people look for an exit. "*Señor*, this is business. We want to do a lot for eight, ten months. Make a lot of money *rápido* and then *finito*. I always pay you, no games. I come here showing you respect, but you don't respect me or my uncle." I hated insulting him, but it was this or nothing.

Carlos stared at me, his eyes wide in shock.

"Translate," I told him. "I don't care. Do it!"

After digesting my Academy Award performance, *El Jefe* cracked a broad smile and answered Carlos in such rapid Spanish I could only pick out a few words. Carlos smiled, then translated for me. "Eduardo, he say you no lie. He look you in the eyes. He say you speak from the *corazón*, the heart."

I looked at *El Jefe*. "*Gracias, señor.* I do."

He rose to his feet to shake my hand and, speaking in Carlos's English, he said "*No problema.* Forever you want."

With nothing more than a gentleman's handshake, we sealed the deal, and a few weeks later, we were on our way. Over the next year we made multiple trips to Boston using various drivers. I had never wanted to make a career out of dealing and never lost sight that one mistake could land me back in the state system—and this time it would not be in a foster home.

Though it was no excuse, our burgeoning operation had kept me from seeing much of Ed and Shirl. During the previous year, Ed's health had deteriorated so much that Shirl had sold the house in Albuquerque and moved back to New Jersey, where it should have been easy for me to run down for a visit after taking care of business in Boston. But it was never convenient; I was caught up in the fast life I was leading. Next trip, I'd promise myself. I did occasionally call, but that was due more to feeling guilt than to making time for them.

For Ed and Shirl, however, it was if they had come full circle, back to the days when they'd first met at the VA hospital and she had nursed him back to health, only this time there would be no recovery. When diabetes finally cost Ed his leg, she had no choice but to put him in a nursing home, their lifetime together ended. Young and selfish and believing I'd always have another chance to visit, I didn't know then that sometimes in life it's simply too late.

Months later when Shirl called, I knew something terrible had happened. "Howie, Dad died last night, a heart attack," she said, crying, her tears muffled by the many miles that lay between us.

Ed, never idle a day in his life, was gone. It didn't seem possible. I listened to the arrangements Shirl had made, but all I could think of was how I would never get to see my dad again.

"Howie, are you there? Howie!"

"I'm here, Mom." In shock, I tried to follow what she was saying. "Saturday . . . Belleville . . . funeral . . . only sixty years old, I can't believe it . . . You're coming, right, Howie?"

"I'll be there, Mom. It'll be okay." I rang off and sat for a long while staring out the window.

Ed's ashes were already waiting at Shirl's when I arrived the evening before the funeral. It had been ages since all of us had been together. Though the mood was somber, we were soon laughing over pizza, Shirl's and my sisters' eyes welling with tears at our Ed stories: about how he couldn't stand to be without some project in hand and what a cheapskate he was.

"Remember how he always said that when he died, just roll him into the gutter?" I laughed. "I can hear him now," I said, slipping into my best Ed impersonation: "'I don't want any of that funeral crap. They just rip you off with overpriced coffins for stiffs who couldn't care less. I'm telling you kids, do me and yourselves a favor and save your money.'" He was getting most of what he'd asked for: a cremation and a modest urn for his ashes.

Reminiscing until far too late, we had to scramble the next morning to get to the cemetery. When we were halfway there, I grabbed the back of the driver's seat and yelled, "Shit! Frank, stop the car! Jesus, we forgot Ed!" In our rush out the door, no one had remembered to pick up the urn from the kitchen table where it had sat while we ate and talked into the night. I swear I could almost hear Ed chuckling.

At the cemetery our forlorn little group picked its way to the plot, our collars turned up against the chilly spring morning. The solemnity of our task engulfed us in silence as we huddled together at the graveside, Frank, Lisa, Robin, and I surrounding Shirl.

The smell of upturned earth blindsided me with regret as vivid memories of childhood gardens surfaced, as if just yesterday Ed and I had worked the soil. So much rebellion and resentment, and for what? To fight a man whose immensity of heart I could never hope to equal, who'd had the courage and generosity to open his home to a strange and broken child who desperately needed a family.

Like a tidal wave churning up the ocean floor of a childhood long past, realization of what this man had done for me, his foster son, crashed over me. All he wanted was that I grow to be strong and whole, prepared for a world often hostile to the likes of me. Adamant that I never indulge in self-pity, he wanted me to learn how to stand on my own two feet and face the world without fear.

Ed was my *real* father, the one who'd guided me and taught me what being a man really meant. Why now, just when I could appreciate the sacrifice he'd so willingly made, was my time with him cut short? When the urn containing Ed's remains was placed in the ground, I staggered with the weight of what I'd lost. This, I realized, was good-bye forever—good-bye to the man who had done everything in his power to give me a fighting chance. Now, when it was too late, I ached to tell him his lessons had been heeded, that his efforts hadn't been in vain. *I'll be okay, I promise. Good-bye, Dad. I love you.*

Tough as I thought I was, I bowed my face to his tombstone and wept.

Home again, I dealt with losing Ed by burying myself deeper in work. I needed the distraction and, fortunately, between scheduling drivers, coordinating pickup and delivery, and managing the considerable stress, I had plenty to keep me occupied.

The sheer volume of cash I was taking in presented a real problem. I had dozens of bank safety deposit boxes all over the place, and more than once I had to ask the bank clerk to leave the vault so I could stand on my money to get the lid on the box to close.

For what would be our last trip, Carlos arranged for his friend José, who spoke little English, and his Chicana wife, Debbie, to drive a shipment for us to Plymouth, Massachusetts. I gave José a beeper number he was to call when he arrived at the Howard Johnson motel where we were to meet, after which I would call him back from a pay phone.

On schedule, I received his call but noticed it was a New Hampshire area code, not the 617 for Massachusetts.

"*Señor* Eduardo, *we aquí.*"

"You here? No, José, you're not here. I'm *aquí.*"

Silence.

"José? Put Debbie on the *teléfono.*"

"Yes, Eduardo?"

"Debbie, where are you?" I kept my voice calm to avoid exciting them.

"We here at the Plymouth."

"Debbie, listen to me. It's just a little mix-up. You're in the wrong state. You're in Plymouth, New Hampshire, not Plymouth, Massachusetts. It's nothing that can't be fixed, okay?"

In the background I could hear Debbie berating José. "You *estúpido*. Is no the New Hampshire Plymouth, is the Massachusetts Plymouth."

Seconds later she was back on the phone. "Ayeee, so sorry, Howard."

"Debbie, it's okay. Do you have a map?"

"Yes, yes."

"All right, it's only a few hours away—don't speed. Beep me when you get here, okay?"

"Okay, Eduardo, no problem."

I hung up, shaking my head in disbelief. Jimmy, who had been listening, had caught the gist of the conversation and moaned. "They went to New Hampshire? Jesus, are you serious? The wrong fucking state?"

"Relax, it'll be fine."

Although José and Debbie delivered the goods later that night, Jimmy and I agreed it was a sign to quit. Our enterprise hadn't made me rich, but the half million or so nest egg I'd stashed in various places was enough to try my hand at something legitimate. I'd still run my modest marijuana operation in New Mexico while I looked for other business opportunities, but I was done with smuggling for my East Coast clients.

SEVEN

EMOTIONALLY EXHAUSTED, ALL I WANTED was to settle down. After looking around, I found a small 1940s New Mexico–style house for sale in Albuquerque's up-and-coming Nob Hill district, a neighborhood that was yuppie personified, with sushi bars, coffee houses, and boutiques all within walking distance. I bought a used BMW and tried to blend in as best I could. A home of my own gave me some sense of security but did little to ease my painful loneliness.

At Tom's invitation, I flew out to California for the Long Beach Grand Prix Formula One streetcar race. For the few days I was there, outside of a nice meal in San Diego one evening and driving around, we kept to La Jolla where he had an apartment.

California was everything the East Coast wasn't. I'd never seen pedestrians wait for a light to change with no car in sight. Who would do that?

My amusement came to an end one afternoon when I was riding Tom's bike through a park overlooking the ocean. The next thing I knew, I was on my back flanked by two men in white shirts. Confused, I felt my arm tighten and looked down to see a blood pressure cuff. I tried to pull away, my trusty fight-or-flight response. Where the hell was I?

"What's your name?"

I stared at the paramedic, unable to speak. Gradually, my head began to clear. "How-ard," I managed to say.

"Howard, you had a seizure. Are you on medication? Have you taken any drugs? A few people saw you go into convulsions. We're going to take you to the hospital, okay?"

"No . . . no . . ."

"Howard, we need to check you out."

"No, I'm fine."

"Howard, you may have hit your head."

"I'm okay, really. I just fell."

Against their wishes and my better judgment, they reluctantly let me go. I have no idea how I managed to get back to Tom's, but a few days later, it occurred to me I'd be an idiot if I didn't get my seizure, or whatever it was, checked out. After some tests that failed to turn up anything suspicious, the doctor pronounced me fine. Relieved, I put the episode out of my mind.

I flew back to Boston for the balance Jimmy owed me, but after finding out he'd be delayed a week, I decided to go to New York and explore the city.

On Fifth Avenue, I got out of the cab and ducked into the hushed lobby of the St. Moritz Hotel. It was the kind of beautiful spring day that made me miss the East Coast's spectacular changing seasons, so after checking in, I crossed the street and wandered through Central Park. Then feeling hungry, I decided to do what every NYC tourist does— have a hot dog. Sitting in the shade of the boathouse by the pond, I savored my lunch as I gazed up at the blue sky rimmed by skyscrapers and treetops. A perfect day, a delicious hot dog—it suddenly struck me. Life was okay.

Shopping was the perfect way to get rid of my small bills, so I doubled back to Fifth Avenue. In Saks I wandered the aisles, aware of the fashionably elegant women and their once-over dismissive appraisals of me. As I watched them browsing for Gucci bags and designer perfumes, their faces taut and unnatural, I pondered the irony that was apparently lost on them. Distorted by face-lifts and thereby robbed of character, their faces were every bit as disfigured as mine.

Out on the street again, I chose the perfect destination—Barney's, six floors of men's fine clothing. Enough of Bement's conservative blue blazers and Docksiders; it was time to move up to Italian suits and shoes. When I completed my classic selections—flashy isn't my style—I paid with my roll of bills tightly bound with a rubber band.

Next on my list, a simple, silver-banded European watch. As I slipped it on, I could hear Ed's reaction. "That much for a watch! So now you're Mr. Big Shot?"

Too nouveau riche to understand what buying meant, I had yet to grasp that there was no need to compensate for my face. My scars were part of who I was, what gave me my character—they were me. Material possessions didn't change anything. I still ate alone, slept alone, and dreamt alone.

When evening came, I strolled down Madison Avenue, pausing occasionally to scan the menus displayed in front of expensive restaurants and simple taverns. In front of a small Upper East Side Italian bistro, I stopped to peer in the window and felt strangely drawn, as if I were meant to eat there, so I entered.

The cozy candlelit tables and vintage black-and-white photographs of New York City, along with the aromas coming from the kitchen, told me I had made a good choice. I requested a table for one.

As I sat down, I couldn't help but notice a young, attractive woman alone at a nearby table. Pretending to read the menu, I discreetly studied her—dark, slanted eyes, high cheekbones, and lustrous auburn hair that fell across flawless skin. Petite and well dressed, she projected an unusual mixture of serenity and vitality, an irresistible combination.

Too shy to dare speak to her, I watched as she sipped a glass of white wine. She must have sensed my eyes on her because she looked over at me, and when I smiled, she didn't turn away. I couldn't believe my good fortune when she spoke.

"How are you?" she asked with an accent I didn't recognize.

"I'm fine, thank you. You?"

Her eyes sparkled. "I'm okay." I wanted to know more but didn't want to appear naive by asking her what her nationality was. "Try the pasta carbonara—it's fantastic!" she said. "You won't regret it."

Could she be Italian? I took her suggestion and ordered quickly, anxious to continue our conversation. "Do you live in the city?" I asked.

"Yes, near Gramercy Park. Do you know it?"

"No, I haven't been down in that area."

"It's a quiet neighborhood with a beautiful garden."

"That sounds nice . . ."

When I told her I was an easterner living in New Mexico, her face lit up, and she asked me questions about Santa Fe, the Native Americans, and the city's reputation for spirituality. I wanted to ask if I could join her but was too afraid to risk rejection; I didn't even know her name yet. I had to do something before the opportunity passed, so I stood and reached across the unoccupied table between us. "My name is Howard."

With a broad smile, she took my hand. "I'm Lena."

"May I join you?" I blurted.

"Yes, of course. Sit, sit," she said, welcoming me as if she were at home.

As I sat down, her meal arrived. "Please don't wait," I said. "Eat while it's hot."

"No, I wait for you."

Happy to obey her "*manga, manga*" when the waiter brought my order, we both dove into our plates of carbonara.

"Is good, yes? I can tell by your face. Good food make anyone smile." She laughed.

"You have a wonderful accent. Where are you from?"

"I have accent?"

"Ah, hmm, a little, yes."

She shook her head. "I do not have accent."

You idiot, I thought, *now you've offended her.*

"I'm from Yugoslavia. You know where that is?"

"Of course. The Baltics, Eastern Block."

"Very good. Most Americans don't know this."

Lena spoke like a seductress in a James Bond film. I loved her charming phrasing and the delight she seemed to take in everything around her. She was mysterious and exotic—and I was smitten.

"What brought you to New York?" I asked.

"I came to study acting."

"Acting?"

"Yes, but it is very tough. Many, many girls."

"I'm sure. Have you been in any movies?"

"No, not yet."

"You will." I believed in her, though I had known her for only minutes.

"Yes, I will," she said, nodding. "Do I have heavy accent or just slight?"

"It's barely noticeable."

She laughed. "Well, *you* noticed. I will work harder." Then she asked me what I did.

Caught off guard, I stammered something about real estate. Luckily we had finished our meal and the waiter arrived, saving me from a detailed explanation.

Over espressos I learned she had lived in Italy for a short while so spoke Italian as well as Spanish, Russian, and a few Slavic languages.

"And English," I said, "with a little accent."

"Yes." She laughed. "A little."

"Do you work also?"

"*Da.*"

I looked at her puzzled, and she hid her face in her hands.

"Yes, I mean. I translate for an office downtown. It's okay."

The meal ended too soon, but when I reached for both checks, Lena protested, insisting that she pay her own way.

"Really, Lena. You've been so lovely. Please let me."

She touched my arm. "Okay, but next time I pay."

Next time! That means she'll see me again! "Please, may I have your number?" I hoped I didn't sound too forward.

Without hesitation she jotted it down for me. Elated, I walked her out to the street and hailed a cab for her. My pulse quickened when she leaned toward me and kissed my cheeks.

"*Ciao*, Howard. Call me. We go out again, yes?"

We both knew I would call. When I returned to my hotel that night, I couldn't get her out of my mind. I realized how comfortable I had been in her company and how I hadn't thought once about her reaction to my face.

The following evening we went to Lena's favorite restaurant, a small place in Chinatown. The packed dining room reverberated, the noise spilling from the kitchen and amplifying as it bounced off the white-tiled walls and bare floors, both customers and waiters vying to be heard above the racket. Despite its questionable sanitation and the smoked Peking ducks hanging overhead, I trusted her recommendation. To me, it felt as if we'd left the country.

Our waiter obviously knew her, and after exchanging pleasantries with him, Lena ordered for us and requested a few other dishes from the menu for me to sample.

"Special for special lady," the waiter said, smiling.

We ate our dinner as a light rain began to fall outside our window-side table. Laughing and at no loss for conversation, I felt my heart soar when she casually described the meal she would cook for me. Now and then, I gazed out at the rain and back to her animated face, an ease settling over me as I listened to her stories. One in particular struck me, a tale of a strange incident that had happened to her in Belgrade.

"I was walking like, how you say, sheets of rain, hard?"

"Yes, sheets."

"Okay, so raining like sheets. So I have my umbrella, but I look for cover from building. What is called?"

"An awning."

"Awning. Awning?"

"Yes, like a canopy."

"I know 'canopy.' So I stand under awning to not get wet and wait for rain to stop. Then I hear music. I think, where can music come from? Then I know is a violin playing Serbian music. I know this song from when I was a little girl. I take my umbrella and follow the music. It is very close, I think. Howard, it is raining so hard."

Lena paused to catch her breath and held her hand to her heart. "I know I must find this music, you understand. This was music I need to hear, from a happy time, so I follow the sound. Howard, it was like the music pulling me. When I turn the corner, I see an old man playing violin all alone. Howard, it was magic, rain all around him, but no rain fall on him! I stand there watching this magic before my eyes. I listen to such beautiful music. He then puts his violin away, opens his umbrella, and he is gone. Is magic, yes?"

I nodded, smiling. Lena was magic herself and attracted magic wherever she went. I knew that the moment I first saw her.

Over candlelight and linguine a few evenings later, I watched Lena's sad eyes as she described her motherless childhood, of growing up with a father trying to cope with his own loss. Moved by her story, I reached under the table and gently took her hand, saying nothing yet everything when her eyes flickered to mine. Afterward, I held her hand while we waited in the dark for a cab and, as if it were the most natural thing, pulled her to me and kissed her tenderly on the lips.

"You will come home with me, yes?" she whispered. It wasn't a question.

In her cramped bedroom, I unhurriedly undressed Lena and ran my hands over her silken skin, wanting to laugh out loud with pleasure. We fell upon each other, each of us fluent in the other's silent language of want.

We spent many more such evenings together, talking and making love, surfacing only when hunger or weather beckoned us. Whenever possible, I flew in from Albuquerque, and it was a rare day we didn't speak on the phone. She never pried for more information about my activities than I offered, and though I always kept to my realtor story, she later revealed she had guessed from the beginning what I was up to.

I fell in love with Lena. In her tiny one-bedroom walk-up, she had made a cozy home full of books on acting and astrology and anything concerning spirituality. A deep believer in prayer, she had surrounded herself with the religious icons that comforted her.

With Lena, giving was unconditional. Her apartment was open to friends and their friends, many of whom she had never met. Upon their arrival in the States, she welcomed strangers into her home, her fellow "Yugos," as she called them. Lena, who was barely scraping by herself, was always glad to help others.

One night when we had ordered take-out, I answered the door. I handed a twenty-dollar bill to the young Chinese deliveryman who spoke little English, and waited for my change from the twelve-dollar tab. When he tried to give it to me, Lena stepped between us and closed his hand in a fist. Smiling, she told him, "Thank you very much. This is for you."

With a grateful, "Tank you, tank you," he bowed and ran down the stairs.

"Who are you, Rockefeller?" I laughed. "He walked half a block!"

She looked at me with a smile. "Howard, you have had a hard life. But here in America, you are blessed. You are free. You may choose your path. You don't know what that man has been through. Many are suffering. Someday you will understand. Tonight we eat and enjoy! Now get the bowls."

Lena nourished my soul with her quiet wisdom and helped me gain perspective. Though only twenty-five years old and three years younger than I, she was more experienced and far wiser. Always, she saw the best in people.

We had been seeing each other for about a year when Lena finally flew out to Albuquerque for a week's visit. Carlos was still my main supplier, but now that I was dealing almost exclusively in New Mexico, my schedule was less hectic. She and I headed up to Taos, where everything seemed to fascinate her: the ancient pueblo by the river; the solar-powered Earthships built of rubber tires and adobe; the brilliant sky and spicy food; the town with its hippies and shy Native Americans peddling their wares of pungent sage and cheap silver and turquoise jewelry. Invigorated by our surroundings, we devoured plates of enchiladas and chiles rellenos while guitarists strummed in the shadows.

Each night we returned tired and happy to our room, where we fell into bed and made love in the chilly air, the dark mass of Taos Mountain visible through the open window.

In Santa Fe, Lena marveled over the New Age bookstores and shops selling herbal remedies and crystals. We ducked into St. Francis Cathedral and loitered in the cool, dark hush, then stumbled out into the blinding light to wander the art galleries on Canyon Road. When the week ended, I sent her home with bags of freshly ground hot red chile for her kitchen. It made me happy that I was the one who had shown her the Wild West of her dreams.

I continued to commute to New York to be with her. One night after the theater, we jumped into the back of a cab, and Lena, picking up on the eastern European accent of our driver, struck up a conversation in a Slavic dialect. I watched her attentiveness to our driver who with his free hand punctuated his terse outpouring.

"*Da, da,*" Lena said, nodding.

I sat quietly listening, understanding nothing but *da* and the universal laughter between them. She made friends with everyone—our cab drivers, waiters, shoe-shine boy—one by one they would open up to her, open their hearts to this petite woman who to them was a complete stranger and who, for me, stood taller than any building in the city.

For Christmas, knowing that Lena loved panthers, I gave her an elegant black-velvet purse subtly imprinted with a black panther. We had planned to stay in that frigid night and watch movies, but when Lena saw the homeless men below on the street, she started a pot of soup and laid out bread for sandwiches. How proud I was of her generous spirit!

As I helped her hand out a warm meal to those unfortunate men, smiling at each and asking how they were, I fell more in love with her. She didn't feed them because it was Christmas; she reached out to others year round and never mentioned it to anyone. Her silence on this spoke volumes.

Lena adored Al Pacino and had studied under his acting coach, Charlie Laughton. During one of my visits, Pacino happened to be performing at the Circle in the Square Theatre in the Village, playing the novelist in *Chinese Coffee* and then King Herod in Oscar Wilde's play *Salome*. Both shows were completely sold out.

I went up to the Marriott Hotel in Midtown to ask the concierge if I could get a pair of tickets. A bellhop pointed out a short, elderly man.

"Yes, may I help you?"

"Possibly. I'd like to buy two tickets for *Chinese Coffee.*

He looked at me suspiciously. "Are you a guest here, sir?"

"No, no I'm not."

"Triple face value, kid."

"Triple?"

"That's it, take it or leave it."

"Well, that's a lot."

"Sorry." He turned and shuffled off.

"Wait," I called out and ran to catch up with him. "Okay, okay. Are they good seats?"

"Yeah, yeah, don't worry."

"Okay, fine, triple."

"Be back here at five." As I walked away, he yelled after me, "Hey, kid, she better be worth it."

"She is!" I laughed back across the lobby. "She is!"

Lena, who never asked me for anything but always gave, couldn't believe the surprise I had for her. I had never seen her so excited.

We sat in the fifth row, so close we could see every line on every actor's face. Overwhelmed by Pacino's performance, Lena was ecstatic. It was worth every penny.

At home again after the show, as Lena filled our cups from a pot of brewed tea, I softly said, "You're always so happy. How do you do it?"

Pensive, she gently blew into her dainty teacup. "Only hope and peace. That's all any of us want, isn't it?"

The last trip I took with Lena we flew to Belgrade for a week and stayed with her father, my first time abroad. Over the next year, we continued to see each other, but we started drifting apart. Stressed out by potential legal problems in Albuquerque, I was too distracted to devote enough time and energy to our relationship.

In truth, Lena was an old soul, and I was immature and unstable, besides being rough-edged, unschooled, and naive in the ways of the larger world. I wasn't ready or even capable of committing myself to anyone. Certainly I needed to tackle the daunting work of self-examination if I were to ever be a decent partner. At least I was honest enough to admit my limits, so we were able to part as friends.

I will treasure Lena forever—she opened my eyes and heart.

"Howard," she said, reaching for my hand, "you know I will always love you."

E I G H T

In ALBUQUERQUE, LATE THAT SUMMER, the noose tightened. Too many of my colleagues were getting busted, and I knew better than to trust any of them. In exchange for immunity from prosecution, they wouldn't hesitate to rat me out—if they hadn't already.

As I drove around town, I started noticing a black Buick following me a few cars behind. At first I attributed it to mounting paranoia, but when I saw the same car parked near my house and again outside my gym, I knew I was being tailed. If things were going south, I decided I should call Shirl while I could.

The same disturbing clicking sound I'd been hearing for some time came on the line when she answered. My phone was being tapped—I was certain of it. As we talked, I kept my end casual. "No, Mom, nothing much going on. How are you?" Several times I had to catch myself from blurting out how much I loved her, which might have tipped my hand to anyone listening in. I couldn't say what I wanted to—that if she didn't hear from me for a while, not to worry. When I hung up, I wondered what I'd accomplished other than getting to hear her voice. It was time to seriously rethink my activities.

When my lawyer called to tell me I was on the hot list and that a vacation might be well advised, I paid attention. What finally decided it for me was a nightmare I had—I was back in my old hospital bed behind bars, trapped with no way out. I awakened in a cold sweat and knew if I waited around for much longer, I might be dealing with more than just a bad dream.

After taking only enough time to dress, I drove to the bank to stash the bulk of my money in a safety deposit box, then returned home. I packed my gym bag, tossed in a fat envelope of cash, and left the house as though I were heading to the gym.

On the way out of town, I dropped six months of mortgage payments in a mailbox before hitting I-25 south. At Las Cruces I veered west and stopped at the nothing town of Palomas to make two quick calls before crossing the Mexican border. The first was to my lawyer, just long enough to tell him I was leaving the country and to ask him to keep watch if my name showed up on a warrant list. The next was to Tom in California to tell him I was going on "vacation." I didn't want him worrying about my disappearance.

"Enjoy yourself," he told me. "A break is just what you need."

There was no need to explain—he got it.

Customs was a breeze, and from there it was nonstop to Mazatlán. Twenty-four hours later I checked into a modest hotel with nothing left to do but settle in for the wait.

I moved around, down to Puerto Vallarta, Playa del Carmen, and then Guadalajara, every few weeks calling my lawyer, who always had the same advice for me: lie low a while longer. Before long, one month had turned into six. My anxiety was gone, but I was bored and doing little more than killing time—swimming, scuba diving, sunning on the beach, and flirting with cute tourists.

On the beach at Playa del Carmen, I made a local contact and was soon in business again, dealing pot to tourists too afraid to buy from a local. Not wanting to run out of cash, I gladly took advantage of the easy nickel-and-dime business, which more than adequately covered my expenses. I spent the rest of my waking hours contemplating my next step, my thoughts always circling back to Tom's earlier advice: use my savings to get into a legitimate business—like real estate.

Finally, my lawyer told me it was safe to return. In two days I was back in Albuquerque.

In the 1960s and '70s, unscrupulous developers bilked fortunes out of unsuspecting East Coast retirees by selling off thousands of plots of desolate property. Albuquerque's West Mesa, cut up into tracts, was marketed with deceptive aerial maps that were dummied up with false overlays of fully developed communities, replete with golf courses. Then, money in hand, these swindlers simply disappeared.

When investors found that they owned nothing more than a bleak patch of sagebrush-covered sand in the middle of nowhere—not the "piece of paradise" they had been sold—they abandoned their properties en masse rather than pay property taxes. These plots, with years of taxes in arrears, were seized by the state and auctioned off at a fraction of their value. I jumped at the opportunity and bought up everything I could. By the late '80s, Albuquerque was rapidly expanding and all that desert land became valuable. Making ten, even twenty times my money wasn't uncommon.

Happy with the way my new investments were going, I took a break to visit Tom, who was still living in La Jolla, twenty minutes north of downtown San Diego. Touring the neighborhood, I felt as though I had walked into an episode of *Lifestyles of the Rich and Famous*. I could only shake my head in disbelief to see parking valets at supermarkets relieving pampered shoppers of their gleaming Mercedes and BMWs.

Everything had a fairy-tale quality, the gardens and velvet lawns so manicured they looked like pages out of *House & Garden*. I was tired of living in the desert, and La Jolla seemed the perfect place to make a fresh start.

Tom was enjoying life. Still dabbling in the marijuana business, he was young, single, and inordinately handsome. The women loved him. Happy to play tour guide, he showed me the sights, chauffeuring me past Mediterranean-style homes nestled on the cliffs overlooking the ocean, one breathtaking vista after another as we sped past opulent, gated estates.

Anonymous behind designer sunglasses, we roared up narrow, winding roads in Tom's classic yellow Corvette with the top down, a blue canopy of sky overhead. "Check that one out—$3.4 million!"

"Must be nice," I yelled over the revving engine.

"See that one?" Tom pointed at a sprawling mansion with panoramic views. "A movie executive lives there. My friend says he's got an indoor basketball court and a movie theater."

"Where the hell do these guys get all their money?"

"I don't know. Inherited, pot, Wall Street guys. Check that one out."

I followed the line of Tom's arm to a palatial Tudor-style estate, the azure sheen of the Pacific glinting below. "I went to a party there once," he yelled over the wind. "Guy made his cash on Wall Street. Mid-thirties. Had a custom-made pool put in for eighty grand—it's in the shape of a dolphin. The guy's loaded. He even had an outdoor pizza oven brought over from Italy."

Boy, would Ed be laughing his ass off if he could see me now. No job, no clock, cruising around in a Corvette convertible with no place to be on a workday. I couldn't help smiling at the thought. "It reminds me of Beverly Hills, only on the beach."

"Yeah, and we're an insignificant spec of sand in their sandbox," Tom said, laughing.

The next morning I picked up the *La Jolla Light* to look for a place of my own, having decided that if I were going to live in California, I'd have to be as close as possible to the beach. After a few calls, though, I realized it wasn't going to be easy. Everyone required a background check, credit report, and employment status, none of which I could provide.

Borrowing Tom's bike, I rode up the beach to get some exercise and almost missed a "for rent" sign on the front lawn of a 1940s, wood-shingled Cape Cod–style house. With only the street separating it from the beach, the location was perfect. Wide brick steps led up to three sets of sliding glass doors, and a wooden porch ran the entire length of the converted duplex; the trim and weather-beaten shingles gave the house a sense of period I liked. Afraid to waste a moment, I peddled furiously back to Tom's.

"Hello? I'm calling about the house for rent on Neptune Street."

"Yes?" answered a well-bred voice.

"How much are you asking?"

"Twelve hundred a month plus a damage deposit."

I knew I needed to make a move right then if I stood any chance at all. "Well, I'm single, no kids, no pets, and I have references."

"What do you do?"

I paused. "I'm an investor," I said, wincing at my hesitation.

"I've had a number of calls on it. Why don't you come down to my place and fill out an application."

An hour later I was sitting at Faye's kitchen table. A La Jolla blue blood in her sixties, she didn't engage in chit-chat. "It says here you're self-employed. An investor you said?"

"Yes, ma'am."

"Would the rent be a problem for you?"

"No, ma'am. I received an inheritance recently." Her expression was noncommittal, all but forcing my next move. "I can pay six months in advance," I said.

"Six months? You haven't even seen the inside yet!"

"I know, but I don't need much and I love the location."

"I'll tell you what. The place is vacant. I'll give you a key. Look around. If you like it, we'll talk."

The sound of waves crashing on the beach receded when I stepped into the living room and closed the rusting sliding glass door. I glanced up at the high-angled ceilings laid with white track-lighting and then down at the brick fireplace at one end. I liked what I saw, despite the worn cream-colored carpet. Through the doors I was glad to note that the thick hedge edging the front porch provided privacy.

Turning away from the expanse of ocean view, I checked out the galley kitchen's dated cabinets and uneven yellow linoleum, so old the plywood showed through in several spots, and stepped out onto a small brick patio at the back where a rusted washer took up one corner—apparently the laundry room. Although run-down and lacking any style, it was a place I could call home and it was on the oceanfront.

I locked up and lingered on the porch, taking in the view. How improbable it would have seemed not so many years before that I would end up here, living on the beach with money in my pocket.

I quickly adjusted to life in La Jolla and its casual wardrobe of flip-flops, T-shirts, and shorts and settled into a daily routine: rise early, wipe off the night's condensation on the glass doors and dining table, and then pad out to the porch to stretch out on an old red futon couch with my coffee and newspaper. Every morning I put aside my reading to catch the early morning show of surfers skimming the long, curling waves.

I was taking it slow, not eager to jump into anything. I joined the Aventine, a state-of-the art private health club offering every amenity, including an Olympic-sized pool lined with replicas of Greek statues—about as far removed from my old YMCA back in Jersey as I could get. After my workouts, I'd head to my favorite sidewalk cafe to people-watch over a coffee.

I had created my own Shangri-La, and from my futon, I had a front-row seat for the ever-changing panorama of sky, beach, and water. When the unit next door became available, I arranged for Tom to move in.

Relaxing on my front steps one afternoon, I heard a voice call out to me from behind the hedge. "Hey, man, can I borrow your hose?"

"Excuse me?"

A young surfer stepped into sight. "Your hose, bro. Can I wash down my board?"

"Sure, go for it."

I watched as the kid carefully rinsed the salt water off his surfboard and disappeared down the street. He must have told his friends because from then on someone asked almost daily to use my water. A few even ventured to knock on my sliding door. "No problem," I always told them. "Just coil it up when you're done."

They had their own surfer clique and a "locals only" territorial attitude. Passionate about their sport, most of them had grown up together and came from generations of surfers. They had their own surf club, the Wind and Sea, named for the stretch of beach in front of my place.

Through Tom I met Jeff, an elder member of the club. "Howard," Jeff told me as we cracked open some beers late one afternoon, "I've been surfing this spot my entire life. If you ever have any problems, you let me know."

I nodded my appreciation and looked away from the ocean back to my new friend. Tanned like leather and a few years into his fifties, Jeff settled his 250 pounds in my deck chair and rested his bottle on his beer gut. Staring out at the surf, he fell silent before taking another swig, then wiped the foam from his heavy moustache with the back of his hand.

"See that square cement block over there with the white railing around it?" He pointed across the street.

"Yeah."

"That's the Pump House. Ever heard of *The Pump House Gang*?"

"The Tom Wolfe book?" I asked.

"That's the one."

The story was about some Wind and Sea friends who went off to fight in Vietnam. One never came back and the others who did return were never the same. Jeff, I learned, had been one of those kids. "All I dreamt about was coming home to this, and here we are," he said softly. I watched his eyes mist as he took a drag off his cigarette.

Every sunset I would settle on my porch for the end-of-day ritual when crowds of locals gathered, all of our lives suspended until the sun concluded its evening performance. Touching down on the horizon, the fiery-orange ball sucked a kaleidoscope of color behind it as it melted into the ocean to the cheers and applause of onlookers.

California, I realized, was making me savor those breathtaking moments I had been too preoccupied to notice.

It became my habit to take long, solitary walks along the beach, removing my shirt only when I was out of view of anyone. I was the same kid who went to summer camp, twenty years later, still afraid to expose all of who I truly was.

On those walks I imagined businesses I could start and the kind of life I wanted to create for myself. I needed a challenge. But what?

Roberta, a New Yorker and good friend from Albuquerque with street smarts to spare, occasionally called to see how I was doing.

"How's La Jolla treating you? Met any beach babes yet?" She laughed.

"No, but I have a great view from my deck."

"Howard, what are you going to do?"

"I don't know, Bert. I need to find something. I was thinking about a small billiards place. Nothing major, just a nice income, simple, no problems."

"I have a friend in Dallas who's owned a few clubs. Do you want me to call him? You never know. He may have some good advice."

"Do you trust him?"

"I've never heard anything bad. I visited his club in Dallas, so I know he's definitely a pro. Look, I'll give him your number. See what happens."

Within days I got a call from Roberta's friend Mark, who lost no time pitching me a quick run-down of his résumé. I thought him pompous, but he did seem to know the business.

"Mark, I'm a layman, okay? Slow down."

"Look, I want to get out of Texas. I could use a change of scenery."

"You in trouble?"

"No, nothing like that. Just an ex-wife, and I'm not too happy right now working for a corporation."

"How's this—if you want, fly out here for a few days. We'll talk and see how it goes, okay?"

A month later when Mark could break away from the club he managed, I opened my door to a big, flashy, round-faced guy, whose mop of dark hair didn't do much for his look. At six foot four, Mark was a muscular 270 pounds, and he could stand to lose 50 of them. Despite his outgoing facade, I sensed he was anxious, which made me uneasy, and his taste in gaudy silk shirts, designer frames, and the gold Rolex he liked to flaunt were a bit much. If Roberta hadn't recommended him, I probably would have ended it right then. I was also put off by how overly impressed he was with my beach house. "It's only a rental," I told him.

"Yeah, but it looks like you've made it."

"Believe me, I'm just living my life."

I realized he saw serious potential in a partnership, but there were issues that concerned me.

"So Mark, you don't have a club now? Why's that?"

"We all hit hard times. Business in Texas got slow . . . a divorce. I'm basically starting over."

"So what you're saying is, you have no cash to put in?"

"No, not now, but I do have friends who might be interested. Howard, I'll give you all the references you want."

He explained OPM to me: using other people's money to create a general partnership whereby we could both draw a salary. This I liked. What I didn't like was his financial situation, but at the end of a long night of serious talk, I was convinced he knew the business.

"Listen," I said, "if you want, we can look for a space and see what happens."

"You won't regret it, Howard. You start looking. If you see something that might work, give me a call."

I began driving around San Diego's Gas Lamp district, stopping to peer in windows of buildings available for lease. The area was in the throes of revitalization, and rents were still reasonable. The district could use an infusion of new restaurants and nightclubs.

When I called about a space that looked promising, I got a realtor named Rob on the line.

"Have you ever owned a club?" he asked.

"No."

"Well, it takes a lot of money and a lot of experience. This isn't a business you can just start up."

"I have a partner who's been in it for twenty years."

"What's your interest then?"

"Financial. Look, if you don't want to show me the space, forget it. I'll call someone else."

"I'm sorry, I apologize. I get a lot of calls. Are you guys ready to seriously look for a space?"

"We both are."

"When your partner comes to town, give me a call."

"No, Rob, you show me what's available, and if I think something has potential, *then* I will call him." By his silence, I knew he was wondering whether to brush me off. I told him to pick me up at my place in La Jolla.

He arrived in a new model silver Lexus. Middle-aged, with a forced smile pasted on his face, he reminded me of a game show host. For the entire day I had to listen to his incessant talk about himself, the people he knew in San Diego's elite social circles, and the deals he'd closed, all the while checking his hair and teeth in the rearview mirror.

As I rejected one place after another, Rob's grin began to turn into a grimace. At the end of the tour, when his interest was seriously flagging, he showed me a basement space only half a block from the downtown plaza. Access to the historic building was by way of a long brick alleyway that ran along a wall of eight-foot-tall windows. The place was beautiful! Brick masonry and stunning three-foot-thick archways separated three large high-ceilinged rooms. The open floor plan would be perfect for a billiards hall. Rob, who smelled a commission, agreed.

When I called Mark in Texas and described the space, he got excited. "We need to jump on this," I told him. "I have a gut feeling this is it."

Mark flew in a few days later, and we met Rob for lunch at a popular La Jolla bistro. It turned out that the consortium Rob worked for owned the space. "Well, guys," he said, tapping his knife on the white tablecloth, "we can offer you a fantastic price. And we're willing to talk about perhaps putting up a small amount of money for tenant improvements. But first, we'll need financial statements, bank records, and tax returns to feel comfortable about your ability to finish this project."

If I'd learned anything from all my wheeling and dealing, it was how to bluff. I assumed my best poker face and assured him that was no problem.

For the next several weeks, the three of us negotiated over the phone while privately Mark and I did all we could to stall, wondering how in the hell we were going to produce records we didn't have. The whole thing was mushrooming out of control.

During a conference call with Rob, when Mark and I were about to give up, a commanding baritone voice interrupted Rob. "How you boys doing?"

Mark and I looked at each other. "Who the hell is this?" I asked, annoyed at the interruption.

"KC," he said, chuckling. "You boys hungry? Where do you live? I'll come pick you up."

A short while later a long black Mercedes sedan pulled up in front of the house. Just in case, Mark and I had reviewed our game plan: he was operations and I was financial.

"Hope you boys are hungry," KC said as I slid into the front seat. Shaking hands, we both tried to get a read on the other. An uneasy tension filled the car as we pulled away.

KC reminded me of Gordon Gekko, the corporate raider in the film *Wall Street*. Fit and polished, he looked the part: a strong, square jawline, neatly trimmed thick mustache, and a full head of groomed silver hair. I took in his finely tailored blue suit and, when he gestured, caught a glimpse of a Philippe Patek watch. This guy was a heavy hitter.

Settling back in the sumptuous leather, KC turned to me. "So, from back east, you said?" He reached over to lower the volume of the classical music playing on the radio. "How do you boys like California?"

"I love it! Land of opportunity," said Mark.

A chuckle escaped KC. "It can be, it can be. Who's the one with the club experience?"

"I am," Mark piped up from the backseat. He began reciting his credentials while I watched KC scrutinize him in the rearview mirror.

"So, Howard, what's your end in this deal?"

"Strictly financial."

His eyebrows lifted, his eyes calculating like a cash register.

Before long we pulled into La Costa, a tony resort about half an hour north of La Jolla. By the way the valet spoke to him, it was plain KC was a regular.

We were shown to a table in the lounge area overlooking the golf course. I scanned the crowd—and saw their glances at my face as I took in their conservative blue blazers, khaki pants, and silk golf shirts. Overdressed as we were in our Italian finery, no one would mistake us for the country club set.

As we waited for our drinks, I watched KC intermittently surveying the room before returning his gaze back to the two of us, trying to determine, I imagine, if we could swing it as tenants in such a large space.

I kept quiet. I sure as hell didn't want KC asking me questions I could not or did not want to answer. As he and Mark began discussing the project, I noticed KC relax. Mark laid out our plan, projecting that the club could realistically pull in five million a year.

"Boys, this sounds good," KC said. "But what about the money?"

"We have it," I said.

"How much?"

"Enough to get started, and we'll raise the rest."

KC took a long, deliberate draw of his cigar and looked around the room again, then back to me. "So you're the money guy? Hmm." He pursed his lips as he nodded. Abruptly, he waved the waitress over to our table. "Honey, we would like to eat downstairs."

"I'm sorry, sir, the restaurant is booked."

KC chuckled and paid the tab, adding a very generous tip. "C'mon, boys." He rose from the table.

Mark and I looked at each other. Who was this guy?

KC led the way down to the formal dining room, confident as a general leading his troops to do battle with the "fully booked" enemy. At the entrance we watched him discreetly palm the maître d' a hundred-dollar bill. It was clear they had an arrangement because in one sweep of his hand, the maître d' motioned us to follow. The picture of entitlement, KC was clearly accustomed to getting his way.

After a round of drinks and some small talk, he selected a $200 bottle of Opus One to have with our meal. When I said I'd never heard of it, he laughed and slapped me on the back. "It's the good stuff. Better get used to it, kid!"

His face turned serious. "Can you two pull this deal off? It's a hell of a big space—a lot of money, boys."

Mark assured him we were up to it, and the conversation once again drifted to lighter subjects.

"You don't play golf?"

We both shook our heads.

"It's California and a gold mine. Lots of business done on the course, I can tell you that." He paused. "You boys got the money?"

"Yes, KC," I replied politely, "we have the money."

Another raise of his eyebrows was followed by a few minutes of silence as his eyes darted around the room, momentarily lingering on various patrons. What was he doing? Looking for women, potential investors, associates?

KC finally redirected his attention at me as he leisurely sipped his champagne. "Look, guys, if you don't have the money, that's okay. We had a nice meal, good company, and we'll stay friends. Just let me know. No harm done."

Enough of this shit. I leaned toward KC and gestured for him to lean in close. The smirk on his face spread as he drew near. "You asked me the same question four times," I said, my voice low and hard. "What do you not understand?"

Surprised, he rocked his head away from mine, a slow smile spreading across his face. Sitting back, he let out a great laugh. "Kid, I've been threatened by the best. That's good!" Then, without any compunction whatsoever, he asked, "You boys got the money?"

I sighed. "Yeah, KC, we've got the money."

He laughed again. "All right, let's see what we can do. You boys like King Louis?"

"Absolutely!" said Mark.

"What about you, kid?"

"Never had it."

"Cognac. Top-shelf, kid."

KC, I was sure, was top-shelf himself.

KC's office building sat atop a hill overlooking La Jolla just a few blocks from my gym. I parked next to a row of luxury cars and found his office suite, marked by a brass plaque on the door that read "CAMBRIDGE CAPITAL GROUP." An attractive receptionist led us from the tastefully appointed reception area down a hall past a large conference room, small kitchen, and half a dozen private offices.

"C'mon in, boys. Good to see ya!" Elegant as always, he wore an expensive black suit, a long-collared white shirt, and a black silk tie.

His office, the size of a small hotel suite, made me feel I had stepped into New York's Upper East Side. From behind his immense mahogany desk, he waved us in and motioned for us to sit in the oversized red leather armchairs. An expanse of windows at his back looked out on a hillside of tile-roofed houses and royal palms.

Rob slipped into the room looking none too happy. With the cocky demeanor of a used-car salesman, he pitched the good deal they were offering us. Though he did most of the talking, I knew who ran the show.

Mark and I had agreed beforehand to play good cop/bad cop. He would take the easygoing role and then, well, there was me.

We negotiated hard. It was crucial to get free rent while the renovations were being done, and furthermore, we needed KC's group to pay for such things as installing a heating and cooling system and retrofitting the structure against earthquakes.

"How much are we talking here?" Rob asked.

Without hesitating, Mark said, "Six months free rent plus $350,000 in tenant improvements."

"Absolutely not!" Again Rob brought up the financial statements we had yet to produce.

At that I jumped in. "Well now, Rob, do you have any other prospective tenants?"

"Well, I'm, uh, talking to . . ."

"You're talking to us," I said.

At my remark, KC guffawed, then quickly got serious. "You say $350,000?"

"Yes. And we want a long-term lease—say, twenty years."

KC nodded. "Howard, can you put up some money to make us feel more comfortable?"

"Absolutely. I will write you a check right now for $50,000 if we can agree on some general terms."

This caught KC's attention. Over Rob's rumbles of protest, we proceeded to hash out a price. To our astonishment, KC discounted by half the one dollar a square foot he was asking. He seemed eager to do the deal, but Rob erupted with another barrage of protests.

KC held up his hand. "Robbie, it's okay. These are good boys."

"But they don't—"

KC calmly rose from his chair and asked Rob (who was looking decidedly disoriented) to join him in the next room. "You boys talk this over. We all need a few minutes. Help yourself to the bar, the phone, anything you need."

A hangdog expression on his face, Rob trailed out after KC. A few minutes later, KC returned without his cohort.

"Ah, Robbie's a little disappointed. I can't say I blame him. The deal we're giving you guys will cut his commission a little, but he'll survive."

Now that we had settled the price and the concession of three months' free rent, we were happy. Only one detail remained. "KC, what about our financial statements?"

"Kid, can you cut that check today?"

"Yeah, sure."

"Well then, don't worry about it."

I was puzzled. Why was he being so generous? While writing out the check for $50K, I snapped to what might have been his angle. "KC, who do I make this out to? Cambridge Capital?"

He laughed. "Just make it out to me, kid—Ken Claudett."

I hesitated. "To you personally? That's a little unusual. Don't you agree? What happens if this deal falls apart?"

He scribbled something in a leather-bound notebook on his desk, and then slid a slip of paper across to me—a personal guarantee of $50,000 plus interest should the deal go south. I had Mark witness and date it.

After the meeting, when we had crunched the numbers, Mark was elated, convinced we couldn't go wrong. Worst-case scenario, he said, we could sell the lease down the road for a profit. But we needed another four months' free rent as a cushion. In our favor, I now knew KC was out for himself, which was okay with me. Problem was we had yet to sign a lease, and Rob was still a major concern.

Under the auspices of his group, Cambridge Capital (so named, I'm sure, to convey an aura of old money), KC ran a small army of realtors, mortgage brokers, appraisers, and budding venture capitalists. His company appeared solid, except for the fact that he was siphoning off money from all angles. Over time, I noticed he always had someone else in the group sign any legal documents. That way, he could maintain a paper fire wall of protection so that if his hand got caught in the till, he could at least feign ignorance. It was also clear to me that Rob had no authority.

"Look, Mark," I said, "about KC, I know how this guy operates. I'm going to meet him for a drink and offer him a side deal." There were too many variables in this deal, any one of which could kill it, but I saw a way to influence the odds in our favor.

The next day I met KC for lunch at a small Irish pub downtown. Anticipating he would be well dressed, I wore a nice single-button, dark blue suit. When I arrived, KC was already waiting for me in the back area, looking as if he knew something was up, a cigar in hand and a bottle of red wine on the table.

As I approached, he stood and gave me a hearty handshake like we were old friends.

"Kid, love that suit. Where do you shop?"

"I got this one at Barney's, in the city."

"Oh yeah. Nice cut, kid, nice cut. Do you know Morrie? Morrie, he's been there for years, best tailor in the city."

"Sorry, I'm not a regular."

"Hands like a sculptor's. Sometime we'll take a trip. Sit down, kid. How's everything going?"

"Good, KC."

"So what can I do for you? Here, have a glass of Chianti. It's a decent bottle."

I took a slow, deliberate sip, then set the glass down and smiled. "First of all, I want to thank you for everything. You've been very gracious."

"My pleasure, kid."

"I need to talk to you about the lease."

"How can I help you boys?"

"Mark and I are concerned that Rob could present a problem for us down the road, and, we have yet to sign a contract, so I thought . . . well, I'd like to offer you a gift so maybe you and I can work something out." I slid a bulky white envelope across the table.

Tucked inside was $10,000 in hundred-dollar bills.

"Kid, this isn't necessary, really."

"KC, I'd like to have a long-term relationship with you. Personally."

He picked up the envelope, discreetly thumbed through the crisp green notes, and gave his now familiar chuckle. "Anything else?"

"We want a guarantee for the tenant improvements."

"Not to worry. I'll draw it up tonight, and you can have any attorney you want look at it."

"I appreciate that. Just one more thing—we may need a few extra months of free rent. From what Mark tells me, the liquor license process could take some time."

He took another puff of his cigar and motioned for the waiter. "This is very generous of you, but don't worry about a thing. It's done. And don't worry about Robbie, I'll handle him."

With my money in his hands, I was sure he would.

Waiting for our meal to arrive, KC said, "Kid, I like you. I come from the streets. I can tell you did too."

"A little."

"I started out in Jersey, worked in a meat factory in Hoboken, paid my way through NYU. Kid, we're not like these La Jolla blue bloods."

I nodded.

KC refilled our glasses. "Listen to me. Always stay hungry and never be satisfied. We gotta stay moving."

"I understand."

"I know you do."

Walking back to my car after lunch, I felt lighter than I had in months. Going on the offensive with KC had been the right move. Sure, $10,000 was a lot of money for me, but it was cheap insurance if it would get him to push this thing through.

The next morning Mark and I met KC for breakfast, this time at La Valencia, a landmark hotel in downtown La Jolla. From our table overlooking the hotel's sweeping lawns and the Pacific beyond, and fortified with gourmet coffee and freshly squeezed orange juice, we reviewed KC's proposed deal laid out before us on the starched tablecloth. Satisfied, I nodded at Mark and allowed myself a brief self-congratulatory moment while he pulled out his preliminary sketches for the project. Although we had yet to sign, the fact that we'd gotten as far as we had bordered on the miraculous.

Our plan allocated half the space for a nightclub, which Mark had convinced me was where the money was because we could charge at the door, and the rest for a restaurant and a speakeasy-themed billiard room. I flushed with pleasure when KC cast an approving nod at me at the mention of the sushi bar Mark said was my idea. If all went well, we could become owners of the biggest club in the downtown area. All we needed was a lot more money, the one detail I had failed to mention to KC.

With our attorney's approval and Rob conspicuously absent, we signed the contract on Christmas Eve in KC's office. As I leaned down to sign, I almost laughed when I saw only Rob's signature. But the terms were what we had agreed to: half the going rate on a twenty-year lease with four small, incremental increases, including the guaranteed $350,000 in improvements and six months' free rent. It was all I could do not to shout with joy. Smiling, I tried to slip a second envelope to KC, which to my surprise he refused. "Kid, it's Christmas—it's on me. Let's have a drink."

Mark and I gathered around as KC broke out a bottle of King Louis he had locked away in the bar. Lifting his glass, KC smiled at me. "Here's to a long, fruitful, and lasting friendship. It's been a pleasure, kid."

"I'm not a golfer," I said when KC called some weeks later to go hit some golf balls.

"It's a beautiful day—let's get some fresh air. All you have to do is make contact. It'll be great! I'll pick you up at your place in an hour."

"Okay, okay." It was hard to turn him down.

When he pulled up in a limousine, I had to laugh. Only KC, I thought, shaking my head as I jogged down the porch steps and climbed in the back.

Reluctantly, I took the scotch he insisted I sample and settled back on the cushioned leather. After a few belts, KC said, "Kid, what I'm going to tell you is just between us, okay?"

"Sure."

"I got out of prison a few years ago."

Somehow I wasn't surprised. I *was* surprised that I hadn't landed in there with him! I shrugged. "I don't care. It's got nothing to do with me."

"I know you wouldn't rat me out."

"We're friends—just shoot straight with me. Your other deals are none of my business."

"I was tops. I had a big law firm, dozens of attorneys under me. I had a few associates and clients the feds wanted. Securities, stock deals. I wouldn't cooperate. They framed me. It was a political vendetta."

"Really, you don't have to—"

"It's okay, kid. They took it all. They backed up a couple of U-Hauls, cleaned out our office." He paused. "Ah, I was in the *Wall Street Journal.* I represented the big guys." Taking a sip of his scotch, he looked out the window and got quiet.

"Ever heard of Roy Cohen?" he asked.

"The attorney?"

"Yeah. I knew Roy. He was the best of the best. If he couldn't beat it, he'd fix it. Oh yeah. He knew every judge in the city and had dirt on everyone. You know, I once worked a case with him." KC raised his hands and gesticulated, his voice mimicking Cohen's. "Your honor, my client has been maliciously, shamelessly persecuted without a shred of evidence by the district attorney."

He shrugged, his body still as he sat staring unseeing at the scenery passing by. Shaking his head, he turned back to me. "I really didn't do it," he said, his eyes filled with sadness.

"I'm sure, KC. I'm sure."

He shook himself like a wet dog and perked up. "Well, at least I got caught up on my reading. While I was inside, I read five, six books a week." His tone took a serious turn. "Always carry a book with you. Whenever you have time to kill, go to a bookstore. I'm telling you, knowledge, kid, knowledge. Expand your mind—keep it healthy. This is valuable advice I'm giving you. Keep things on the straight and narrow. Believe me when I tell you it ain't worth it. It just ain't worth it."

I hadn't known KC very long, but in a strange way, we clicked. Not that I trusted him, but I was smart enough to know he had plenty to teach me. It was more a feeling that he saw something in me that made him want to look after me, and I was listening.

While I was living and breathing almost daily meetings with our contractors, marketing firm, and architect—and loving every minute of it—Mark had finally finished putting together our prospectus for the half million we needed to raise. And as luck would have it, at the gym I had recently struck up an acquaintance with a guy about my age, Craig. Without any intention of soliciting investment, I casually mentioned I was building a club downtown.

"Howard," he said, "if you're looking for an investor, let me know."

He wanted to see the space we'd leased, so I walked him through it a few days later. "Nice," he said. "Tell you what, give me a few days to read the prospectus, and I'll get back with you."

A week went by. I didn't see Craig at the gym or hear from him, and then I got a call that he wanted to meet Mark and me for lunch.

"I gotta say I like what you guys are doing," he said, leaning back in his chair. "It's a good investment. I can put up the entire half million. All I want is that everything be on the up-and-up and that the books be signed. And I want to be a silent partner."

I knew he had something going on that wasn't exactly kosher, but his money was as green as mine. Mark didn't have much to say—he was in shock.

"Craig, that's fine. I just don't want any problems," I said. "I don't care how you got your money, but don't jeopardize the club."

"Howard, I don't want any problems either. The money's legit—I have my own personal reasons."

We needed the money, and with no other potential investors, we agreed to a partnership. Driving back to my place afterward, I tried to ease Mark's concerns that we were taking a huge risk with just one backer. "Look, we need this guy. One partner is better than ten. Ten partners, ten problems. You know I'm right."

Mark grudgingly agreed, and besides, he had nothing to lose. I did.

Craig kept his word. When the entire amount had been wired into an escrow account, I thought about what KC had told me—to keep it straight and narrow—which was exactly how I wanted it. But this whole deal was getting more complicated by the moment. Still, I was in, and there was no turning back.

Our project was going well—we'd secured the licenses and a graphic designer and were making nice headway on the remodel—but we desperately needed the $350,000 KC owed us. For months, despite going out of my way to be overly polite with him, I couldn't get him to pay up. We had taken money from Craig, and I had to live up to my end of the deal and get the club running. I had gone through all my own money as well.

KC not delivering was *not* an option—he was stalling, and I had to find a way to corner him.

With his charisma and savoir-faire, KC was an expert at manipulating a conversation and was close to impossible to pin down. I needed some leverage, so I called a guy Lena knew in New York and told him to find out what he could about my uncooperative associate. No doubt KC had played this game before.

According to my contact, everything KC had told me about his connections was true, although his bit about being framed, if that was the case, wasn't the whole story. He was ultimately convicted of insider trading—to the tune of millions. Those who knew him well considered him verging on brilliant, but that intelligence hadn't saved him from his egotistical belief that he could outsmart everyone. I also discovered he had been married three times and had six children, none of whom he'd ever mentioned. But the funniest information to come to light was a photo of KC that revealed a severely receding hairline, meaning that the thick mane I'd so admired was a toupee. I wondered what else was smoke and mirrors.

That he was a masterful hustler who had conned even sophisticated investors and that he owed a lot of money to a lot of people came as no surprise. But now I was much more concerned about ever getting paid. Too afraid of what he'd do (or not do) if I pissed him off, I was desperate to figure out how to proceed.

Ultimately, I decided to ingratiate myself as much as possible with KC to coax the money out of him. Almost daily, I spent hours in his office, reading the paper or talking with him about sports or whatever topic came up.

His entourage of old friends from New York also hung around there. These guys looked like characters out of *On the Waterfront*. Tony— "Fat Tony," as KC aptly called him (though never to his face)—a giant oaf of a guy, six foot five and between 375 and 400 pounds, wore an absurdly small hairpiece atop his enormous head. Mornings, KC often brought in donuts for the staff, but Tony usually got to them first. Once, when KC offered me one, he looked inside the nearly empty box and sadly shook his head. "This fucking Tony. This guy, he takes all the ones with sprinkles."

Then there was Johnny, an alleged hit man for the Irish mob in New York. I never asked, but talking with him left little doubt that he was connected. Small and wiry, he was barely five foot two and looked like someone who belonged in an Irish pub on the West Side. KC called him Johnny Shades because he never took off his rose-tinted glasses, even at night. Johnny and Tony were office fixtures, like the furniture, and passed the time reading racing forms and drinking coffee.

Rounding out the cast was Frankie, a six-footer who weighed little more than Johnny. Painfully crossed-eyed and always with a cigarette dangling from his fingertips, he'd show up wearing one or another of his pastel leisure suits, all of them smelling of mothballs and looking as if they'd been saved from the 1970s. Frankie was KC's chauffeur and gofer, the one who picked up the dry cleaning, made liquor runs, and placed bets for KC at the Del Mar Racetrack. "Howard," he explained, "I would do anything for KC. He got me off once."

"What for, Frankie?"

His face went blank. "I can't remember, but I was gonna do more time, I know that much."

Frankie was constantly popping pain pills, and a drink was never too far from his hand. What was really scary, though, was that KC would send him out high as a kite to pick up clients. This group was a circus of clowns, and KC was the ringmaster.

Periodically he recruited Mark and me to meet him and some of his prospective investors down at our club while it was under construction. KC laid it on, telling them how he owned the building and a percentage of our club (which was untrue), pointing out all that he had done for us. Mark and I backed him up with over-the-top testimonials. Since we had yet to collect our money from him, we fell over ourselves trying to keep him happy. As I later learned, for the minimal amount he had put down on the building, he then had sold shares for 150 percent of it. These offerings, compounded with his other properties, came to millions.

Most of his investors were aging wealthy women and almost always divorced or widowed. Knowing KC, I didn't think this was a coincidence. And the ladies loved him. "Oh, KC, such a wonderful man! So smart and worldly, you have no idea. And what a gentleman!"

Mark and I would smile and nod. "Oh, KC's smart, all right," I'd say when pressed. It was all I could do to keep a straight face.

Mesmerized by his charms, they flew him to New York and Vegas and not infrequently to Europe to meet their wealthy friends—anything they could do to help him find investors. "Honey," I heard him say on the speakerphone once, "my secretary has my wallet. Just put it on your credit card and I'll pay you later." One detail he always failed to mention was his beautiful twenty-something Italian girlfriend he kept in a condo on Coronado Island. Had KC been legit, he could have run a Fortune 500 company.

Browsing the *New York Times* one morning as I waited for KC in the reception area outside his office, I looked up to see an expensively dressed Middle Easterner barge through the door with two large men in attendance.

"Where's KC?" the foreigner barked at the receptionist.

A moment later KC appeared. Completely unflappable, he opened his arms as if he were delighted to see the visitor. "Hey, good to see ya."

"Bullshit. I want my money." Gesturing to his associates, the man glared at him. "You understand?"

"C'mon, relax. Everything's great. We're about to make a killing." He put his arm around him and escorted him back to his office.

"No more, KC. That's it!" I could hear the man threatening and KC cajoling as their voices receded down the hallway.

Five minutes later, KC returned with his arm still around the man's shoulders. "It's going to be fine. We're both going to do very well on this thing. Relax."

You poor bastard, I thought. Just try getting anything out of KC. It wasn't comforting to think I was in line behind oil sheiks, or whoever he was.

"Okay, KC, give me a call if you need anything." Beaming, the foreigner turned and strode out the door.

As soon as the door closed behind the trio, KC turned to me and nervously straightened his tie. "Whew! That was a close one, kid! Let's have a drink."

The man who had come in like a pit bull went out like a lapdog. For all the nail-biting KC was putting me through, I couldn't help but admire his skill.

As much as it was in his interest to do so, KC had also taken a personal interest in me. Quite unintentionally—but mutually understood—I had become his protégé of sorts, and exasperated though I was, I welcomed it.

One morning I walked in to find him ashen-faced and uncharacteristically pouring himself a scotch on the rocks, something I'd never seen him do before lunch. "You all right?" I asked.

He shook his head and took a few swigs, his hand visibly trembling. "This fucking Frankie, he almost clipped the Admiral."

"What are you talking about?" I was well acquainted with the Admiral, or "Skipper," as he was affectionately called. He was another fixture around the office, a distinguished-looking retired rear admiral in his eighties who over the past fifty years had put together an impressive portfolio of properties he'd bought up around San Diego. KC had convinced him to borrow against his holdings so they could make millions in one of KC's schemes.

"That fuckin' Frankie." He shook his head. It seemed Frankie had been showing his revolver to Zipper Tits (our name for one of the shapely blonde secretaries who periodically had her breasts augmented with ever larger implants) as the two of them stood in the hall just outside KC's office. "Kid, I heard the gun go off. I know that sound. I thought it was a drive-by so I hit the floor. You never know. I looked up at the Admiral who was just standing there, looking down at me as if I'd lost my mind. What could I do? I'm yelling at him, 'Skipper, hit the deck, incoming!' Well, you know how he's hard of hearing, so I guess he didn't hear any of it. When he asked me what I was doing on the floor, I said I was looking for my contact lens. Jesus, if Frankie had clipped the Admiral, we were all gonna get pinched. And I mean hard."

Hearing this latest office insanity made me break out in a sweat, and this time I was the one who shook my head. All I needed was KC getting himself killed.

Days later, we still didn't have the money. After reminding myself before entering his office to behave like a gentleman, I approached him for the umpteenth time.

"KC," I said, "this is imperative. We're over budget on this thing. We really need the $350,000 now."

"No problem, it's on the way."

"I'm sure it is, but we need to pay the contractors. We have a partner. We could be sued and lose everything."

"Listen, you have my word. Believe me when I tell you I'm here for you. Tell you what, just between us, I have a lot more than that coming in. When I get flush, I'll lend you boys whatever you need."

Classic KC, offering more than he owed. He even had me thinking about it.

After another couple of weeks and no money from KC, Mark and I were in a full-blown panic. The only solution Mark had to offer was suing him.

"Are you out of your mind? You want to sue this guy? He'd have us tied up in court forever!" Pacing my living room, I raged on about what I'd like to do to KC.

Mark had seen what I was like when I lost it. "Howard, whatever it is you're thinking, *don't* do it."

Two more sleepless nights, and that was it. No way would I let this guy put me back on the street. I didn't care who he was or who he knew. He'd made a deal and he was going to deliver.

I drove up to KC's and walked past the secretary into his office. Fat Tony and Johnny were there, reading their race forms with donuts and coffees in hand, and KC was on the phone. When he saw me, he quickly hung up.

"Kid, relax." Smiling, he rose from his chair and came around the desk. "I told you it's on the way. I'm even working on the extra credit for you guys."

"Forget it—just the money you owe us."

"C'mon, I'll pour you a drink."

"Forget the drink. I want my money. *Now!*"

Tony's and Johnny's mouths fell open, which in Tony's case was not a pretty sight. Both guys got to their feet. Tony I wasn't worried about; he couldn't have dropped a donut. Johnny was at a distance to my right, and KC was directly in front of me, about ten, twelve feet away. My adrenaline racing, I was too angry to be afraid. I owed them nothing.

The smile disappeared from KC's face. "Kid, no one's talked to me that way in twenty years."

"If you don't write me a check right now, you won't have to wait another twenty!"

KC's eyes locked on mine. He was in great shape, but I also knew I could hold my own.

He came at me, and I pulled back my right fist. When just inches away, he abruptly stopped, then put his arm around my shoulder and broke out in a chuckle. Turning to Tony and Johnny, he drew me to him. "Look at this fucking kid. I love him!" Laughing, he walked over to the bar. "C'mon, you got it. Let's have a drink."

He poured us each a scotch and sat down at his desk. Taking a key from his pocket, he unlocked the center drawer and pulled out his checkbook. Swiftly he wrote out a check for the entire amount and signed it with a flourish. I wasn't ready to celebrate, because too many times I had heard him instruct recipients to hang on to their checks. "It's not a bad check," he'd tell them. "It's just not good yet."

KC handed over my check. "Kid, this one's good."

We were friends again. As he did with everyone, KC tested me relentlessly, perhaps to see what mettle I was made of or to determine my breaking point. But that I got the check proved to me I had passed. Without KC the club never would have happened. No one else would ever have done a deal of that magnitude with two young guys like us.

N I N E

WITH ALL THE CRAZY BEHIND-THE-SCENE machinations out of the way, our club finally opened on July 21, 1994. When I called Shirl to tell her it was actually happening, she had me smiling ear to ear like some dopey little kid. "Howie, that's just great! I'm so proud of you!"

To accompany me opening night, I'd asked Lena to fly in from New York City. "Are you nuts?" she said, laughing. "I wouldn't miss it for the world!" Our breakup had not affected our friendship, and I wanted to share my big moment with her. She, more than anyone, knew what this meant to me.

On the big night, Lena, who looked stunning in a black silk pantsuit, and I, in a six-button black suit, were about to walk in like I owned the place, which in fact I did, when a bald and very large doorman stepped in front of us, blocking our way.

"Sir, one moment, please. Are you on the guest list?"

"You know, I don't think so, seeing that I'm one of the owners."

"What's your name?"

"Howard Shulman."

Our man ran his oversized finger down the page. "Sorry, sir, your name's not on the list. Guests only."

Well aware I wasn't one of the beautiful people on the club scene or one of the social elite, I wasn't worried about getting in. I just didn't want to make a scene for the grand opening. "Look," I said, "you know Mark, right?"

Jumbo started getting irritated with me. "Yeah, I know Mark—he's my boss."

"Okay then, call him on your walkie-talkie."

"Sir, you're not on the list. Please step aside so others can get in."

At that, Lena burst out laughing. I, however, was getting perturbed. Moments later, Mark bounded up the alleyway steps looking mortified that I had been refused entry.

"No, no," he said. "He's my partner. Let him through. It's okay."

The doorman cringed, fearing his first night would be his last. "Sir, I am so sorry. I, I . . . didn't know."

Given my face, I can't say that I blamed him for barring my way. I was so used to being on the outside of the velvet rope that the episode didn't surprise me. Quickly the doorman unhooked the rope and we were in.

The place was packed. We pushed our way slowly through the crush of in-crowd types: long-legged, overly made-up women in short, revealing dresses hung on the arms of posturing men, whose unbuttoned Versace shirts showed off tanned, muscled chests. Intent on networking, they dealt out business cards with one hand as they preened their gelled hair with the other. Lena laughed at the sequined women milling around us, whispering in my ear that they looked like Christmas trees with fake boobs.

Out of the corner of my eye, I saw Rob the realtor wave us over. Loudly congratulating me, he slapped me on my back. "Hey, we pulled it off!" *We*, Rob? I turned away.

As we made our way through to the chic sushi bar done in black terrazzo and leather, I glanced approvingly at the waitresses, who looked sharp and sexy in short black skirts, white blouses, and black high-heels. Their youth and long legs turned heads as they efficiently tended the crowd. Lena, I was pleased to see, seemed impressed when she saw the mounds of seafood displayed in the glass cases that rimmed the massive three-sided bar. All fifty seats were filled, and people were waiting three deep for their turn.

Pressed by the crowd, I took Lena by the arm, guided her through

one of the glass-brick archways that separated the restaurant from
the billiards room, and laughed with pleasure when she admired the
bar that I admit looked sensational: padded with cobalt-blue leather,
it was straight out of a Prohibition-era speakeasy. We skirted the grid
of blue-velvet-covered pool tables and headed to the lounge area at
the other end. Glasses and billiard balls clinked as blues played in the
background. Over the raised voices of a crowd of well-wishers, I made
small talk as best I could, then excused myself and guided Lena to the
nightclub across the hall.

She laughed, her eyes widening. "Howard, it's fantastic!"

We pushed through the crowds to one of the circular bars, where I
ordered her a glass of white wine. Shouting to make myself heard above
the music, I couldn't help but brag to Lena that we had the biggest and
one of the most exclusive clubs in the district. Pounding music bom-
barded us as we circled the dance floor, our eyes hypnotically drawn
to the crush of dancers gyrating under the strobe lights, their writhing
bodies fragmented in a kaleidoscope of light and color.

In the next day's social column, an entertainment reporter wrote
of the grand opening:

> It's after 11:00 p.m. and the line outside the club stretches all
> the way up the block to 5th Avenue. The buff Citified Group
> is eye candy: lots of tailored suits, lots of cleavage and curls;
> daringly high heels and skintight short skirts over black sheer
> hose; hair layered and moussed to gleam in amber light like all
> the pendants and earrings. It's a lean, mean partying machine
> of a crowd.

For me, the night was a comedy. Between air kisses and handclasps,
the Beautiful People paraded, while I retreated for most of the night,
preferring to hang out with KC, Jimmy, Tom, and a few friends from
La Jolla. KC and Lena, I was pleased to see, hit it off immediately.

"She's a good girl, kid," he told me, nodding in her direction. "Smart,
smart."

Amused, I watched KC work the crowd. Determined to take ad-
vantage of new blood, he adhered to his usual modus operandi of lay-

ing the groundwork, deftly moving about as he zeroed in on the high rollers, his game just another surreal facet of the night.

Introduced to everyone as one of the owners, I was lavished with unaccustomed attention. "Wonderful job you've done here!" "Amazing!" "Beautiful suit!" With dollar signs in their eyes, they fawned over me, calculating my usefulness for their own financial gain. If nothing else, maybe I'd be good for some free drinks or perhaps a VIP card. From hot-plate meals in my New Jersey walk-up to an endless flow of sushi and drinks, the contrast was making my head spin. Although I was enjoying myself, I also knew in the back of my mind that the only party I would be invited to might not be worth the price of admission.

In the beginning I went to the club daily and played the game. My favorite subterfuge to get dates was to have the hostess sit me next to a row of single women at the sushi bar, whereupon the sushi chef and I would launch into our routine.

"Welcome, Howard-San."

Casually I would leave for a few minutes while he served a round of sake to the ladies, telling them it was compliments of the owner. It was a devious yet effective way to meet women, who had their own tactics—it was open season on both sides. I had come to the conclusion we all use whatever assets we have to draw upon, whether looks, money, or influence. It sure as hell was not going to be my looks that would get me laid in San Diego's world of hot singles and eligible bachelors.

For the first six months I was like a kid in a candy store, singling out women standing in line and directing the doorman to let them in. I ran up obscenely high tabs for food and drinks, which I gave away by simply signing my name. Mark was even worse with his entourage of hangers-on.

Though eye-opening, the novelty of one-night stands soon faded. I met a few women who wanted to pursue a relationship, but I never felt connected to any of them. Eventually I woke up enough to realize that the superficiality of the scene I was steeping myself in had left me emotionally on empty. These women had no real interest in finding out who I was, and I was equally indifferent about them.

My enthusiasm for dropping by the club waned when I realized that whether I was surrounded by crowds or with a woman on my arm, nothing relieved the loneliness. Once, during dinner with a beautiful woman who was actually very nice, I couldn't get over the nagging feeling she had a hidden agenda. I recall looking at her over platters of sushi and thinking, what the hell am I doing here? I didn't need a Southern California reality check to understand why I had a string of women. No club, no money, no women. It was that simple.

Business was good. I was doing all right financially. So, despite my reluctance to endure more surgery, I decided this was the time to have my lips reconstructed to make them more uniform. By some inexplicable shift of attitude, the face I had long considered a misfortune I now believed to be a gift. My decision to have another operation was not based on a desire to look like everyone else, which wasn't even possible. I simply wanted to achieve some modicum of normalcy. I had grown immune to the stares for the most part, and while I knew I would always get second glances, I still had a few basics that needed to be fixed.

I chose Dr. Robin Yuan, a highly sought-after plastic surgeon in Beverly Hills, and arrived early for my appointment. His very attractive receptionist asked me if I'd like a soda, a juice, or perhaps a Perrier, and then handed me a Lucite clipboard and silver pen. So accustomed was I to public clinics that when I turned to take a seat, it was impossible not to compare the expensive furnishings, glossy magazines, and fresh flowers to the sad waiting rooms I had known growing up. That world of battered clipboards and plastic pens was a far cry from the one I could now afford.

After filling out the forms in my usual abbreviated manner (simply writing "N/A" in the space for "Previous Surgeries," not having enough paper to list all my previous work), I sat back and pondered the pretty blonde teenager across from me. What she was doing here I couldn't imagine. Breast implants? Nose job? What were her parents thinking? All that pain. And for what?

To her left, a forty-something executive type sat leafing through a magazine. Obviously, he was overweight with a bit of jowl, but hey, come on. What about working out or eating a little less?

I took a sip of water and studied the elegant older woman sitting rigidly at the end of the room, a grande dame socialite, perhaps, pink nails matching her Chanel suit, her eyes studiously averted. It was sad, really. Whatever happened to aging naturally?

Punctually, I was shown into the doctor's office, where Dr. Yuan performed a thorough examination and then outlined the procedure. To make my lips more symmetrical, he explained, he would laterally slice my oversized lower lip, flip it up, and attach it to my nearly non-existent upper lip. After five weeks he would then proportionately divide my sealed lips in two, leaving me with what I hoped would be an evenly shaped mouth.

It would be best, he advised, to spend the first week after my operation recuperating at a private center in Beverly Hills, a time when I could use assistance with eating, tending my stitches, and keeping my swelling down to a minimum. In Southern California, where raw chemical peels and bruising were commonplace, going about in public as I normally looked, compounded by one massive lip sewn together, my face swollen, and my eyes blackened from surgical trauma, would have been pushing it, even for me. His office would make all the arrangements.

Anticipating the improvement in my appearance that the procedure would make (despite the painful associations it triggered), I was eager to get on with the operation. Nervously I awaited my appointment.

The surgery went well. Before my grogginess had a chance to wear off, a private nurse escorted me down to the underground parking and to a sleek black Lincoln Continental with tinted windows waiting to whisk me away. Within minutes we pulled into Le Petit Ermitage's massive garage, where a nurse coaxed me out of the car and led me as if floating through a private garden of trickling water and sweet-smelling flowers, an Eden hemmed in by high walls and Tudor-style architecture.

Exhausted, I gratefully let myself be helped into bed and gently eased back on a stack of oversized down pillows positioned to cradle my head. Scanning the room, I took in the French provincial décor, flowing draperies, and large vase of flowers. When my eyes lit upon a silver champagne bucket filled with bottles of Evian water, I fell asleep.

Dreamless, I slept through the night, not waking until late the next morning when I rang the nurse's buzzer, which promptly brought an attractive nurse to my door. Instead of the old Jell-O and carton of milk delivered on a plastic tray, she offered me a fresh fruit smoothie with protein powder. After gently applying small ice compacts to my lips, she helped me into a plush terry-cloth bathrobe with the Le Petit Ermitage insignia on the pocket. The Bronx's thin hospital gowns seemed a world away.

As I sat overlooking the lush garden, I carefully sipped my liquid breakfast through the hole in my lip the surgeon had made to accommodate a straw. Wincing, I tried to ignore my stinging mouth as I studied a woman sitting quietly in the garden, her long, shapely legs revealed by the part in her robe.

Disguised by bandages and black wraparound sunglasses, she was most likely an actress or a Hollywood executive's wife in for a tune-up that would stave off the advances of middle age. Only the wealthy could afford a place like this, and I had to admit luxury made convalescence much easier to bear. I laughed to myself, careful to keep my mouth immobile and not pull out any stitches.

A week later, after nothing but smoothies and pay-per-view TV, I returned home and holed up for the next month. To avoid drama, I had told everyone I would be out of town, except Tom, who knew me so well that nothing shocked him. A true friend, he took over all my shopping and errands.

With my mouth sewn shut I had no choice but to stay on my protein smoothie diet. Under strict orders to avoid the sun, I had to wait until nightfall to walk down to the beach, where I'd sit for hours on end gazing out over the vast prairie of water, the sea breeze moistening my sealed lips.

Secluded and unable to communicate, I took advantage of my near-hermitic existence to reflect on my life and all that had transpired in the past year. It was then that I began to practice my version of silent meditation, though at the time I didn't have a name for what I was do-ing. The irony of my situation didn't escape me: here I was a partner in a thriving nightclub and living in a beach house in La Jolla, and yet I was sitting alone day after day with the curtains drawn, hiding my unsightly face from society. Fortunately, I hadn't made the mistake of taking all the fawning over me seriously. It would run its course and I was along for the ride, nothing more. For all the energy I spent on chasing money, sex, and prestige—none of it filled the emptiness I felt.

In my surgical mask, my eyes still bruised, I returned to Los An-geles to have my stitches removed and checked into an exclusive hotel in Beverly Hills. Unable to speak, I indicated with my hands to the desk clerk that I had a throat problem. He looked at my photo ID and then dubiously back at me, but recovered nicely and welcomed me to the hotel.

In the elevator, just as the doors were closing, a group of giggling beauty pageant contestants crowded in with me. In the crush of sash-emblazoned chests, I retreated to the corner and lowered my head, making myself deaf to the whispers. As the elevator purred upward, I could see them stealing sideways looks at me, their curious faces re-flected in the polished steel walls. I'm sure they didn't intend to be rude, but how much more irony could be held in a six-by-six-foot enclosure?

Obsessed as they were with appearance, I wondered if in the pres-ence of someone like me, they were able to recognize their own per-fection. They fell silent while I prayed their floor would arrive before mine and spare me the torture of passing through a gauntlet of teen-age scrutiny. My prayers were answered—the doors opened, and the girls, anxious to get away from me, quickly exited. I lifted my eyes in relief as the last contestant stepped out and was surprised to see her smile at me, signaling, I like to believe, that I hadn't been disquali-fied as a person.

To pass the time, I wandered down to watch wannabe starlets mince around the pool in bikinis and stiletto heels, self-consciously parading before an oil-lathered audience. In tiny Speedos, the men sprawled in chaise lounges, cell phones going off as they wheeled and dealed with one eye on the girls.

I could take only so much before returning to my room to watch a mind-numbing amount of television, alternating talk shows with Aleksandr Solzhenitsyn's memoir that I'd brought along. In some strange way I found comfort in his account, trying to imagine how he survived the brutal hardships of a Siberian gulag. It gave me some perspective, especially since I was reading his story on a full stomach in the comfort of room service and air conditioning while nursing my small, temporary problems. That I had the resources to help myself while so many others were caught in an endless cycle of hopelessness made me profoundly grateful.

T E N

MARK HAD GONE FROM SLEEPING on my couch to buying expensive sports cars and acting like king of the district. I can't say that he had changed—all I knew was that he was going through money like wildfire. A national motorcycle magazine did a spread of him straddling his customized Harley-Davidson as he angled his diamond-studded Rolex toward the camera. He'd even had a bracelet made that spelled out his name in rubies, probably so that with his ballooning ego he could remember who he was. With little in common between us, I deliberately distanced myself, and when we did get together it was only to take care of business.

Saturday nights the club was packed. I still showed up, but the novelty was wearing off, and the incessant patronizing was beginning to grate on me. "Nice suit!" "You working out?" "You look great!" It was all part of the game. These people were acquaintances at best, and most of them would not have given me so much as the time of day if I hadn't been a partner.

The harsh truth was driven home one night when a woman I approached at the bar ran her eyes up and down me as if I were a side of spoiled beef that had failed FDA inspections. Signaling with her entire body her utmost contempt, she cut me dead and turned her back to me. I brushed her off. Conditioned my entire life to brace myself against such moments, I scarcely registered the insult, but the rudeness of it never failed to unnerve me. Just then, in a gratifying twist, a woman I knew joined her and introduced me as one of the owners. When she turned back to meet me, she lost her composure, her face registering her shock.

"Oh, uh, you're an owner here?"

It was impossible to keep the smirk off my face and not feel perverse satisfaction in her discomfort. I shook her hand, then called for drinks to be brought before I disappeared into the crowd laughing.

Later that evening, when I was standing at the main bar nursing an Evian and trying to rid myself of the bitter aftertaste of my unpleasant encounter, peals of laughter drew my attention down the bar to a small group of young women. Bathed in the amber light of the low-hanging lamp was a girl with the most beautiful hair I had ever seen; it gleamed like chestnut satin and fell halfway down her back. Rooted to the floor, I watched her, mesmerized.

Without thinking, I moved toward her, drinking in every detail of her animated face, her embroidered white blouse, the delicate necklace lying in the V of olive skin, her simple tan corduroy trousers. As her friends maneuvered toward the bartender, I swiftly stepped to her side. "Please," I said as she turned toward me, "allow me to get you a drink. What would you like?"

"That's so nice of you, but no, thank you. I'm fine, really."

"It's okay, I work here. It's no trouble at all."

She hesitated. "Well, okay, a Coke?"

I laughed. Invariably, the women I approached requested champagne and usually wanted the same for all their girlfriends. This woman was different—she was a delight, a flame, and I a moth. Instantly captivated by her, I looked into her hazel eyes. "I'm Howard." I gently shook her hand, reluctant to let go.

Her eyes sparkled. "Hello, I'm Sabrina."

Unable to hear her over the music, I invited her to move into the VIP area. Nodding, she motioned to her friends to follow and allowed me to guide her to the relative quiet behind the velvet rope.

Fearing she might think I wanted to impress her when she asked me what I did, I played down my role and tried to steer the conversation to her, but she insisted I tell her about myself.

"New York? I've always wanted to go there! Howard, have you been to MoMA, the Museum of Modern Art?"

"Well, yes."

"Central Park? Chinatown?"

I couldn't contain my laughter. "Yes, yes," I said, nodding.

Her friends and skepticism seemingly forgotten, she leaned forward, intrigued by my stories about mornings in Washington Square Park, where people of all ages gathered to watch chess matches, and by descriptions of my favorite haunts, the theater, and street musicians.

I had never met anyone so full of life. From the moment we first spoke, I knew she was the real thing, nothing like the crowd on the prowl who frequented the club, myself included. What a refreshing change! She was an open book, there only to have a night out on the town with her friends.

"Enough, Sabrina," I said, laughing. "No more about me. I want to know about you!"

The noise of the club and the people around us fell away as Sabrina told me her story of growing up in San Diego, of being one of five raised by her single mom and her grandparents. In school to get her teaching certificate, she was working with special needs students, "my kids" she called them.

"I hope you know how fortunate you are that you've found your passion," I said, envious that someone in her early twenties had what for me was so elusive. "Do you realize how few people love their work as you do?"

"But look at you! You have this amazing club!"

How could I explain to her that this was what I did, not what I was?

When her friends wanted to move on, I felt a teenager's awkwardness in asking for her phone number. We were polar opposites. Naive and beautiful, she had clarity about her path in life, whereas I was still wandering, traveling paths that she, God willing, would never know. So when she jotted down her number on a bar napkin and handed it to me, her eyes smiling, I was elated. Carefully, I tucked it into the inside breast pocket of my suit, determined to safeguard it. After only one evening together I wanted to protect her, a feeling I didn't quite know how to handle.

After that we met frequently—for dinner at the club or at my place—and before long she asked me to come out to visit her. Nearly drunk with new love, I turned my Mercedes into the steep hills and headed for her barrio. Though only a few miles from the club, her house was light years away from the world I inhabited. As upscale restaurants and boutiques fell away, I left sedate La Jolla behind and entered a world of saturated color. "La Raza" painted on a wall in vivid greens flashed by my window as I passed bodegas covered with murals, in front of which old men basked in the sun, dozing in their woven-vinyl chairs as newspapers lay forgotten in their laps.

Despite my being marginally tolerated in the La Jolla of wealth and status, I felt the all-too-familiar pangs of exclusion as I entered Sabrina's world—it was the feeling of being a foreigner in my own country. Whether it was Bement, New Mexico, or even the countryside of New Hampshire, I had always felt like an outsider, always searching for acceptance, trying to appease a yearning I didn't know how to satisfy.

Women and children outside a community center receded in a stream of color, disappearing in my rearview mirror along with taco stands and small shops, their signs hand-painted with names like *La Esquina* and *Tito's*. I slowed, knowing I was nearing Sabrina's, and smiled when I saw her sitting on her stoop with an elderly woman.

I quickly maneuvered into a parking space in front of a turn-of-the-century Victorian, whose shingles, long ago painted gray, were now cracked and faded. As I locked the car I heard her call my name and turned to see Sabrina running toward me, a radiant smile lighting up her face as she flung her arms around me. Laughing, she pulled me impatiently toward the porch and introduced me to her friend. "Howard, this is Teresa, my landlady I told you about."

Teresa wagged her finger at me playfully. "No, no, more like your *abuelita*. So, Mister Howard, you are Sabrina's new friend?"

"Yes, yes I am. So good to meet you."

"*Bueno*, you take good care of my Sabrina, she is *muy especial*. She takes care of me, she's *mi familia*."

"I know. I assure you I will."

Sabrina wrapped her arms affectionately around the older woman's shoulders. "We take care of each other, don't we, Teresa?"

Smiling, Teresa rose from her armchair and, with one hand clutching Sabrina's arm, opened the screen door. "*Pásale, pásale. Sientese.*"

While listening to what little of their Spanish I could decipher, I looked around the small living room filled with a small forest of yellowing family photographs. A momentary lull in the conversation brought my attention back to Teresa, who was gazing fondly at Sabrina. "Look how young and beautiful Sabrina is," Teresa said. "*Mira*, you both are!"

Delighted to see Sabrina blushing, I smiled as we said our good-byes. From the porch stairs, I followed her up to her apartment. I wanted to laugh out loud with joy when I walked through her door. Every detail had her mark on it. Wall hangings and Mexican folk art popped against deep wine-colored walls, and eclectic yard-sale finds and small saints were scattered everywhere. Except for a cross that hung above the headboard, the tiny bedroom held nothing more than a rocking chair and a bed covered with a handmade quilt that Sabrina said her *abuelita* had made for her. The kitchen, tiny and cluttered with an odd assortment of colorful tableware stacked in green cabinets, had just enough room for a small table and mismatched chairs. Stacks of books and school papers cluttered the living room.

"Do you like it?" Sabrina asked, craning to read my face.

"I love it! It's perfect!"

We sat side by side on her small couch and talked for hours. It was all I could do not to reach out and touch her long, silken hair that fell in a curtain between us.

For some time Sabrina had wanted me to meet her young friend Susie, whom she often helped care for on Saturdays. I happened to be visiting one morning when Susie was dropped off, and went out to meet her. Seeing only a mop of curly red hair hiding behind Sabrina, I watched as Sabrina kneeled down beside the child.

"Susie, I want you to meet my friend Howard."

Slowly I kneeled down beside Sabrina. "Hello, Susie. How are you?" I asked, gently touching her small hand.

The young girl, her face hidden and her arms tightly wrapped around Sabrina's neck, refused to look at me.

"Howard's my friend, too, Susie. Can you say hello to him? We can all be friends."

It wasn't until Susie reluctantly peered out at me that I saw the small pale face dusted with tiny freckles and on it the unmistakable stamp of Down syndrome.

"It's nice to meet you, Susie. Sabrina's told me all about you."

The child kept her eyes on the floor and turned back to the safety of Sabrina's arms.

Later, as I sat watching Sabrina and Susie make cookies, the two of them laughing as clouds of flour settled on the little girl's face and bare arms, a sharp pang of regret struck me—of all that I had missed out on for so much of my life. It was abundantly clear that I had my priorities all wrong. How could I have lived my entire life without knowing what was truly important? It was almost painful to see the strong bond between them.

Sabrina had this incredible life. Her calling was to help others. What was mine? I smiled wistfully when the cookies cooled, and Susie rubbed her hands in glee. What could compare with this beautiful child? Certainly not sushi bars or fancy meals at the club or anywhere else. More than cookies it was love that was concocted in that tiny kitchen. And it was love that I yearned to give and to receive.

Sabrina's world humbled me, and on the drive back to La Jolla, I had to admit to myself how little I had contributed to anyone's life. I had always been so self-centered that I hadn't realized what I was missing. And now, with hopes that something enduring could develop with Sabrina, I could see other paths, other possibilities. Even so, I was still up to my old tricks of evasion. While she gave and received, I barricaded myself, afraid that if I opened up and told her the truth about my past, I would lose her.

It was Sabrina's spirituality and high morals that made me adore her. We had spent the night together on several occasions, but I had never dared take it further than holding her in my arms, thrilled just to be with her and watch her sleep. But one night as I lay holding her, overwhelmed by feelings of fear and love, and terrified by my desire for her, she awakened and kissed me. Thirsting for her, I kissed her lips, hands, and cheeks, feeling as if I had arrived at an oasis.

She ran her hands tenderly over my scarred chest, then turned my face to hers. Holding my gaze, she whispered, "It's okay, Howard. I want you." It was as simple as that. All my masks, insecurities, and false bravado fell away. She wrapped her arms tightly around me and carried me to a place I had never known before—a place called hope.

The following week I arranged to pick up Sabrina after school was out. As I walked down the empty hallway to the sound of echoing footsteps, I studied the students' artwork that hung on the walls, wondering if any was done by Sabrina's students. As I neared her classroom, I could hear laughter and low voices within and was about to enter when I stopped mid-stride. Unseen from the doorway, I watched as Sabrina guided a seeing-impaired child around the classroom.

"Here are the desks," she said, placing his hand on the flat surfaces. "Yes?" She then led him to her desk and gently ran his hand slowly along the front edge. "See the difference? Let's go to the windows, okay? You're doing great!"

I could see the boy gaining confidence before my eyes.

"Can you feel the breeze? Doesn't it feel good?" she asked.

"Yes, Sabrina, it feels good."

The afternoon sun poured in through the windows and burnished her hair. I froze. I had seen beauty before—but nothing like this moment. To witness Sabrina's tender connection with that blind child made me want to weep. In silence I watched the woman I loved in the act of changing a life as she had changed mine, simply by being herself. Feeling my presence, Sabrina turned and smiled, and the moment passed. My composure regained, I emerged from the doorway, feeling as if I were stepping out of the shadows and into her light.

On the way out to my car, we paused to sit in the shade and enjoy the schoolyard glass murals. "It must have been hard for you," Sabrina said softly.

"It's fine. I'm blessed, believe me."

But I knew, next to hers, my world was colorless. I had no knowledge of what or who I came from; for me there was no continuum or connectedness. "You're in my life now and that's all I need," I told her. She said nothing, but I saw her eyes mist as she silently laid her hand on mine.

We cancelled our plans for the evening and drove back to my place, where I left her on our favorite perch of high flat rocks jutting above the beach. When I returned with glasses and a bottle of wine I'd retrieved from the house, there was Sabrina silhouetted against the flaring sun, dancing alone, the tide lapping at her feet. I quietly scaled the rock, wanting nothing more than for her dance to never end.

Sabrina was busy, and I was happy, proud even, that she wasn't changing her life for me. Insisting that nothing get in the way of her time with Susie, Teresa, her family, or work, I saw her whenever she was free. We let our growing attachment unfold naturally and soon had our favorite places in La Jolla—one, a rotisserie restaurant where a fit, well-dressed crowd in European linen suits and $300 Prada loafers dined under the shade of palm trees, slumming it by La Jolla standards with fifteen-dollar plates of chicken and black beans served by surfer girls in tight short-shorts and T-shirts. During conversations loud enough for anyone to hear, the women talked about their personal trainers, weekends in Cabo San Lucas, Gucci bags they just had to have, or the "fucking maid" who had screwed up yet again. We laughed at the air kisses and snatches of inane posturing. "Darling, you look wonderful!" "Love your shoes!" "We should all go to Europe together this summer."

As much as Sabrina enjoyed our outings, she was aghast at the money I spent and the phoniness of the club scene. "Please, let's just go home," she'd say. "It's so much nicer."

One night when she fell asleep to the sound of the surf pounding through my open doors, I stroked her hair, careful not to awaken her. Though I loved her with my entire being, I felt she was slipping away from me, that somehow what I had to offer wasn't what she wanted. Her simple need of family and community was too complex for the guarded man I was—even craving it as I did. I never doubted that our paths were meant to cross, but I also knew we were meant to part. She had no affinity for La Jolla—and that she knew the difference between our disparate worlds was the very thing that I loved about her.

"Howard, would you mind if we didn't come here anymore?" Sabrina asked one evening over dinner at the club.

"Sabrina, what are you saying?"

"It's just . . . well, I feel like I lose my identity when I'm here." Quietly she added, "It's not who I am."

"Sabrina, it's okay. Coming here doesn't matter to me. Look around. Do you really think I care about all this? I don't belong here either. I want more than this—something real—family, work that *matters*, friends who care about me. You have that. You know who you are and what's important to you. Never forget that, promise me."

Back in her apartment, we settled on throw pillows piled on her floor. Sabrina lay still in my arms. "Howard?"

I remained silent, knowing she had something important she wanted to tell me.

"Howard, the people at the club have nothing I want."

"I know that, Sabrina. Just stay true to yourself. What you have they will never know."

"That's what my mom says."

"Well then, you should listen to her. She's right."

Jumping up, she hurried over to her small stereo. "You have to listen to this song by Alanis Morissette, 'Right Through You.'" She glanced back at me, her eyes sparkling. "When she sings, it's like she's singing to me."

I settled back on my cushion to concentrate on the lyrics, welcoming anything I could learn about Sabrina. The words swept me up.

"Howard, now listen to this one. It's called 'All I Really Want,' and it's what I want too!" She laughed.

When the last notes faded away, she turned down the volume. "Yes," she said, "what I really want is an end to the crazy conflicts and pretenses." I grinned at her, blown away by how much she understood. Sabrina saw right through everything, including me.

"I love that song," she said. "It reminds me of my kids."

"How so?"

She sat on the floor and crossed her legs. "Michael, for one. He has behavioral problems and was labeled as incorrigible." As Sabrina spoke of her student, I saw myself, back in the misery of my first school in New Jersey, the one with the chicken wire embedded in the windows.

"All he needs is encouragement and understanding," she said. "He tries really hard. He can do it!"

I took her hand in mine. "And so can you, Sabrina. Like what you've shown me tonight, what Alanis was saying. What you're doing is important, Sabrina."

"Howard!" She laughed, her eyes wide. "You understand me!"

I'd been wanting to do something special for Sabrina and to give her a well-deserved break. "How does San Francisco sound?" I asked one evening as we lay curled together on my deck.

"San Francisco? Yes, yes!" Clambering over me, she hugged me repeatedly, laughing with excitement.

I wanted her experience of the city to be perfect, so I booked a room at the St. Francis, a landmark hotel deserving of her. When the taxi pulled up to the hotel, she gasped. "Howard, it's beautiful!"

We passed under the oversized red awning that faced Union Square and entered the grand lobby. Sabrina craned her head to take in the soaring, fluted columns that supported a canopy of murals lit with immense chandeliers. Beaming, she nudged me to notice the curving red-carpeted staircase and antique bar.

Hungry from the trip, we ventured out at the concierge's recommendation to a little place known for its clam chowder and sourdough bread. Over dinner Sabrina bandied about ideas of all we could do. "Howard, can we go to Chinatown? I want to see the Golden Gate Bridge, museums. Oh, and ride the trolleys!"

We spent the day playing tourist: strolling around the city checking out storybook Victorian architecture, visiting Golden Gate Park, lunching in Chinatown, and at dusk, feeding the seagulls on Fisherman's Wharf. While Sabrina was in the shower getting ready to go out to dinner, I ducked out to try to get tickets for a show in the theatre district. The concierge arranged for me to meet a scalper who had tickets for *Phantom of the Opera*, a coincidence I found more than a little ironic: a masked man hidden from society meets a beautiful young woman, who through love brings out his inner beauty.

I returned to find Sabrina waiting for me in the lobby and saw her as if for the first time. In a simple black satin dress and black heels, she looked like a Mayan princess with her almond-shaped eyes, high cheekbones, and rippling, silken hair falling over her shoulders.

"Sabrina . . . you look beautiful."

"Thank you! Do you like my dress? I made it myself. Is it okay?"

Acutely aware of the figure I cut, my malformed face in stark contrast with the perfection of my double-breasted black suit, I was the Beast offering his hand to Beauty.

As arranged, we met the scalper at a coffee shop close to the theatre, in a booth at the back where he said he'd be. Right off, I got a bad vibe from his unkempt appearance and paunchy gut hanging over his belt.

We had barely slid into the banquette when he waved the tickets at me and quoted double the amount I'd agreed to pay with the concierge. I politely countered that the price was not my understanding. "Don't waste my time!" he snapped.

I tried to reason with him, but it soon became more a matter of principle than of money. Where Sabrina was concerned, money wasn't an issue if I could make her happy. He switched tactics and came on with a tough-guy act, mistaking me for some joker yuppie he could intimidate. When he became belligerent and foul-mouthed in front of Sabrina, I exploded. Lunging over the table until my eyeballs were nearly touching his, I grabbed his shirt and yanked him toward me. Livid, I twisted his shirt tight and screamed at him. "Don't you dare talk that way in front of her, you understand me?" As I pushed him away, I saw fear in his eyes, as if he were dealing with a raving lunatic.

"Okay, okay, I'm sorry, I didn't know. Here, here, take the tickets."

I threw the money on the table. "Now get out of here!"

He leapt out of the booth and scampered off like a kicked dog.

"Howard, you didn't have to be that way. That wasn't right," Sabrina said softly, her eyes lowered. She was visibly upset.

Sabrina knew I wouldn't take crap from anyone, but she had never seen me behave like that before. She was embarrassed for me, and worse, I had scared her.

"Please, Howard, I just want to go back to the hotel."

"But the play?"

"I don't want to go."

My heart sank. I felt ill. "Sabrina, I'm sorry, please, just listen . . ."

"That was wrong, Howard."

"But he tried to—"

"What does it matter? You shouldn't act that way."

I had never felt so humiliated in my life and wanted to sink through the floor and disappear. "Sabrina, I'm sorry. It's over. Can't we forget it happened? Please?" I was like a child begging his mother to be given another chance.

As she pondered me, I cast my eyes down in complete submission and awaited her verdict.

"Okay, Howard," was all she said. I took her hand and walked with her out into the fog-shrouded San Francisco night.

The grandness of the San Francisco Opera house temporarily distracted her from the scene I'd made. We found our seats, and Sabrina, awed by the red and gilded opulence, couldn't contain her excitement. In the darkened theatre I watched as she sat entranced, delicately biting her lower lip, her eyes wide with wonder. Beautiful Sabrina was slowly, lovingly, peeling away my phantom's invisible mask.

The incident with the ticket scalper was never mentioned again, but I knew my behavior that night had done irreparable damage to our relationship. After San Francisco, Sabrina seemed to distance herself, and a reserve crept into her that hadn't been there before. Though I knew she was slipping away from me, I was too afraid to do anything about it.

The fault was mine. How could I ask her to give everything when I wasn't forthcoming myself? I chose to fool myself by believing she would grant me time to redeem myself. How ironic that just when I felt I could risk opening my heart, and the invisible cage within that had kept me imprisoned and unable to fully connect with others was slowly beginning to unlock, I seemed determined to drive away the very person who had helped me find the courage.

My entire life I had fought and clawed, searching for something I could never identify, only to be hopelessly lost when I had it within my reach. I can't say I found myself that night—or even saw a light—but I did recognize that I had found someone who truly accepted me, something I hadn't yet learned to do for myself. And now, I feared, I was driving her away.

After that night we got together less frequently, on top of which her car had broken down beyond repair. But like everything else in her life, she took it in stride. "It's not so bad. I get to see lots of people on the bus and save on gas," she said, shrugging.

I knew if I offered help she would refuse outright, so I went ahead and bought an inexpensive used Jetta without consulting her and invited her over for lunch. Afterward, too excited to wait any longer, I took her by the hand and pulled her up. "Sabrina, close your eyes. I have a surprise for you!"

She gave me a curious wide grin. "A surprise?"

Taking her by her arm, I led her through my long, narrow kitchen into the brick patio and out through the rickety gate that led to the street. On the sidewalk I stopped her. "Are you ready?"

"I think so . . ." She leaned into me and nervously laughed.

"Okay. Open them!"

She opened her eyes and squinted in the bright sunlight, looking at the car in front of her with an expression of puzzlement before it dawned on her what the surprise was. When the realization hit her, her hands flew to her mouth. "Howard, no! You shouldn't have!" Laughing and jumping up and down, she flung her arms around me.

"Here's the key. Get in!" I said.

She ran around the front of the car and jumped in. Smiling, she ran her hand over the dashboard and turned to survey the backseat. Then, like a child, she pretended to drive.

"Do you like it?"

She stopped moving and got very quiet.

"Sabrina, honey, what's wrong?"

"I don't think I should accept this."

"It's okay. Really. I got a very good deal. It cost almost nothing, and you need a car."

"I shouldn't. It's too expensive a gift."

"Please. I'm lucky I found it."

She furrowed her brows. "What if I buy it and make payments?"

"We'll work it out, okay? Just do me a favor. Take your kids on a picnic."

She smiled but was still reluctant. "Okay, but I want to—"

"Sabrina, we can settle it later." Her reservations I could understand; I knew how she was.

When she spotted the clutch, her face fell. "Howard, I don't know how to drive a stick shift."

Her concern wrung my heart. "Sabrina, please don't worry. I can teach you."

We switched places, and I drove to a vacant parking lot so she could practice. Sabrina, who could make anything fun, had me laughing as we lurched along in fits and starts, the car shuddering and stalling as she struggled to get the hang of the clutch. She was having a hard time but persisted while my frustration only mounted.

"Jesus, Sabrina, let the clutch out."

"Howard, you're making me nervous."

Finally, when I'd lost all humor and patience, she figured it out.

The next day we hit the side streets of La Jolla. Everything was going smoothly until she tried to downshift to get up a small hill. Grinding the gears, she nearly brought us to a halt as cars behind us honked, trying to overtake us on the narrow road. It didn't help that I overreacted as I always did by yelling and screaming. "Jesus! Shift. Shift. Shift!"

"Howard, let me do it."

I'd never seen Sabrina so agitated. The problem was not her driving but my destructive temper. I had so shaken her self-confidence that she missed a sharp corner and jumped the curb. The car came to a jolting halt in a flower bed. Sabrina was embarrassed, and I was incapable of seeing the humor of the situation. Savagely, I reached over and turned off the ignition. "Sabrina, enough, get out. I'm driving."

"Howard, just take me home, please."

Rigidly silent the entire drive, she seemed unmoved by my repeated apologies and still wouldn't look at me when we pulled up in front of her house. "Howard, I want to return the car." Her face, usually so animated, was unrelenting.

I felt panic rising in me. "Sabrina, look at me. We'll go out for dinner, somewhere quiet where we can talk, okay, honey?"

Her voice subdued, she turned to me. "No, Howard. I can't do this anymore. I'm sorry."

"Sabrina . . . just give me another chance. *Please*, don't do this!"

"I still love you, Howard, but it's over." She touched her forehead to my shoulder and then shook her head. All I could do was watch as she got out of the car and walked away.

That night I wept, not only for myself, but also for causing her unhappiness that she didn't deserve. My temper was destroying everything dear to me.

I waited a few days before I trusted myself enough to call her up and ask if she would stop by my house. There was none of our usual banter as I led her to the futon that faced the ocean.

"Sabrina, about the car, it's a gift. I gave it to you from my heart. Please keep it. I respect and love you so much, honey. Please, I'm asking you not to let this come between us."

Her head was down, and I knew it was over.

"You're an amazing person," I said, my tears welling up as I gently raised her chin. I wanted her to look me in the eyes and see the love I felt for her. "You're young and beautiful with your entire life ahead of you. I know you have to go your own way. I know that." I paused, my voice breaking. "You know I will always be here for you. Listen to me. You've changed me for the better, Sabrina. That's something I can never forget."

We embraced, and then I let her go. Through Sabrina, I had been awakened to a new way of being in the world, and there was no going back.

ELEVEN

OR SEVERAL WEEKS I WAS too depressed to do little more than shuffle around in my bathrobe or stare blankly at the TV while the take-outs I ordered sat spoiling on the counter. Unable to sleep, I turned to Joni Mitchell, music being the only thing that gave me comfort. "A Case of You," which I had played I don't know how many times over the years, brought back memories of Sabrina bent over her sketch pad late at night, drawing by the TV's light so she wouldn't disturb my sleep. "In the blue TV screen light . . ." The lyrics broke my heart yet somehow helped me through my pain.

That I had failed Sabrina was disturbing enough, but now that she was gone, I was no longer able to deny the meaningless direction my life was heading. She had made me want to be a better man, and I was, but the guilt I carried for what I had taken from her gnawed at me, knowing that my personal growth had come at the expense of her innocence. I had been happy to attach myself to a life that represented everything mine lacked, sharing in her dreams, only to repay her with explosions of temper erupting from a lifetime of simmering anger. That it had nothing to do with her didn't matter; she had not deserved that.

Memories of Sabrina flooded over me, of her in San Francisco, the bathroom door ajar. I could still see her reclined in her bath, a circle of candles forming a halo shimmering over her wet skin. I remembered the hairpin she reached up to remove, her hair let loose in a dark cascade that tumbled over her shoulders, and was sick at heart.

Life resumed, but I could feel myself retreating to the safety of old strategies designed to keep my world compartmentalized. My hiding behind Italian suits was another mask, hardly different from the bandages I had once hidden behind. I knew the time had come for me to face up to my demons, but how did I find the courage to shed the image I had of myself, of being the selfish, rebellious loner who refused to conform to other people's rules? Was I capable of anything more than acting out of self-interest? Was I really so weak that I couldn't find one thing within me to offer up for the greater good? I was tired of always feeling shallow, of skating on a thin, superficial surface, yet was strangely relieved that Sabrina no longer had to suffer my volatile moods.

What panicked me, though, was the fear that never again in my life would I experience the light she had brought to the intolerably dark place I inhabited and hated. What if my time with her had been like being struck by lightning, a once-in-a-lifetime occurrence?

Many weeks later, just before the evening rush, I was killing time at the bar in the club's billiards room, chatting with the bartender, when I casually glanced down to the far end of the bar and noticed a sultry, raven-haired beauty leaning on the padded railing and deep in animated conversation with another woman. Tall and buxom, she wore a long, form-fitting black-velvet dress slit up the side, a vintage number that revealed a shapely leg that would have stopped traffic. Her deep, lusty laugh floated down to where I sat perched on my stool, discreetly watching her in the mirror as I sipped my Evian.

She reminded me of Rita Hayworth, almost as though she had stepped off the screen onto the red carpet, lacking only a cigarette artfully trailing from her fingertips and a ribbon of smoke exhaling from her full lips. This young woman emitted a formidable presence and had the kind of beauty that hints of mischief.

My reverie was interrupted when I realized she had caught me watching her and was returning my admiring gaze with a radiant smile.

The look we exchanged was more than mere eye contact—I was being invited into her realm and I accepted, without a word spoken. We continued to look at each other as she continued her conversation, our smiles broadening to full-on grins until finally I made my move, the attraction intensifying with each step that brought me closer. *Having fun? Been here before? What are you drinking?* I knew she had heard it all before. In the end I'm not sure I said anything. I just remember grinning as if we were old friends meeting again.

Helena lived in Chula Vista, a coastal town just a short drive from the Mexican border. When she told me she was a schoolteacher, I almost slapped my forehead. *Not again!* Somehow I had managed to meet another beautiful Latina teacher with incredible energy. As she spoke of her love for teaching, her students, and community, I knew instantly that she, like Sabrina, was a grounded woman.

There the similarities ended. Far from innocent and shy, Helena was fiery and sophisticated, a vivacious Latina loaded with street smarts, her zeal for life as apparent as her beauty. I gave no thought to a one-night stand with her or any psycho-spiritual connection. Our meeting simply felt right.

"I love this song. C'mon, let's break a sweat!"

"No thanks, go ahead. I'll wait here," I said, laughing.

Grabbing her friend's hand, she laughed back at me over her shoulder, her eyes sparkling. "See ya when I get back!" she yelled over the music.

I waited, knowing my instincts were right when she returned as promised, her skin dewy with sweat.

"You still here?" She smiled.

"I told you I'd wait, didn't I?"

"Well, now, that calls for a shot!" She slapped her hand down on the bar.

"Tequila, I presume?" I asked, playfully arching an eyebrow.

"Of course, what else?"

"Tequila it is." I ordered a round.

"So, you don't have to pay?" she asked when the bartender made no effort to collect.

"No, I work here."

She gave me a quizzical look and dramatically raised her glass. "I propose a toast."

"To what?"

"To new friends!"

Helena was the first to finish her shot, tossing it down without a wince. "Time to go home to my man," she said, reaching for her purse.

Of course! I realized. A woman like this would have a boyfriend or husband, though I'd noticed no ring on her finger.

Quietly I said, "Tell him he's a very lucky man."

"Thank you, I will. In fact, he's at home waiting for me. In bed."

"Well, that's exactly where I would be," I said, smiling.

She threw her head back and erupted with a hearty laugh, her eyes dancing mischievously. "No, it's my son. He's five and gorgeous. My little man."

I asked for her number but wasn't surprised when she turned me down. "No, you give me yours. I'll call you." I knew the nightclub code, "Yeah, right, pal. In your dreams." With nothing to lose, I jotted down my number on a bar napkin and made one final appeal. "Come up next week and have some sushi with me."

She leveled her eyes at me and smiled as I watched her tuck the folded napkin into her purse. "I will."

At the end of the week she called. I hadn't given any thought to her, but neither had I forgotten our encounter. It was in her hands.

"Hey, it's Helena. Up for sushi tonight?"

Wanting to amuse myself and hear her reaction, I deadpanned. "Helena? Who?"

There was a momentary silence followed by an incredulous, "It's me, Helena. You don't remember me?"

I couldn't hold back my laughter. "No, no, I was only kidding. How could I forget you? You know you're unforgettable."

"Damn straight, mister." She knew her worth, no doubt about that.

At the club over dinner that night, she cajoled me into having some sake, calling me a wuss when I showed reluctance. Fearless and playful, I loved her gusto and respected her unbridled frankness.

"So, Mr. Nightclub Guy, how did you end up here? Let's have it."

Resorting to my customary diversionary tactics, I redirected the conversation back to her, though she made it abundantly clear I wasn't off the hook. As I listened to her speak of her world of students, I watched a myriad of emotions flicker over her lovely face and saw in her expressive eyes her depth of passion. I saw myself as a young boy, back in a classroom with thirty kids who were not half the rebellious handful I was. Was I supposed to be sitting across from her for a reason?

"Howard, are you listening?"

I shook off my dreamlike trance. "I'm sorry. Really, I'm listening. Go on."

"I had no plans to become a teacher," she said. "I was in college studying pre-law, planning to become a civil rights attorney. I wanted to work with migrant workers for immigration rights and reform laws so that Mexican American kids would be afforded the same rights for education and healthcare as any kid born in the US. *Sí se puede. ¿Comprende? ¿Habla español?*"

"*Poco.* I'm impressed." And I was. Her goals were lofty, and she was ambitious. Another teacher. A coincidence? I began to wonder. "So how did you go from pre-law to teaching?"

"More sake first."

Unable to keep pace with her, I poured my sake into my water glass when she looked away.

"I loved the law, but something never felt right. You know, in my heart."

I nodded, knowing what she meant. "The heart never lies."

"Exactly." Shifting to the voice of a storyteller, she said, "So one night I lit a candle and began to pray. I prayed and prayed with all my heart. I asked God what he wanted me to do with my life, not what I wanted for myself." She fell silent, staring at her cup.

"And?"

He said, "Teach."

Thinking she was joking, I laughed.

"Don't laugh. I'm serious."

"Sorry," I murmured, but I couldn't help asking, "Did you actually hear his voice?"

"I did. I heard it deep inside me and felt a peace like never before. I knew right then and there my prayers had been answered. So now I'm a teacher! And so much happier." Pausing, she distractedly took a bite of sushi.

"So now you're going to change all the stigmas and stereotypes of Mexicans and Mexican Americans?"

"Hell, yes!" At that moment I felt sorry for anyone who got in her way.

Helena did have a boyfriend as it turned out, but that didn't deter us from pursuing a friendship we both felt was important. We managed never to allow more than a couple of weeks to go by without seeing each other, and every once in a while, we took along her son, Brandon, a sweet, little dark-eyed kid who loved basketball. The three of us would pile into my car and head to a nearby park, where we would run crazily around the basketball court chasing him as he ran after the ball. He and I would team up against his mom and soundly trounce her. Helena, laughing and on the run, didn't have a chance. Swooping down on Brandon, I'd fly him up to the hoop and in would go the ball, his roars of delight reward enough.

Those outings were a treat for me, so rarely was I around children. Afterward, we'd stop for tacos or ice cream before going back to my place to sit on the beach and talk while Brandon ran barefoot back and forth, dodging the surf until, finally exhausted, he returned to collapse in the sand beside his mother. Helena had big dreams for her son and was determined he go to college. Listening to her, I couldn't help but reflect how different Brandon's expectations were from mine when I was his age, when all I thought about was self-preservation.

We broke away for lunch one day and went up the coast to a rustic place in Malibu called Gladstone's. When our shellfish and Coronas arrived, Helena couldn't hold back her excitement any longer and blurted out that she had been admitted to a master's program in teaching, and when she finished that she planned to get her PhD.

"I'll have to call you Dr. Helena."

"No. Just Doctor will be fine," she said, her voice sincere.

Like Sabrina, she was passionately connected to her community. On a quest to expose me to Mexican culture, she took me to museums in Los Angeles to see paintings by Diego Rivera, Frida Kahlo, and others. Through her I learned about lesser-known poets and writers, and saw flamenco for the first time at a dance studio run by her cousin. I even met her *abuelita*, who was a respected *curandera* (natural healer).

It was at Gladstone's that Helena tried to pin me down; she hadn't forgotten. "Where did you go to college? Did you get your MBA?"

"What do you say we play Guess a Stranger?"

"Guess a what?" she asked.

"Guess a Stranger. We pick out someone and try to guess what their story is."

"You're doing it again," she said, frowning and shaking her head. "Every time I ask anything about you, you change the subject. You're not getting out of this again. You're not."

She was cornering me, but I was determined to sidestep her questions. The truth was, I was profoundly embarrassed, not just for my lack of education and checkered past, but for not having a family that connected me to something larger. She was a single mom who didn't just talk about what she was going to do, but was actually doing it. Next to hers, my ambitions seemed frivolous.

"Later, I promise. Now, let's play. Enough of the serious talk."

I jerked my head toward a beefy guy in a new "I Love LA" T-shirt walking toward us, obviously a tourist, judging by the camera dangling from his neck. "I know. He's from Iowa, here for a plumbers' convention, using his company credit card. Tonight he's going to Hollywood to check out the strip clubs. Wait. He's going to try to hide it on his expense account. How's that?"

"Howard!" Helena erupted in laughter. "You're so bad."

"Your turn. Let's see how intuitive you are."

"Okay, you're on." She scanned the room and pointed to an older woman sitting in the corner. "Her, the one with the teased hair and too much makeup. She's a judge for Little Miss Beauty pageants. She spends half her paycheck on hair products and makeup. Buys hair spray by the case and was once a showgirl in Vegas in the '70s."

"Wow, you're good. Maximum points for creativity and originality."

It puzzled me that Helena was single. She was a fascinating, desirable woman who could have easily found someone to take care of her and her son—someone who could offer her security. When I shared my thoughts on the subject, she shrugged. "I'm not interested if they don't get me or what I'm about."

Over a game of pool one night, I was getting a kick out of her competitive nature and her skills with the cue stick when I heard a familiar voice. "Hey, kid, how about a game?" I turned around to see KC standing behind me, impeccably dressed as ever.

"KC, good to see you! Where have you been keeping yourself?"

"You know me, kid, gotta keep moving," he said, erupting in his signature chortle as he patted me on the back.

Insisting he join us and let me buy him a drink, I introduced him to Helena. We resumed our game, the mood light while KC entertained us with stories that had us in stitches.

I looked up to see Mark strutting through the crowd toward us, camera in hand, his chest puffed out, as a couple followed in his wake. When they drew closer, I recognized the actor Tony Curtis with a lady friend on his arm. His companion, a tall, painfully thin woman with inflated red lips and bleached hair, possessed the most enormous breasts I'd ever seen. In a skintight red dress that left little to the imagination, she minced along on stiletto heels, her breasts bobbing ahead of her like Jessica Rabbit's. That she didn't pitch forward defied physics.

I turned to see both Helena and KC staring. For once, KC was speechless.

Tony, very much the gentleman and a genuinely nice guy, accepted my offer to join us for a game of pool, while his date, occupied with a flute of champagne, perched on a nearby couch. Sidling up to me, Helena ribbed me with her elbow. "Can you believe Tony's toupee?" she whispered in my ear. "It's so obvious!"

"Well, look at KC's rug."

"No, he's got one too? You're serious?" Helena was enjoying herself immensely, her eyes darting back and forth like she was courtside at a tennis match.

"KC's is more subtle, more Frank Sinatraesque," I said. "Don't you think?" Just then I heard KC wrapping up an investment pitch to Tony, who was showing no interest whatsoever.

Helena, unable to contain her laughter, excused herself to go to the ladies' room. Casually, I mentioned to Tony that I'd recently been to an exhibition of his paintings and was an admirer of his work.

"Howard, right? You've got a beautiful club here, and I have to say I'm having a marvelous time." Between shots he regaled us with stories of his early days in San Diego and his time filming *Some Like It Hot* on Coronado Island. "Say, where's your girlfriend gone off to?" he asked, looking around for Helena. "She's a lovely lady."

"No, no, Tony, we're only friends." I could see his interest piqued. "Really? So is she single?"

I knew Helena was on Tony's radar, and wanting some comic diversion, I thought, why not?

"She is, actually. She's a fun, wild one, that girl." It was clear Tony's curiosity ratcheted up a notch.

When Helena returned, I invited KC to a game of pool and left her with Tony. As I lined up for the winning shot, I glanced over to see her tightly wedged between Tony and his companion's chest. The look of dumbfounded shock on her face made me quickly wrap up the game with a deliberately bad shot. "Good game, KC. Let me buy you a drink."

I felt a solid punch to my shoulder and turned to see Helena. "I can't believe you left me alone with them!" she said. "Do you have any idea what they wanted?"

"Hmm, a new adventure?"

Helena's eyes bore into mine, and as we turned toward the bar, I heard KC's fading voice, "So, Tony, how long are you in town for?" I could imagine what was coming.

That was one of the last times I ever saw KC. A few nights later, Mark, the ingrate, came crying to me. "You have to talk to KC. He's got $5,000 on tab." I had approved KC for an open tab, feeling it was the least we could do, and he hadn't been shy about putting it to use.

"Mark," I said, "it cost us what, twenty, thirty cents on the dollar? If it weren't for him, you and I wouldn't be standing here now."

To placate Mark, I met KC for a drink and explained the situation. As always, he was his usual gracious self. "Kid, this is not a problem," he said, patting me on the back. It made me feel bad to have to collect because, despite his questionable dealings and shady maneuvers, KC had a big heart in his own way. He'd taken me under his wing in ways far beyond that of a business associate, and for that I was deeply appreciative.

Not long afterward, I heard KC had left town. The news, while not surprising, made me regret I hadn't been given the chance to say a proper good-bye. Still, I had to admit that his disappearing was a fitting end to our relationship—his exit, like our first meeting, was abrupt and without explanation. I think we each intuitively knew we could ease a gaping void in the other: me, the young, fatherless protégé anxious to learn, and he, the brilliant outcast, protective and wanting to redeem himself. Between us was a tacit understanding that didn't require words. We both understood the other's need to keep moving.

I never in my life wanted to see another pair of surgical gloves or again smell the caustic odor of hospital disinfectant. I'd seen enough plastic name tags ending with MD to last me several lifetimes. I had thought I was through with surgeries—not because I was happy or even satisfied with my appearance, but because I was done with being cut, molded, and stitched. However, my lack of a lower right eyelid was becoming more than a nuisance. Aggravated by the salty air, my eye wept all the time, and I was fed up with incessantly having to wipe away tears. Though my condition had never been a priority on my surgical to-do list, I was now willing to try an experimental modification, hoping that a simple nip and tuck would take care of the problem.

I settled on Dr. Stephenson, a respected specialist in eye modification. He practiced out of an office in La Jolla that reflected the cachet of his address, and once again I was offered the obligatory bottle of imported water.

Looking around at the all-too-familiar setting, I sat with my legs dangling off the end of the examination table and was besieged by a flood of memories that thankfully was interrupted by the doctor's arrival. I liked him immediately, even though his large hands were an unpleasant reminder of Dr. Gratz's. Head back, Dr. Stephenson peered down at me through his tortoise-frame glasses and studied my eyes. In his, I saw a spark of genuine concern and knew that I was in the hands of someone with compassion. I wanted to tell him I felt as if

I were trapped in a revolving medical door that never slowed down long enough to let me exit, but instead asked, "Just how complicated is this going to be?"

"It's a significant surgery, but it should resolve your problem."

Should? I felt my hopes plummet. "What do you mean?"

"As you well know, given your medical history, I can't make any guarantees. Nonetheless, I feel confident."

He explained that the surgery would require two phases. First, he'd construct a lower eyelid by grafting skin from my upper right eyelid and attaching it to where my lower eyelid would normally be—essentially the same process used in my lip procedure the previous year. Rather than being on a liquid diet for eight weeks, I would only need to wear an eye patch. A pirate with no ship. I couldn't hold back my sigh of disappointment; it would not be the simple nip and tuck I'd hoped for.

"And part two?" I asked.

"In the second phase, we will insert a small plastic tube inside the corner of your eye to act as a duct, providing your tears with a drainage cavity so they will flow more naturally."

As usual my mind raced to seek the most efficient and proactive course. "Can you combine the two procedures?"

"I've done that before, but I can only make that decision once I get a good look inside." When he saw the disappointment on my face, he assured me he would go in with that aim, but that was all he would promise.

That was enough to sell me. "Fine, let's do it."

"Howard, don't you want to take a few days to think it over?"

"No, not really. I need an eyelid, and you build them. I trust you." I shrugged. "That's about it."

A few weeks later I arrived before dawn at Scripps Hospital in La Jolla and was soon prepped for surgery. "Listen," I told my newest anesthesiologist. "First, I'll need some Valium, and then please be sure to remove the air tube from my throat before I wake so I'll avoid choking."

Perplexed, he looked at me as if unsure who was wearing the name tag. "Anything else?" he asked.

"No, that about covers it."

Helena somehow got me home from the hospital. Half conscious, I was in no shape to be of much help, but she managed to get me settled in bed before I fell back into a drugged sleep.

When I woke up, the room was dark except for a pool of light where Helena sat reading, curled up in my desk chair. In a sedated dream, I drifted in and out of sleep, struggling to keep my one eye on her and anchor myself to her calming presence.

I woke again to the feel of a steaming cloth and saw Helena smiling down at me, her face full of concern as she gently wiped the blood off my face. "Hey, you. You awake? How do you feel?" she asked. "How about some tea?"

I nodded, my throat still sore from the breathing tube. For nearly a week Helena played nurse, bringing me all my meals and changing my bandages. Being in her presence was the best medicine I could possibly have had. Except for Sabrina, I had never before allowed any woman to see me in such a vulnerable state. Ironically, when my sight was impaired, I could see more and more.

"Howard, hold still."

Though I had hoped I'd never again hear the sound of scissors snipping at stitches, it nonetheless signaled a rite of progress—the desired outcome was in sight. Like a vacuum-packed seal opening for the first time, I felt my lower eyelid release from the upper one.

"Hold on, your lid is a bit stuck. I'll clean it with some peroxide."

I felt queasy, the odor triggering memories I'd rather forget, and had to remind myself to breathe.

"Okay, Howard, open your eye. Slowly now."

I did as instructed, forced to obey by the harsh overhead light. The room was fuzzy, but I could see Dr. Stephenson's blurred features just inches from mine. Seconds later, the world came into focus and my sight returned to normal.

"Looks great," Dr. Stephenson said, beaming as he stepped back. After briefly studying my eye, he offered me a hand mirror. "Would you like to take a look?"

Carefully, I examined the reconstruction. It was surreal to see a lower eyelid where none had been before. What the surgery had done to improve my looks was emotionally overwhelming. I wanted to convey to Dr. Stephenson my gratitude but was too choked up to speak.

"You're just fine, Howard. How about we give the tube a test run!" He tilted my head back and deftly squeezed a few drops of artificial tears into the corner of my new eyelid. "That's good. Now pinch your nostrils together for me and inhale."

Amazed, I felt a whoosh as the tears were sucked into the implanted tube and disappeared into the cavity, followed by a novel sensation of water trickling down my throat. It worked! I gave a sigh of relief and thanked Dr. Stephenson, this time shedding a few tears of my own.

My delight was short-lived.

Only days later, when I stood before my bathroom mirror applying the eye drops that kept the tube clear and working, no liquid slid down my throat after I'd done the disappearing sniffing trick. Nothing. I tried repeatedly, squeezing and sniffing harder and harder, only to have the artificial tears pool and spill down my cheek. I panicked and grabbed a Q-tip to see if the tube had become clogged but couldn't feel it catch on the rim or feel any sign of its presence.

I looked in the sink. Could it have gone done the drain? I dashed to my bed and frantically searched my sheets, finding nothing. "Shit! I can't believe this." I slammed my fist into the mattress. I dropped to the floor and combed the rug on all fours. "Please, God, don't do this to me."

In the nap of the carpet, my fingers grazed the tube. Holding my breath, I went back to the bathroom and washed it off with sterile artificial tears before trying, unsuccessfully, to reinsert it myself. Defeated, I was soon back on Dr. Stevenson's examination table.

"Howard," he said, "you have to understand. Sometimes they slip out."

"Slip out!" I forced myself to calm down. This man was my eyelid specialist—I needed him. "Why didn't you *tell* me this could happen?"

"In your case, I didn't think it would be an issue."

Somehow I restrained myself from screaming out what I wanted to say: *Maybe your surgery caused permanent scarring of the tissue— ever think of that? Why the hell didn't you tell me what could go wrong?*

"Howard, let's do this. Let me try to insert it and then see what happens." The good doctor leaned over me and started working the tube into my sensitive canal.

"Shit! Stop!" I yelled. Determined to bear the pain in exchange for a functioning eye, I grasped the sides of the table and dug my fingernails into the thick leather. I took a deep breath and told him to try again, but after a few excruciating seconds, I couldn't take it anymore. "Stop, *stop!*"

He looked almost as frustrated as I was. Of course, he couldn't know that my emotional pain was even worse than the physical. "Howard, this is too much. Let's try a local anesthesia." When the second attempt was no more successful, he suggested that we wait a few days and try again under general anesthesia.

"Fuck. Shit. Fuck. Fuck." I was on the brink of losing it and had no words to express my frustration and disappointment. I thought I was going to break down. My tears that had no place to go welled up. "I can't take it anymore," I said half to myself. "I just can't." One straightforward surgery had turned into a nightmare torture session. I looked up at him and told him through clenched jaws, "You got me into this—*now get me out.*"

"The only thing left is to take some X-rays and possibly make a custom tube for you," he said, his face clouded with concern.

With no other option, I agreed. The following week I was back under general anesthesia and fitted with a new standard tube that had to be adjusted every few hours. I trained myself to periodically check its position with my index finger and push it back in place if necessary. It worked and that was all that mattered. I just needed to constantly keep my finger on the problem. Literally.

The ordeal with my plastic tear duct wasn't over. I noticed it missing one morning when I leaned into the mirror while brushing my teeth and saw tears pooling behind my lower eyelid. Pinching my nostrils to suck them down had no effect. I checked in the mirror again—not even a ripple of liquid. Dejected, I stared down the drain.

A referral from Dr. Stephenson led me to a Dr. Hornblass in the Bronx, back yet again to where my saga had begun. As it turned out, the pain this new doc put me through was for nothing, because only days later, I was tubeless again. Beyond the physical inconvenience, my lower eyelid had begun to droop, exposing my lid's red interior and reminding me of a fish on a hook gasping for air.

I called Dr. Stephenson in California and through clenched teeth made myself clear. "I don't care where I have to go—London, Rio, Paris—whatever it takes! I'm in hell. You took me here, now get me out!"

As promised, Stephenson's secretary called me with the names of two well-known specialists: Dr. Wobig in Portland, Oregon, for my plastic tube, and Dr. Anderson in Salt Lake City, who reconstructed eyes. Wobig would custom fit me with a Jones Tube, a device invented by the doctor Wobig had trained under. If he couldn't help me, I was screwed.

While my custom tube was being made, I checked into the Shady-something Motel in Portland. Situated on a slab of baking asphalt, it didn't have a spec of shade. The night before my surgery, I smoked a joint and popped a Valium, terrified that I was at the end of the line for help. This was about functionality—nothing cosmetic about this one. Emotionally spent, I dropped to my knees and, with my elbows sunk in the polyester bedspread, made a last-ditch pre-op plea. To the din of rain drumming on the metal chairs outside my motel room, I prayed for God to please let my new tube stay in this time. Desperate, I apologized for everything I could think of that I'd done to disappoint him and promised to do better, then dozed off in a drug-induced slumber.

Miraculously, my Jones Tube worked beautifully, and when it still appeared to be functioning after a few months, I flew to Salt Lake City to meet Dr. Anderson.

Once again as in Portland, I put myself through the paces: motel, Valium, joint, prayer, repentance. After the insertion of an artificial strip inside my lower eyelid to provide support, I was left with a reasonably shaped lower lid. It didn't match the other one, but it kept its form. What mattered was that my eye functioned and I could see without obstruction.

Drained from the emotional roller coaster I'd been on, all I wanted was to retreat and get my head clear. Tahiti, faraway and exotic, seemed the perfect place for a complete break. Deciding to forego amenities and live simply, I rented a bamboo-and-frond hut on the beach and spent my days soaking up the sun, eating fresh fish and an array of fruit I mostly didn't recognize, and putting miles on my rented bicycle on short excursions I made around the island.

Gradually I ventured further inland. One day on a hike through rugged terrain, I picked up a steep path that led through lush foliage and followed it zigzagging up the mountain. At the top, I scrambled up a massive rock and found a perch from where I could gaze out at the world below. Small dots of emerald extended to the horizon and seemed to float on an expanse of sapphire blue. Not long before, with my bandaged eye, I would have gotten only half the picture.

I next discovered diving (my tightly fitted goggles safeguarding my precious eye tube) and spent hours exploring a world I'd hardly imagined to exist. Never had I felt so free as I did swimming in those waters of flickering light and shadow—not just in body, but in spirit. There was nothing to weigh me down—no surgeries, no bandages, nothing dreadful on the horizon. Only beauty.

I surfaced and headed for the shadow of a wind-swept palm. After flinging myself on the sand, I heard shouts and ripples of laughter and turned to see a group of bronzed bodies descend noisily to the beach. From the shade I watched as they excitedly unpacked a picnic and set up a volleyball game. Young and old darted from beach to water and back again, their shrieks carrying down the shore. Feeling my mood plummet, I turned away. At issue wasn't my face. What deflated me was my lack of connection—a lack that robbed my life of much of its pleasure. I had come a long way from where I had started, but I had yet to find my true moorings.

From Tahiti I flew on to Jamaica, working—or, more accurately, playing—my way home. On the beach a few days later, I happened to strike up a conversation with some friendly young locals who invited me to a beach party they were throwing that night. Gladly, I accepted.

Night had fallen by the time I arrived, and after consuming too many swigs from a communal bottle of Jamaican rum, plus taking several hits off a massive joint being passed around, I was thoroughly stoned, happy to stare at the sparking fire. In a near trance, I smiled at my new friends dancing wildly around the bonfire, their bodies bathed in firelight. Reggae, weed, and jerk chicken spread contented grins across their faces.

Out of nowhere, melancholy descended on me like a great weight. I wandered alone down to the shoreline and waded in until the gentle waves lapped at my scarred calf, the tug of the Caribbean pulling at me as music flowed around me and out to sea. I shoved my hands deep in my pockets and stood staring at the watery path of light that led to the moon, wondering how it would feel to know my heritage and the people I came from, to have a sense of community.

Why this nostalgia for something I had never known? I was here, I was alive, and I had made it this far. That was something, wasn't it? I scanned the pinholes of light piercing the night sky, then took a slow draught of rum and went back to the bonfire.

In Miami, with a few hours to kill before my connecting flight to San Diego, I called my sister to tell her I was back. "Howard . . ." I could feel Robin flailing for words and knew something was terribly wrong. Bracing myself, my forehead pressed against the phone booth's glass, I held my breath. "Howard . . . Mom died." I shut my eyes. "Leukemia. It was so quick . . . We couldn't wait for you—nobody knew where you were. I'm so sorry."

I managed to get out a few words before hanging up. Then I drifted dreamlike down the concourse to my gate, where I took refuge by the wall of windows until my flight was called. Before me a steady parade of jets lumbered across the tarmac—it was unfathomable that the world could go on as if nothing had changed.

Guilt-ridden and numb, I mercifully made it home before shock turned to grief. There are no words to describe the feeling of losing that one person upon which everything else depends. My mom, my anchor, was gone. She had loved me unconditionally since I was a child, accepting me for who I was, disfigurement and all. It broke my heart—I had heaped so much rage and rebellion on her for no reason, and she had borne it all. I'd had plenty of setbacks, and I always knew I could count on Shirl. Who was going to be there for me now? That sounded so selfish, but I had no idea how I'd manage without her. I was scared. I didn't want to go through life alone.

Anger fought with grief—rage was my trusty substitute for emotions I couldn't risk feeling. All I knew was that my mom had been sick, and where was I? Lying on a beach, oblivious to anything but my own selfish wants, that's where! But not being allowed to bury her, or even say good-bye, felt too unfair a punishment. With Shirl's passing went my last chance to let her know how much she had meant to me. Did she have any idea of the depth of my gratitude? My mom, who nursed me, prepared me for the world, and showed me how to love, had mothered and fought every inch of the way for the monstrous child she had been handed. She *raised* me—and now she was gone.

It was unbearable to remember the angry child I'd been and all I'd put her through. God, the horrible things I said to her when I was young, the hurt she must have felt when I turned on her, raging how hateful she was and how she wasn't my real mother. Was this my punishment? That I could never tell her that without her I would have been truly lost?

Almost by osmosis, I had absorbed my most important life lesson from her: the power of love. I believe Shirl understood it was love above all else that would heal me. There's no arguing I needed her nursing skills, but the most perfect face in the world wouldn't have made me whole if I were to grow up unloved. I saw the sacrifices she willingly made for Ed and the four of us children, and as much as I felt undeserving and perversely fought it, it was thanks to her the conviction had gradually taken root that I was as worthy of love as anyone else.

At night I escaped to the beach, where I struggled to come to terms with her passing. I remembered everything I could, back to the very beginning: her tying my shoes as I sat on the stairs, peering down through the banisters at my first home; the many games we played to teach me arithmetic; her sympathetic ear when cruelty threatened to crush me; her relentless optimism. I remembered the way she rolled her eyes and her dry humor that kept our family on track and put everything in perspective. My grief grew quiet, but the unfairness of losing her was hard to accept. Shirl, who'd spent a lifetime caring for others, should have been spared the cruel irony of fighting her own battle.

Not for the first time, it staggered me to think of the courage it must have taken to bring a broken child into her home. What in me made her begin to love me? Or was it equally something that sprang from her? And why had she thought I was worth the effort? Love? What other possible reason would make a person never give up? I could see her shaking her head. "What kind of question is that? You're my Howie!"

She was my nurse, but foremost she was my mom, the first to see beauty in me. Beyond my deformities and behavioral problems, she saw a child desperate for love, whose greatest disadvantage was to have begun life handicapped by its absence.

I remembered her stories of amputees and burn victims, her examples not meant to frighten, but to give me perspective: that I was smart, strong, and capable—with challenges, yes, but none insurmountable. When school bullies tormented me, I know she suffered with me. She had no real solutions, but I knew she believed I'd find a way to survive it—and I did. Most of all, I remembered her making me feel there was a place in the world that was mine. Where was my place now? In every sense that mattered, Shirl had given me my life. What had I given her? I wanted her forgiveness, to tell her I was sorry. I wanted her to know she had saved me. Overwhelmed, I buried my face in my hands and wept.

Many, many nights later, I wandered the beach in front of my house, trying to see the stars through the lights of the city when I felt a shift, as if the bands constricting my heart loosened. Above all else, I wanted to make Shirl proud of me. If I could find a way to be more giving, like she had been, rather than always taking, maybe I'd find what I was searching for.

When it occurred to me that I already had Shirl's forgiveness, it wasn't because I wanted to absolve myself, but because that's the person she was. She would want my efforts, not my guilt. The experience of being Shirl's child changed my truth—she was the game changer who had quietly led me out of my wilderness by simply holding up a mirror in which "invalid" or "unlovable" were never reflected.

Arriving at the water's edge, I looked up to ponder the night sky and was comforted by the thought of Mom rolling her eyes, telling me not to worry—we do the best we can, and if we're lucky we learn something along the way. "I'm trying, Mom," I whispered, and then smiling, I turned for home.

T W E L V E

HAD GROWN TIRED OF THE pretentiousness of La Jolla and had little to show for my time spent there in terms of people I could honestly call friends. The club was a success, but I was stagnating and needed something new to do, though I had no idea what that might be. I found myself missing the East Coast—the seasons, the directness of people, their energy—so I decided to move to Manhattan. The Big Apple. Why not? I'd never lived there, and where better in the country to get my blood pumping. Helena was getting more serious with her boyfriend, which meant less time for me. With no real ties holding me back, I announced my plans to her over lunch.

"Mark is already pretty much running the club without me as it is," I told her. "If I'm hardly there anyway, I might as well be in New York."

"Howard, that's a great idea! Whether you're out east or here, we're friends—nothing will change that. We'll be fine. You should go!" I knew I could count on her support, as she could on mine, and I was relieved she didn't think my idea was ludicrous.

Two weeks later, I was on a plane heading east. As we banked into the sun, I smiled at the sight of downtown San Diego nestled below, realizing how much I had grown and accomplished since moving there. I knew I was making the right decision, breaking out of my comfort zone and seeking something that couldn't be touched or bought, something undefined but growing within me.

I bought a one-bedroom apartment on the thirty-third floor on the Upper East Side, with a kitchen the size of the tiny bathroom I'd had in La Jolla. The living and dining areas were long and narrow, but the place had lots of windows and a balcony with magnificent views of the city. When the windows were open, the distant sound of traffic drifted up from the street below. It was about as far from trendy La Jolla as one could get: instead of surfboards, bikinis, and sand, I saw briefcases, high fashion, and concrete. It was overpriced and undersized, but it was Manhattan.

My first several weeks there, I spent nearly every waking moment exploring the city that never sleeps: riding my bike through Central Park, taking the subways, and watching the infinite variety of people. Recharged, I wanted to get involved in something worthwhile, so I volunteered at a center for the blind, whose clients were mostly teenagers. For the first time in my life, I was with people who didn't "see" me as different. Like able-sighted kids, they flirted and gossiped and compared notes about their favorite musicians, movies, and sports teams. In a music store we visited once, I was touched when they insisted I listen in with them on their headphones. I couldn't help but think of Sabrina with her blind student, and I wanted to be giving like her, but for me, unfortunately, altruism wasn't second nature.

Since leaving San Diego, I noticed that my share of the profits from the club had steadily diminished, and knowing Mark as I did, I was confident it wasn't a coincidence. I'd given him the benefit of the doubt for too long and decided it was time to give him a call.

"So, Mark, how's business?" I asked, keeping my suspicions to myself.

"It's slowed down. A few new clubs have opened up, and there's the whole dot-com bust, as you know. But, hey, that's business."

I played along, damned if I would give him any heads-up.

"Howard, trust me, I'm doing all I can."

When he said that, alarms went off, and I knew I needed to make a surprise visit.

Timing my return so I could see how "slow" the club was on a Saturday night, I got a hotel room a few blocks away and arrived unannounced. Not surprisingly, the line outside the club was as long as it had ever been. I chatted with the doorman and asked about business. "Howard, it's always good," he said. "You know that."

Inside, the same familiar faces greeted me as I made my way to the main bar. There I cornered Phil, who had bartended for us from the beginning, and off-handedly asked him for a quick rundown. According to him, business was excellent. Feeling like a covert operative, but leery of raising any suspicion that I was checking up on my partner, I casually asked, "So, how's Mark doing?"

"You know Mark—he's always up to something," Phil answered, stirring a cocktail while I wisely nodded my head, acting as if I knew what he was talking about. "Did you see his new Bentley yet?" he asked.

"Yeah, I heard about it. Incredible! That's Mark for you." I laughed, playing along.

"He's out of town pretty regularly, so I don't see him around here too much. He was just in Hawaii, and I know he goes up to Vegas a lot."

"He's something, that Mark," I said. "I wish I had the time to do all he does."

We talked a bit about New York, when Phil suddenly asked, "Are you going to be a partner in Mark's new club?"

"New club?" I hoped I didn't sound like an idiot.

"Yeah, he's opening an even bigger one."

My mind raced. "Oh yeah, he mentioned something about that. No, one's enough for me. How's that going?"

"He said he'd be open in a few months. Said he was going to be taking a few employees with him to the new place."

I was almost shaking with anger but kept my composure. What else was he moving? It was blatantly clear he was riding high on my money.

Back at my hotel I took my time digesting everything I had learned and carefully thought through how I was going to handle the situation.

The next morning I called him up. "Hey, Mark, I'm in town." I could hear his breath catch.

"You're here?" he asked.

"Yeah, I was at the club last night and wanted to surprise you, but you weren't there."

"I was, uh, not feeling well, so I called it an early night."

"Well, do you feel good enough to get together for an update?"

"Update?" The alarm in his voice wasn't my imagination. "Can't it wait?"

"Mark, c'mon. I flew three thousand miles to see you." He knew me well enough to know I'd go over to his place if he didn't come to me.

I was waiting in front of the club when he arrived, and before he could turn the key and punch in the security code, I stared straight at him and told him how great he looked. He stiffened but said nothing—I could tell he knew something was up.

An empty nightclub has a distinct feel; in its silence, two people can somehow fill an immense space. Mark, playing the role of gracious host, stepped behind the bar and got us each a cold bottle of water. When we had settled into a booth, I let him squirm, his charade of nonchalance failing miserably. His face was taut, like he was bracing for takeoff.

"So, Mark, I don't get it."

"Get what?"

"Well, you say business is slow. What I mean is, I'm told the numbers have dropped since I left, in only a few months." I kept my voice calm, matter-of-fact.

"What are you saying?"

"What I'm saying, Mark, is you're driving a Bentley, taking bigshot vacations, and now you're opening a club. How's that?" I asked, keeping my eyes trained on his.

"Who told you?' he said, alarm in his voice.

"Are you kidding? Who doesn't know? What amazes me, Mark, is you tell me over the phone how bad business is but you forget one thing—YOU'RE OPENING A CLUB. WHO TOLD ME? WHO DOESN'T KNOW?" I was screaming at him now.

"That's my business," Mark snapped.

"No, Mark, it's mine. You're commingling funds and employees."

"Hey, check the books if you want."

"Check the books? That's rich, Mark. It's all cash. You're clipping the joint."

At that, he puffed up like a cartoon character in Italian loafers and played his contract card. "Listen, Howard, I'm the managing partner and I act at my discretion, so you'll just have to deal with it." He sat back and spread-eagled his arms out across the back of the booth, a look of smug triumph on his face.

I laughed in his Gucci glasses. "Hmm, deal with it, right, Mark? You slept on my couch, I gave you money to buy a couple of suits before we opened, and I'm supposed to deal with it? How do you figure that?"

"I'll get a lawyer and put a restraining order on you!" He took a swig of water that didn't seem to go down too well.

I paused. I knew him through and through, and when it came down to it, he always choked. I leaned toward him. "I have a better idea. You want to hear it?" He sat motionless, a peevish, pinched look on his face. "Since you're going to continue to rob the place blind and I'll essentially be insolvent within six months, I figure I have two options. Number one, you buy me out."

"Are you crazy? I don't have that kind of money."

"Hold on. I haven't told you your second option."

"You can forget it. I'm not buying you out." He licked his lips and downed his water like a parched animal.

"Okay, so here's option two: I go to the Alcohol Beverage Commission and rat you out for money laundering."

"No way," he said, his jaw clenched.

"Mark, sell your Bentley or a couple of pinkie rings, I don't care." I watched his face turn from red to scarlet. "And did you maybe forget that the liquor license is in my name too? As I see it, I have nothing to lose and you have everything to gain. You'll be Mr. Nightclub, or Nightclubs, I should say. You deal with it."

"Fine, okay, good. How much are we talking about?" he asked, looking as if he were bracing himself for a nasty dose of medicine.

I gave him the healthy six-number figure I had arrived at before our meeting. "I'll call my lawyer and draw it up."

Angrily he got up and stormed into his office, while I leisurely finished my water, the last I would have at the club. As the doors closed behind me, I had no regrets. It was the end of a chapter whose time was over. I *had* seen the other side of the velvet rope. And I wasn't looking back.

THIRTEEN

AFTER RETURNING TO NEW YORK, I felt adrift, once again not knowing what to do with my life. I hadn't seen Helena while I was in San Diego—mostly because I was too busy extricating myself from Mark and his sticky fingers—but I'd been reassured by how happy she sounded over the phone. At least one of us was on track.

I had faith that a new calling would show itself soon. In the meantime, I was living the California lifestyle in Manhattan. Every morning I strolled to H&H Bagels to have my coffee and read the *New York Times*, after which I put in a good hour working out at the gym.

Afternoons, I liked to browse the eighteen miles of shelves at the Strand Bookstore in the Village at Twelfth and Broadway. I hadn't forgotten KC's advice to read, read, read every chance I got, and I did just that. I perused the memoir and biography sections for hours, trying to make up for my rebellious youth spent sabotaging my education. I wanted to bring my mind up to the same rigorous discipline I demanded of my body.

I began with *The Diary of Anne Frank*. How, I wondered, at such a young age and in such devastating circumstances, could she write so eloquently and articulate her feelings so well—even risking her life and that of her companions to do the forbidden and draw back that curtain just to see a single flower growing below her window?

I immersed myself in books like Nelson Mandela's *Long Walk to*

Freedom and Booker "T" Washington's *Up from Slavery*. Nelson Mandela's ability to use his mind to see beyond the concrete walls of his prison cell astounded me. Because he refused to renounce his political convictions, he was imprisoned for twenty-seven years yet held no hatred toward his captors. And Washington, a former slave who became a teacher, worked in a salt furnace and coal mine as a young boy and traveled five hundred miles predominantly on foot to get a college education.

Though they were a world away in space, time, and circumstances, their stories spoke directly to me. Where did they find the strength and inner fortitude? As I read their books, I began to appreciate all that I had been blessed with, grateful that I'd never had to suffer such hardships. What Lena years before had tried to make me understand began to take on meaning beyond mere words.

On a lovely spring morning, I set off toward Greenwich Village. Feeling buoyant with new possibility, I wove through the crowds as the cries of street vendors hawking their knock-off designer watches and handbags rose above the traffic. For a moment I paused in the stream of pedestrians, undecided where to go, when I noticed a narrow, one-way cobblestone lane off the main thoroughfare. In the mood to explore, I turned onto it and soon felt I had stepped into a bygone era of smaller buildings and tighter streets. I was perhaps halfway to the next cross street when I passed a bookstore nestled between two brick townhouses.

Under the grime-coated window, blocking the narrow sidewalk, a long, heavy-legged table was haphazardly piled with stacks of books, the overflow contained in wooden crates beneath. Slowing down, I skimmed the titles as I walked by and stopped when I reached the last stack. Why I felt compelled to browse through the end pile I can't say, but after removing a few volumes from the top, I froze, my hand in midair. Silence flooded my ears as I slowly picked up the slender volume. Scarcely breathing, I studied the photograph of the young girl on the cover, whose face was obscured by a piece of wrinkled cellophane.

The world around me disappeared as I registered the title. *Autobiog-*

raphy of a Face. Right there on the sidewalk, I began to read the book, a hunger surging through me like a charge of electricity. I skimmed page after page, words jumping out at me like "skin grafts," "scars," "embarrassment," "face." My heart raced and the realization grew that in those pages was a theme consistent with my life.

I quickly went inside and paid the clerk, and on the first quiet stoop I found, I sat down to read. Starting again from the beginning, I devoured every word of Lucy Grealy's memoir. She told the story of the rare cancer that had attacked her jaw and gradually eaten away at her face, and described the innumerable surgeries she endured as a child and young woman, the physical and emotional pain she experienced, the struggles to keep going. It was as though I were reading my own story, my own pain.

When I had finished the first chapter, reading as fast as my eyes and mind could absorb the words, I stood and headed for the subway. Oblivious to my surroundings, I read on, only coming back to the present when I heard the conductor announce, "Next stop, 79th and Lexington Avenue."

Back in my apartment, I stretched out on the couch and continued reading. I was stunned to learn how Lucy employed the same survival tactics I did. We had both honed the skill of avoiding eye contact: dipping our heads to avoid the gaze of strangers and picking up speed when passing others, not wanting to give them time to register our deformity. At our beck was a litany of excuses for not being photographed or doing anything that would subject us to needless exposure. I related to Lucy and felt for her—how she hid, often behind animals, especially horses. They were her refuge where no one judged or stared.

Her alienation, loneliness, and pain were palpable. I couldn't fathom how a petite young woman like Lucy had survived the cruelty and maliciousness she had suffered. As a man I could physically defend myself and over the years had developed a mindset of never allowing anyone to intimidate me, even if I had to use my scars as a prop for self-defense. My tough-guy facade was a shield to hide my vulnerability and discourage anyone who might think I was easy prey.

How, I wondered, could Lucy defend herself? All of society was against her, brainwashed by magazines and movies filled with images of the ideal woman, one who starved herself and hid behind a mask of cosmetics. In the elusive quest for perfect beauty, an impossible standard had been imposed on all women. What chance did *she* have? I wanted to protect her, comfort her.

"Life in general was cruel and offered only different types of void and chaos," Lucy writes. "The only way to tolerate it, to have any hope of escaping it, I reasoned, was to know my own strength, to defy life by surviving it."

I was profoundly moved when I read that passage, comforted in ways I'd never felt before. But sadly for her, that void was never to be filled. She died too young, of a heroin overdose, most likely heartbroken and alienated from the world, through no fault of her own. With Lucy I found kinship with a woman I'd never met, someone who had experienced and understood what I had faced—and still faced.

FOURTEEN

ONE NIGHT, AFTER HOURS OF trying to fall asleep, I turned on the TV and mindlessly watched *From Here to Eternity*. As I was drifting off, a commercial roused me: "Find your long-lost loved ones! Call now! 1-800-SEARCH." Half asleep, I fumbled for the remote and turned up the sound as smiling men, women, and children ran toward each other across the screen. Radiant with joy, they embraced in a meadow of wildflowers, the empty void in their hearts filled. "Call now and find that special someone today!" I scrambled to find a pen and jotted down the number.

The next morning when I saw the number lying on the coffee table, I sat down and eyed it warily, as if it were some creature that might bite. My mind raced as I stared at it, wondering what I would do. Call? Toss it in the trash? Tuck it away and let it nag at me like a splinter? An unpleasant tightness in my chest made me realize I was holding my breath. *Do it!*

If only to end the suspense, I picked up the phone and dialed. Casually, I gave the information requested: date of birth, social security number, place and date of birth, my biological parents' full names as stated on my birth certificate, and my credit card number for the fifty-dollar service. Had Big Ed's suspicion that I came from a Jewish family been right? After informing me that I would receive the results by mail within six weeks, the operator wished me luck and rang off.

In a daze I hung up and began pacing my apartment, pausing every so often to stare unseeing out at the city.

I had never intended to track down my birth parents, but like Lucy's book, this ad had found me. Apart from desperate times in childhood when I had ached for my birth mother, I had mentally banished her and my father from my life. My attitude was, if they didn't care enough to seek me out, to hell with them. But now, with that one call, I began to imagine my parents. What would they be like? How would they react to my contacting them? Did my mother have an emotional breakdown over my disfigurement? Had it psychologically incapacitated her? Had my father forced the decision to abandon me? A "him or me" ultimatum? Imagining one scenario after another consumed me, each playing out in my head until finally, overloaded with pointless speculation, I put it all out of my mind.

Weeks later the envelope I'd been waiting for arrived. I anxiously tore it open and pulled out a short stack of computer printouts. It was an almost out-of-body experience to gaze down on columns of Shulmans listed in New Jersey with their phone numbers. I was thirty-eight years old and had never before met a Shulman, and now somewhere among the names I held in my hand, there might be the ones I sought.

Ed and Shirl, from the time I was old enough to ask, had given me what information they had, which was little more than their names. Knowing that Leonard and Sarah were my parents' names, I focused my search on the *L*'s and *S*'s. I began dialing the first *L* but hung up when it occurred to me that it would be best if I had an opening that didn't make me come across as weak or needy.

"Hello?" I practiced, clearing my throat to find the right pitch, "Is Leonard or Sarah in? Please, may I—my name? It's Howard, your biological son." No, too contrived. "Excuse me, my name is Howard and I'm looking for my biological parents." No, too abrupt. "Excuse me, my name is Howard. Did you by chance leave a baby in the hospital?" Okay. Again. "My name is Howard Shulman. I'm looking for a Sarah or Leonard Shulman. I was wondering if you might be my birth parents?" This was ridiculous!

On the first call that someone answered, angst set in. The woman said she knew of no such people. The relief I felt made me wonder if I was ready for this.

Determined, I took a deep breath and dialed the next number, and the next. With each call I made, though I received the same reply, I expanded my questioning, asking if they might be related to anyone named Leonard or Sarah. "Sorry, no," they each answered. After a series of dead-end calls, my anxiety began to subside. Becoming resigned that my search would lead nowhere, I was thinking that I might just forget the whole thing, when a young woman answered. "Who's calling, please?"

I had to grope for words. "Um, well . . . my name is Howard Shulman. I, uh, got your number from a family search agency, and I was, well, put up for adoption, well, sort of, and now . . ."

"Hold on a minute, please."

I held my breath. In the background I could hear voices, an exchange with another woman I strained to hear. An eternal moment passed.

"Hello?" a woman answered, her voice cautious.

"Is this Sarah Shulman?" *She knows who's on the phone. I can feel it.* Suddenly I was wary.

"Yes? I'm Sarah."

"I think you may be my birth mother," I said, my voice quiet. Time slowed down as a deafening silence filled the connection between us. I waited, every fiber of my being tuned to the other end of the line. In my state of hyper-awareness I could hear her strained breathing and the unmistakable sound of tears choked back. Gently, I broke the silence. "Are you okay?"

A long pause. "Yes, I'm fine."

"Are you sure?"

"Yes, thank you."

"I don't want to disturb you."

After a lull, I heard her whisper, "I always knew you would call."

I was stunned. Unable to respond, I could only listen to her faint crying.

What had I gotten myself into? What had I done? Phoning numbers like it was a crapshoot? For the first time, it fully dawned on me that this was more than just about me. I wanted to say that I hadn't meant to upset her. How could I tell her I had never intended to make this call in the first place and was no more prepared than she?

Unprompted, she began talking of Leonard, who had passed away a few years earlier.

"I'm sorry, I would have liked to meet him."

"He was a good man," she said, her voice trailing off.

My mind raced full throttle. *How good of a man could he have been, being party to giving his own son away?*

She regained her composure and opened a floodgate of questions about my life. "Are you married? Any children?"

"No, no. I've had wonderful women in my life, but no." I needed for her to know that I wasn't a social outcast and functioned fully in the world. Fearing she might hang up at any moment, I blurted, "What's my heritage?"

"Why, you're a Russian Jew."

"Russian Jew?"

"Yes, on both sides. Third generation. Your father's side was in the garment trade."

Well, at least my call had been worth something.

"Are you a practicing Jew?" she asked.

Startled, I laughed. "No, that I'm not." For me, the question was absurd. She assured me that it was all right, but I could sense her disappointment.

At her urging, I briefly touched on the main events of my life, conveniently omitting the nefarious details. I knew that children's records were sealed and that she had given up all rights to me once she had signed on the dotted line, but I couldn't help wondering what she knew of me. More than anything, though, I thought it odd that she had not asked a single question concerning my health or medical status. Were the words "face" or "nose" taboo?

Her discomfort and fright were transmitted over the phone and made me rush to reassure her again. And then, without intending to, the question that had festered inside me my entire life shot out of my mouth. "*Why* did you give me up?"

I heard her breath catch, but she made no response. When she didn't answer, I broke the tension by suggesting a reason, as if I could know. "I understand it was a different time, with all my medical issues."

"No, it wasn't that," Sarah said, retreat in her voice. I could sense her anxiety mounting.

"*What* then?" I asked, desperate to understand.

"It was a very difficult decision. Please, don't make me feel guilty."

I decided it wise to back off if I didn't want her hanging up on me. "Do I have any siblings?"

"Yes." Relief and pride filled her voice as she began to speak at length on a subject obviously dear to her heart. "David, the oldest, is a lawyer. He's married with children and . . ."

Her words became a blur. I wondered what had been the point of initiating this surreal conversation. So that I could feel invisible? A nonentity? *Sarah, are you that insensitive? Don't you realize the more you praise your "true" children, the more you exclude me?* Bewildered, I hardly knew how to respond. I could feel my anger rising but held my tongue.

"My daughter, Linda," she continued, "is also married and is now expecting. And Joseph, my youngest, is a lawyer as well, still single." Her voice trailed off, as if Joseph's bachelorhood were the only thing that marred her contentment.

Struggling to disguise the hostility I felt, I asked, "So David is my older brother?"

"Yes, he's always been aware of everything. The same with all the other children." As she spoke, the image of my birth certificate loomed in my mind's eye, the names Leonard and Sarah Shulman officiously typed under the heading of parents, an *X* in the married box.

I needed answers and returned to the only question that mattered to me. "Why did you give me up?"

I thought I would crush the phone her pause was so long, my hand turning white as I waited for her to tell me the truth. I was owed that much.

Finally, in a voice unsteady and barely audible, she answered. "We couldn't handle *it*."

Couldn't handle it! What the hell was "it?" Social stigma? Financial? Medical? Family pressure? Maternal guilt? What? Was I even human to her? She couldn't? Or wouldn't? I was shaking, enraged. I had never cared before; survival had always been my focus for as long as I could remember, but now I had to know more. I closed my eyes and fought to calm myself. If I didn't regain control, I knew what little headway I had made would evaporate. My next question was nothing I had intended, but it flew out of my mouth. "Can we meet sometime?"

She hesitated. "Perhaps. I'm quite busy right now."

"I understand." I didn't, actually. Her dismissal felt like another abandonment. I let it go and thanked her for her time.

"Call me again if you wish," she said. Then the line went dead.

I sank down on my couch, stunned. Sarah's mixed messages confused me and were too much to process. On the one hand, she had taken the time to speak with me and had left the door open for future contact; but on the other, she was cold and distant and evasive. Cruel even. When she proudly told me how wonderful her children were, she didn't think enough of me and my feelings to care what that implied: that I wasn't one of them and certainly no one to brag about. A discard.

I passed the week in a fog. I paced, worked out at the gym, kept to myself (uncharacteristically drinking a few bottles of wine), stayed up too late, and woke up exhausted each morning to pace some more. What I had put in motion was upsetting my equilibrium, and although there was familiarity in the darkness I felt, this involved others who shared my blood. TV, reading, even simple cooking were beyond me. I couldn't focus on anything and was torn between wanting to walk away from the emotional quagmire I'd gotten myself into and the need to see it through—whatever I had started with my birth mother. I changed my mind almost hourly. I would call—I wouldn't call—my resolve ran in circles.

I had to contact her again. I was emotionally stuck. I couldn't go forward and couldn't go back. The limbo I was in was exhausting. When I finally made the call to ask Sarah to meet me for coffee, she laid out the terms.

"Not if you insist on continually lashing out at me." Articulate and obviously educated, she was determined to defend herself.

"Sarah, I don't know what to say. I'm not trying to hurt you by opening up old wounds, and I get that you don't want to dwell on the past. I understand that. But surely you understand that thirty-eight years is a long time to not know. My questions are nothing more than my attempt to understand what happened."

"Howard," she asked, her voice tired, "what do you want out of this?"

What did I want? I closed my eyes and took a deep breath before answering. "Sarah, initially I would have said I didn't want anything. I had no agenda—it just happened. But now everything's changed. I want answers."

Like a mother exasperated with her tedious child, I heard her sigh. "Howard, there is nothing more I can add to what I've already told you."

I knew we were at an impasse and backed off. At a loss for what to do, I tried to mollify her and directed the conversation back to "her" kids.

She had no trouble talking about David, her firstborn, who worked as an attorney for New York City, and her middle child, Joseph, born after me, who specialized in immigration law. As she boasted of her children's triumphs, her mood lifted, which only made me feel more rejected. *Couldn't you be proud of me for surviving, Sarah? Isn't that at least some accomplishment?*

Having heard enough, I changed the subject. "Did you tell your children about our conversation?"

"I did."

"And?"

"They said they supported me in my decisions."

"You're lucky," I said.

"Yes, I am. Would you like to speak with them?"

Her question threw me. Never once had it occurred to me to contact them. As it was, I was on emotional overload dealing with Sarah's maneuverings. I wanted to exorcise my resentment and anger towards her, to let it go, but I couldn't, and I didn't know why.

"They would like to speak with you."

"Really?" I didn't know what to say.

"They're good people."

Sarah obviously wanted me to meet my siblings, perhaps to prove to me that she was a good mother. Whatever her reasons, I couldn't summon any feeling whatsoever for them. They had played no part in the choices Leonard and Sarah had made. "That would be nice," I said, surprised by the direction our conversation was taking. We ended on a positive note, which was progress.

David called the following night, and right away I knew I was talking with the head of the family. When the obligatory pleasantries were out of the way, his tone changed as the guise of cordiality dropped and suspicion revealed itself. He made me feel like a thief lurking around the family silver. Like Sarah, he asked me what I wanted, as if I were a threat to *his* family or, worse, trying to latch onto his inheritance. Seeking compensation by means of Sarah's guilt, perhaps.

"Howard, you have to understand you came out of nowhere. All this is very traumatic for Mother. I can tell you, being a few years older than you, I remember everything." I listened carefully to David's very different piece of the puzzle that gave shape to Sarah's vague allusions. "Mother and Father agonized over their decision. You will never know what they went through."

I couldn't help myself. "And you do, David?" When he used the word "mother," I realized I felt absolutely nothing. Shirl was the only association I had with "mother."

Joseph called soon afterward. From his first words of greeting he struck me as genuinely concerned, and I was touched when he asked if there was anything he could do for me. He asked how my health was, if I was still undergoing surgeries, and never once did he question my motive for contacting Sarah. "I can't imagine what you went through, Howard," he said, which made me appreciate that he wasn't going to try to guess how I felt. He gave me his number and told me to call anytime I wanted. When I hung up I had a smile on my face.

Next was Linda. I had a hard time getting a read on her, but after a short exchange that felt unnecessarily forced, I politely ended our conversation that was going nowhere.

I allowed enough time for her kids to bring Sarah up to date before I called her back to ask, once again, if we could meet for coffee in the city. This time she agreed, and we settled on the 2nd Ave. Deli on Thirty-Third Street near Lexington. When she described what she would be wearing, I made no move to offer the same; we both knew I'd be easily identifiable.

I wanted her to know I wasn't crawling to her with my hand out, none of that pauper business of returning to my princely birthright to avenge my betrayal, like some character out of a Greek tragedy. I wanted her to know I was doing fine. More than fine. I decided against wearing a suit—too obvious that I was trying to impress her—and settled on a pair of pressed dress jeans, a plain white shirt, and a pair of polished black leather dress boots.

After a restless night I awoke early, in a state of nerves I didn't expect. I was emotionally invested and didn't understand why. How had an impulsive call to an 800 number gotten so out of hand? I was a grown man, and Sarah, who played no part in my life, had triggered emotions I didn't realize I had. The thing that kept me going was that I knew I had done nothing wrong. My conscience was clean. Was hers?

I toweled dry and stepped before the fogged bathroom mirror. As I wiped away the steam, my reflection cleared, and I was taken back to the devastation I felt twenty-seven years before: the awful moment when I'd viewed myself in the three-way mirror at the men's store in Greenfield. That boy was gone, and in his place was a man with a face I'd grown proud of. Critically, I studied my odd, asymmetrical nose and uneven lips and eyelids, then cast my eyes over the seams of scars. In deliberate, circular motions I polished the mirror until my chest came into full view—more scars, still rough after what felt like a life-time. As my gaze returned to my face, a John Lennon refrain popped into my head. "Mother, you had me, but I never had you . . ."

Taking a deep breath to calm my nerves, I slowly buttoned my shirt. A sense of queasy excitement was building in me, the kind that propels you forward while some rational part of you drags your feet. I wasn't about to forget that it's only a fool who lets sentimental longing cloud what years of experience have otherwise taught him. Inarticu-late thoughts of betrayal and fate filled my head, flitting out of reach as fast as they surfaced. Why was I feeling so much stress? What was there to regret about the life I'd been forced to create? But no amount of internal dialogue could alleviate the tension I felt steadily mounting.

I had no illusions of walking into a joyous reunion like the ones I'd seen on 1-800-SEARCH. This reunion would not undo thirty-eight years of longing. It would not make up for the loneliness I had suffered as a child or make the darkness go away. This, I knew, would be no fairy-tale homecoming. All I wanted was my due, to have my questions answered, face-to-face. I deserved that much. But how to collect would be another matter.

Apart from the sound of my boot heels striking the pavement and the tension I felt in my body as I paced the curb to flag down a taxi, I remember little except a mother and her child waiting in front of my building. I felt like a child myself, running off to find Mother. I had to remind myself to breathe.

"Lexington and 3rd," I shouted, jumping into the cab.

The short trip down to Midtown to meet Sarah was dreamlike. By the time we pulled up in front of the deli, my heart felt as if it would leap out of my chest. I took my time paying the fare and, as calmly as I could, stopped to peer into the chrome interior, my misshapen nose all but pressed to the window. Seeing no one who fit her description, I took a deep breath and entered. Inside, I scanned the diners and settled on a petite woman halfway down the aisle. She sat alone and faced the entrance. Without looking at her clothes, I knew she was Sarah.

As I approached her, I was startled to see she was older than I had imagined. What had I expected? Sitting straight, her shoulders back, she sat stiffly waiting for me, her face tense. Noting her tailored light-brown jacket and white satin blouse, I thought she must shop at Saks or Ann Taylor. Almost four decades had passed since that day my fate was sealed, when I was made a ward of the state of New Jersey, and I was critiquing her wardrobe? My attention shifted to her dark coiffed hair streaked with gray, and at that moment I realized that she, too, had spent time preparing herself for the occasion. "Sarah?" I heard myself ask. My birth mother . . . This was my birth mother!

"Yes?"

"I'm Howard."

"Yes, I know."

How could she not? With her eyes absorbing my face, I could barely follow what she was saying. We tentatively shook hands.

Facing Sarah, I settled myself in the booth and took measure of the stranger sitting across from me. Tired and drawn, with deep shadows under her eyes, she betrayed her studied composure by nervously fidgeting with her coffee cup.

"You look good," she said, her voice quavering.

I'm sure I do, compared to the last time you saw me—bandaged, hooked up to tubes, fluids, and God knows what else. "Well, I'm still here."

She sighed but kept her eyes on me, then acknowledged my cutting attempt at humor with a wistful smile. As she searched my face, I got the distinct impression she was evaluating my surgical alterations, comparing what she saw seated before her against what she remembered of me at birth. Her expression hovered somewhere between stoic and vulnerable, like hot and cold water running into a plugged sink—a lukewarm temperature that could go either way.

"I want you to know I never hid anything from my children," she said, her eyes filling with tears. At "my children," I sucked in air, cut to the quick. What was I doing? Ill at ease, she kept changing her position in the booth, as if some comfort might be found there.

More out of manners than compassion, I tried to ease her distress and not make her more upset than she already was. I changed the subject and launched into bits of my history she'd already heard from our phone conversations. But the burning question of why she had abandoned me refused to stay bottled up and was making my stomach churn.

Before I even knew I was forming the question, it slipped off my tongue. "*Why* did you give me up?" I asked again, the urgency I felt evident in the force of my question.

She dropped her head and stared unseeing into her untouched coffee. *You continued on with your lives while I began mine with strangers? Answer me!* I bit my tongue but pushed on. "Why didn't you ever try to contact me? Why, since your family knew about me?" Saying "your family" to the woman who gave birth to me was surreal in itself.

"I thought it would be best for you that you start over with a new family," she said, her shoulders sagging.

Best for who? You and Leonard? "My new family? I don't understand."

"You were adopted, right?"

"No," I answered haltingly, "never formally."

A shocked look came over her face. "But . . . but they told us you were adopted!"

"They? Who's 'they'?"

"The lawyer."

"Lawyer?" Now I was totally confused.

Sarah's hands lay still, as if what held her up had deflated. Shaking her head, she finally continued. "Leonard and I hired an attorney to look after you. He told us you had been adopted by a nurse, a nice family in the Midwest."

Nurse? Could that be Shirl? "Midwest?" I had to laugh out loud. "The family I was placed with was in New Jersey."

"Where?"

"I lived in Morristown, Summit, Randolph."

Her eyes widened. It was too much for her, and she slumped back against the booth. In some detail I told her of my childhood, growing up in the Garden State.

"You lived in Summit and worked at the Office restaurant?"

"Yes, you know it?"

She covered her face with her hands, her fingers splayed so I could see her eyes tearing up.

After some time she lowered her hands and placed them palms down on the table. "We . . . Leonard and I would eat there on occasion." Her words were tremulous and distant.

It was my turn to lean back and catch my breath. I saw myself, washing their dirty dishes, the closest I would ever be to them since the day I became an *it* to her. The irony of my scraping their discards in the back room, bussing their table, or redoing an order they might have sent back to the kitchen—like they sent me back for failing to be good enough—made me sick to my stomach. I wanted to walk out then and there, leaving her the way she did me.

Instead, I resolved to finish what I had started.

We sat some moments in silence before she began to speak of Leonard, how he was a self-made man who owned a clothing store with his brother. She told me what a hard worker and honorable man he was. More than ever I wanted to meet him so I could ask him how such an "honorable man" could abandon his second-born son.

I pictured the five of them living in an affluent, predominantly Jewish neighborhood in the suburbs, with matching cement lion heads flanking their double-door entrance, a Mezuzah nailed to the door frame. Her version told of a close-knit family with each of their lives neatly planned out, except, of course, for my coming along and messing up their perfect picture. "We simply couldn't handle *it*" was the extent to which she could explain the event that framed my entire life. Imaging "her children's" trust funds, European vacations, and college funds was excruciating for me, though I had no idea if, in fact, any of that even existed.

When Sarah told me how she and Leonard had started a program to help Jewish children in need, I was dumbstruck by her callousness—cruelty, really. Proud of her charity, she prattled on. My body temperature soaring, I abruptly rose and excused myself to go to the men's room. Reeling, I dropped my forearms to the rim of the sink and cradled my head in my hands, utter disbelief at what I had just learned sucking the wind out of me. Insult added to my years of injury, was there no end?

Get a grip, I told myself. This was her guilt, trying to save thousands when she'd turned her back on saving her own son. Little good it had done me.

My jaw clenched, I returned to our booth for round two. I needed to rise above her insensitivity and regain my composure. How could I fight with an elderly woman? But sadly, my anger got the better of me. "Do you have any regrets?" I asked, my voice steely.

Without emotion or hesitation she answered, "No, I don't. I did what I had to."

Oddly, that was the only thing she'd said that I could relate to. But how she could see herself as a proud mother, benefactor, and devoted wife and still look me in the eye? She expected me to be satisfied with her refusal to explain her decision to walk away from me, her baby, her blood. I was incensed.

Her lips quivered as tears resurfaced and streamed down her cheeks. "Howard, I can't do it anymore," she cried. *Tears, Sarah? You have no idea the tears I cried for you when I was a child.* Suddenly indignant, she straightened up and said, "I will not relive this again. What's done is done."

I nodded in complete agreement.

Having exhausted any shred of mercy, incapable of holding my peace after so many years of pent-up anger, I pressed on. "How could you have done that to a baby? Forget me—*any* baby?"

"Howard, I've punished myself enough. No more." She was now in full retreat.

I felt no satisfaction in seeing her cry. The woman who had been in control was gone, and in her place sat a pathetically guilt-ridden one, burdened by a lifetime of crushing denial. At that moment the depth of her distress suddenly struck me, and I apologized over and over, swearing to her that it had not been my intention to hurt her. My quest had gone from curiosity to attack—with an aging woman who could never defend her actions or dare to revisit the past.

The table between us seemed to broaden as the distance between us grew, the air suddenly as stifling as our conversation. I made a feeble attempt to reach out to her. "I'm having a hard time understanding this, you know."

Like the stranger she was, I thanked her for her time and escorted her outside, where I flagged down a taxi for her. There was no feeling between us—nothing. The ties of blood were evidently not enough to bridge the gap. Drained, we could do nothing more than shake hands and say good-bye. Alone on the sidewalk, I watched her taxi pull away.

Our meeting replayed in my head as I struck out towards home. I had poured my heart out, venting frustrations buried so deep I didn't believe anything could ever have awakened them. I had barely refrained from lashing out that she was a God-fearing, synagogue-attending, do-gooder, Jewish hypocrite, all of which would have served no purpose and would have done nothing for my anger. I arrived at my apartment emotionally and physically spent, taking no comfort from the thought that blocks away she was probably experiencing similar emotions. Sarah, too, I realized, had suffered her own torment. How had she always known I would call?

Sarah and I talked several more times, and although conversations with my siblings were awkward on both sides, we made the effort. For our next meeting, the whole family would come. I chose the place, the Oak Room at the Plaza Hotel. I knew my brothers were successful attorneys, but I had had some successes of my own and wanted to meet them on equal footing.

Dressed in my best suit, a white shirt, and conservative striped tie, I felt I was preparing myself to enter the lion's den. I had reserved a table but planned to arrive ten minutes late so I wouldn't be the one waiting. Plus, I wanted the chance to size them up.

When I strode through the stately doors of the Plaza and crossed the plush carpets to the quiet, elegant dining room, I saw Sarah seated by the windows. With her were two men and a woman near my age who looked a bit like me—black shiny hair and brown eyes like mine. I had guessed right that the friendly sibling who smiled at me was Joseph. He stood and warmly greeted me, clasping my hand in his. Well-mannered but cool, David took his turn, his brief handshake stiff and formal. Lastly, I was introduced to Linda, who looked sweet in a red floral maternity dress. I got the impression that she was there only because of family obligation, rather than any real feeling or curiosity about a long-lost brother.

I sat down, and after a few awkward false starts, we began with small talk, all of them discreetly scrutinizing me while I did the same. Though by now they knew my story, they politely asked me about my life: what I did, where I'd lived, pointedly skirting any reference to my childhood except to say, more than once, that I looked good. Who knows what monstrosity they had expected to walk through the door, if they had thought about it at all.

"What is it you do now?" David asked, his eyes assessing me as he absentmindedly aligned his silverware.

"I'm a silent partner in a gallery and art authentication business on East Seventy-Fourth Street," I lied, not wanting them to question my financial stability.

"How did you get into that business?"

"Happenstance, I guess. I've been a partner in several different businesses. A nightclub in San Diego, and before that, I did a stint in southwestern real estate. I have eclectic interests."

"What made you come back to New York?"

"I was ready for a change."

"Mother says you're not married."

"That's right."

From the moment I arrived, I could feel my siblings closing rank around Sarah, the Queen Mother. David, in his role of gatekeeper and protector of the monarchy, ran interference if topics turned difficult. Determined to block my admission to the keep, he appeared to want to hold me responsible for my exile. Linda, as lady-in-waiting, was there to ease the queen's distress and offer moral support, while Joseph, compassionate and kind, acted as ambassador, seeking only to establish peace between the parties. Banned from the kingdom, I knew it unlikely that the moat of starched linen tablecloth that separated us could be bridged, nor was I consciously seeking to do so.

Intellectually, I could understand their distance, but emotionally, it was hard to accept. In spite of my real-world pragmatism, I realized I had lapsed into flights of fantasy, imagining—even hoping—for something more embracing. This was my family after all, despite my own branch having been pruned from the familial tree. Clearly they didn't need me but assumed—or feared—I needed them.

I was getting tired of being cross-examined by David, who was acting as if he were taking a deposition. When he stopped and asked, "Look, Howard, it's all well and good to meet you after all this time, but just what do you expect from us?" I was speechless. They were surely all wondering why I had chosen to show up when I did, and I sensed that they felt threatened, but the thought that they worried that I might have my hand out made me retreat. The last time—and the only time—I had reached out to Sarah, she had walked out of the hospital and out of her newborn's life. It would never happen again.

Shifting my gaze beyond the expanse of windows that looked out on Central Park, I escaped into my private thoughts, the conversation receding into the background hum of low-pitched voices and silverware against fine china. Transfixed by the view, I tried to figure how best to handle this. Suddenly KC came to mind. I could see him, cigar in hand, laughing his ass off, saying, "Fuckin' David, he can't take the heat." To laugh it off wasn't so easy for me; this was, after all, my biological brother I was dealing with. Since Bement days I had felt resentment for the privileged classes' sense of entitlement and took pride in my street smarts, proud of how I had risen from less than nothing.

And now here I was being confronted by my birth family that for me represented everything I'd never had.

Joseph, in an attempt to diffuse David's crassness, tried to make amends. "Howard, just tell us. What can we do for you?"

I had no answer. Betrayal was all I felt. I was alone among a table of five, unable to open up. This was my family and I felt nothing for them—no love or kinship—only the sense that they were all attached by an umbilical cord I could almost see snaking under the tablecloth to Sarah, one that had been, for me, severed from the start. These people were *not* my family.

David broke the silence. "Howard, what is it you want?"

"Don't patronize me," I said. "I've simply invited you here so we could meet and get to know one another. There's no hidden agenda. I'm only curious, nothing more." I hope I was dignified because for the first time I felt completely calm.

Sarah, obviously wishing she were anywhere but at our table, kept her eyes averted, surveying the dining room. Linda, nervously twisting her napkin, stared at her swollen abdomen. Only Joseph showed in his eyes how bad he felt for me. Changing his tone and backing off, David finally seemed to get it that my intentions were straightforward. I had to hand it to them that they had shown up at all, though I knew they'd been recruited to support Sarah. Now it was only Sarah who remained fearful, and I almost felt pity for her. Like a prisoner who can only save face by never admitting to any wrongdoing, she was condemned for a lifetime to her cell of a suburban home in New Jersey—her bars the trimmed hedges of respectability. Her penalty was to sit across from me all these years later and be forced to remember what she had done, all because she couldn't handle *it*.

By the end of lunch we had maneuvered our conversation back to safer ground. As I took care of the bill, they each invited me for dinner at their homes in New Jersey.

Sarah and I met several more times over the next few weeks, both on the phone and on long walks through Central Park. The immovable wall she had erected when it came to discussing my infancy remained difficult to accept, and to try to budge it felt hopeless. Too often I tuned her out, unable to stomach her family stories. She never asked about my childhood and refused any queries I made concerning the choices she had made. Repeatedly she invited me to her home, but only on the condition that I promise not to bring up the past. "Leonard and I punished ourselves for a long time. I can't do that anymore," she said when I pushed.

We kept going around in circles.

"Don't drag me back into something that happened forty years ago. We always hoped the best for you," she said, shaking her head, her mouth a determined line of obstinacy.

I wanted to be considerate and respectful, but the barrier she put up created more and more resentment. What made it even more difficult was her incessant bragging about her other children: what a good job she had done raising them and how much she loved her in-laws and grandchildren. She had love for everyone but me.

I continued to call her, firing more accusations, even though I knew we were at an impasse. "You never even knew what became of me."

"I did get in touch with the agency. I tried. They wouldn't tell us anything except that you were to be adopted by a nurse. I wanted to find out what happened to you."

"After all the state's attempts to find me appropriate homes and all the expense of my reconstructive surgeries," I retorted, "I have no doubt they would have gladly given me back to my real parents. They didn't tell you I learned to read through the bars of a hospital crib?" I spat out. "Or how I was treated as a mental incompetent because of my face? No one ever mentioned to you that I never knew when I was going into surgery? Or how kids called me vicious names when they weren't scared out of their wits at the very sight of me? All I could ever do, Sarah, was try to find a way to simply survive."

I wanted her to hear the truth, but I was making myself into what I most detested from as far back as childhood—a victim. Every conversation with her made me more and more bitter. She knew it too. There was no joy for either of us in what we were discovering. She was always on the defense and I always pushed on the shell in which she had cocooned herself. We were playing a vicious chess game and had come to a stalemate. I had no regrets about having found my birth family, but they weren't my family, not in the sense I understood family to be. Worse, I was regressing, caught up in a futile pipe dream that was destroying everything I had come to rely on in life: my resilience and inner strength. I was *not* a victim. Unable to continue, I held the receiver against my chest. I knew what I had to do.

"Good-bye, Sarah."

"Good-bye, Howard." A brief moment of silence followed, then the connection went dead.

Some months later, I was listening to "Rainy Night House" by Joni Mitchell. I'd heard it hundreds of times before, but for the first time the lyrics spoke to me.

In my own way, I was a refugee from a wealthy family, forcibly ejected from the homeland. And now I had discovered who I was and who I might become.

I have never stopped thinking about Sarah. She had spent hours with me—sitting in the coffee shop, walking with me in the park, introducing me to her children. She had answered most of my questions and told me what was most important to her, painful though it was for me to hear. In the end, for us, a lifetime of separation and hurt was too great a rent to mend. I never spoke to Sarah again.

FIFTEEN

DOWN IN THE VILLAGE ONE DAY, I bought a fiery red shawl that reminded me of Helena. We must have been on the same wavelength because she called the next morning, before I got a chance to mail it off.

"Helena? I was just thinking about you!"

"Everything okay?"

We talked awhile, catching up with each other, when I suggested she come for a visit. "No beaches here, only bright city lights. Do you think you could ever break away?"

"As it so happens, I'm off next week."

Four days later we were sitting together at the Village Vanguard listening to some of New York's best jazz. It was as if I had just seen her yesterday, so seamlessly had we picked up where we'd left off.

Knowing art would be high on her list, I took her to MoMA to see the Impressionists. That night at dinner when she dribbled red marinara sauce on her white turtleneck, instead of rushing to the ladies' room, she laughed. "It's my New York art, don't you think?"

I told her about my meeting with Sarah and about the conflict and anger I felt. She listened patiently for hours while I struggled out loud to make peace with a reunion that had failed to give me the answers I wanted.

"Howard, you just can't imagine the depth of blame that Sarah felt.

Feels," she said softly. "I feel excruciating guilt when I have to leave Brandon for a few days or even if I have to tough-love him for something he's done."

"But that's exactly my point. You *love* him. You couldn't leave him, especially if he was sick."

She paused. "You're right. But I've known a lot of girls who got pregnant young and had to give up their babies for adoption. And I know a lot of others who got an abortion. They get on with their lives, but they never forget." Helena reached over and touched my arm. "Howard, some people can repair that kind of damage, and some can't. But whatever story Sarah told herself, she never forgot you."

The next morning was too beautiful to spend indoors, so we set off for Central Park, Helena striking in the shawl I'd bought for her. In high spirits, we were starting to think about lunch when I started feeling dizzy, the leaves and trees swirling around like something out of *The Wizard of Oz*.

The next thing I remember is waking up in Roosevelt Hospital in a familiarly drab room, confused at seeing Helena sitting by my bed reading. She looked up at me and smiled. "Hey, you. You're awake! How are you feeling?"

"What happened?"

"You had a grand mal seizure, Howard," she said, her voice serious. "You fell in the park, convulsing." She took my hand. "Then these weird Euro tourists crowded around you like you were a breakdancer. When the cops showed up, you tried to punch them out. You were crazy! You didn't want to get in the ambulance. It was scary. But at least I knew you were still the real you." Smiling, she leaned over and kissed my cheek.

Something, I felt, was looking out for me, some power that had brought Helena to me in New York to help me.

Helena returned to San Diego, and I began a battery of tests: EEG, EKG, CAT scan, MRI, blood tests—there seemed no end to them. Even after my neurologist told me they hadn't turned up anything that could explain my seizure, I wasn't mollified. It was deeply disturbing. I had survived everything life had thrown at me. My surgeries were behind me, and I had long since stopped seeing myself primarily as a disfig-

ured man. If I was fine, how could this happen? My unexplained sei-
zure was like a night stalker that threatened my survival yet couldn't
be confronted, and therefore couldn't be overcome. I was no longer a
furious boy who could hide behind a mask of bravado. I was afraid.
Life felt more precious and fragile than ever.

I was forty years old and much as I loved New York, I was getting rest-
less again, maybe in part because of hearing from Helena that she was
getting married. While I was happy for her, it brought home the sad
truth that apart from a little financial cushion, my future held noth-
ing. With real estate booming, I sold my condo and flew out to Albu-
querque to visit friends and consider my next step.

With no intentions whatsoever, I stopped to tour an open house
in Ridgecrest not far from the university and ended up buying it on
the spot—a 1930s New Mexican adobe situated on a large shady lot
behind a wall of wisteria.

After arranging for movers in New York, I flew back once again
to Albuquerque, amazed by how different my life was now from my
first move to New Mexico years before. Back then I'd arrived with
my few earthly belongings stuffed into two cheap suitcases and now,
in what felt like another lifetime, professional movers followed with
my possessions.

Settled into my new house with Big Kitty and Little Kitty (rescues
from the shelter), I felt full of optimism and flung myself headlong
into a new chapter.

Soon after, while I was shopping at Walmart for cat food, the twenty-
five-pound bag tucked under my arm, I found myself waking up on
the floor to see three impressively large women in polyester peering
down at me, their kindly plump faces clouded with concern. "You had
a seizure," one explained. "The ambulance is on its way."

Please, not again! Months earlier, when I had my grand mal sei-
zure in Central Park, I had been petrified that I hadn't seen the last of
waking up confused in random places.

Once again I had to explain my medical history to a bewildered
intern and, after yet another battery of tests, had to wait four nerve-

racking days for my follow-up. Was it too much to ask to live a productive life without medical drama?

By the time I returned to my neurosurgeon's office, I was a wreck. While I waited, I looked around at the solemn faces heavy with worry and wondered how far resilience or faith or determination could ultimately carry any of us. When did it end?

As a precaution I was put on Dilantin, an antiseizure medication, even though the tests had again found nothing. My prescription felt like a second chance at life, and I almost skipped out of the office.

Grateful for my reprieve and determined to curb my self-absorption, I started working as a volunteer at a children's hospital, where I was assigned to read to a ten-year-old boy who had suffered a brain injury. Steve could only communicate through blinking, which he rarely did. For weeks, triggered by the antiseptic odor, cold glaring tiles, and the yellow guideline I followed down the hall to Steve's room, I struggled with a flood of unsettling memories. The hospital, so painfully familiar, put me on edge.

I did my best with Steve, but my efforts seemed pointless. Every day I found him as I had last seen him, lying listlessly in bed propped up on pillows, the life-support machines whirring away. "Hello, Steve, it's me, your volunteer buddy, Howard. How you doing today? I'm going to read to you, okay?" Receiving no indication that he registered my presence, I nonetheless pulled my chair up to his bed and opened a storybook, careful to angle the colorful illustrations so he could see them. After reading a few pages, the uselessness I felt was disheartening and made me only want to finish so I could get away from that claustrophobic room.

Though I dreaded it, I kept returning to read to him. And then, one overcast afternoon as I was turning the page, the clouds cleared, brightening the room. I saw Steve's eyes shift to the window that streamed with light. He was aware! I could see it in his eyes; he had communicated volumes.

All along, the despair I'd felt in his room had been my own. I resumed the story, reading slowly to give him time to examine the pictures. By the tiny movements of his eyes, I knew he saw and heard.

On my way out, the nurse stopped me to tell me how much Steve enjoyed his reading time with me. Profoundly touched, I looked into her kindly face and remembered my nurses who had read to me all those years long ago. Gradually I was beginning to see color emerge from the black-and-white film of my childhood. Why does it take tragedy to recognize the gift of life?

The house on Ridgecrest was spacious and had a large basement apartment with a fireplace, kitchen, and full bath, all of which I had no need for. One bright-blue New Mexican Sunday morning, a woman called in response to my ad, asking if two kids would be a problem. Something about her accent and tone of urgency edging on desperation made me think I'd found the right renter. When a short, attractive woman showed up on my doorstep an hour later, determined-looking is what came to mind. All I could see of the little girl hiding behind her mother's legs was one dark eye peering out at me through long strands of shiny black hair. In front of them stood a young boy, chin up and defiant, his mother's arm draped protectively over his chest. Behind them stood a social worker.

"Gloria?" I asked.

"*Sí.*"

"*¿Y los niños?*"

"Humberto *y* Cristina."

"*Hola. Mucho gusto de conocerles. ¿Son mexicanos?*"

"No. *Soy de Guatemala*," she said, her voice filled with pride. "Do you live alone?" she asked, switching to English.

"Yes."

"Do you have references?"

Surprised, I realized she was screening me. I scribbled down a few names and numbers and handed her the slip of paper.

"How much rent?" she asked.

"Four hundred," I said, immediately knowing it was more than she could afford. "But we can work something out," I quickly added. She looked at me suspiciously.

I didn't know why, but I knew this family belonged in the apartment. Perhaps it was the way she kept Humberto and Cristina close, her head held high as she looked me directly in the eye. I was in awe of how protective she was with her kids, how different she was from Sarah. From my kitchen they followed me downstairs to look at the apartment. When the kids ran off to explore the rooms, Gloria seemed to hesitate.

"What do you say to $350?"

She looked around the empty space. "I don't have much furniture."

"I have an extra bed and a few pieces I can move down here. It'll be fine." At that, she smiled, and as the kids excitedly jumped up and down around us, we shook on it. When I closed the door behind them and looked out the kitchen window into the courtyard, the little family had joined in a circle holding hands, their heads bowed in prayer.

"Howard, you don't have to do this," Gloria said.

The truth was, I was glad to help. The more I learned of Gloria's situation, the more I admired her. Over time she told me her story, how at sixteen she had been married off to an older man, a brute with whom she bore two children, Myra and Mario. When her son fell seriously ill and her husband refused to pay for medical treatment, Gloria wouldn't accept her son's death sentence. Leaving her children in her mother's care, she slipped over the border into Mexico, where she found a job packing fruit, not returning until six months later when she had enough to pay for his treatment. When an uncle in Dallas offered her work, it was an opportunity she couldn't turn down, even though it meant leaving her children once again. It was heart wrenching to see Gloria weep as she relived her decision of years before, and it made me reconsider the belief I'd always clung to: that it was unforgivable under *any* circumstance to leave one's children.

She told me she traveled north by bus and train and got as far as Reinosa, Mexico, just across the border from McAllen, Texas, before she ran out of money. On nine occasions over the next five years, *la migra* caught her and deported her back to Mexico, and just as many times, she found a way to get back. During that period, she had what she called her "youthful indiscretions," which resulted in Humberto and then Cristina.

It wasn't all hardship. She fell in love with a man named Samuel and moved with him to his new job in Los Alamos, New Mexico. Five months later, he lay comatose from a traumatic brain injury—a twisted brain, as she described it. He was unable to eat or breathe on his own, and his doctors gave her the grim news that he would never recover.

Without his paycheck, unmarried, and with no legal rights, Gloria had no choice but to move into a homeless shelter with her two young children. Although they spent every day with Samuel, hoping for some response, in the end their efforts were futile. When I imagined the three of them in a shelter and coping the best they could, it broke my heart.

"One day," Gloria said to me, "I will have *all* my children with me. Eventually, I *will* bring them here, and we will be a family again."

"Gloria, you know you only have to say the word and I'll help you. I'll always be here for all of you."

To make things easier for her, I reduced the rent further, and when her savings ran out, I put it on hold altogether. Watching her struggle with her dignity intact made me admire her all the more and made me deeply appreciate my own good fortune. Her strength of character and loyalty amazed me. Beside Gloria, I measured up poorly.

Soon the young family's living space—and mine—came alive with echoes of children's laughter and the aromas from Gloria's cooking wafting up the stairs. For the first time, my house was a home.

From years of habit in New York and elsewhere, I was accustomed to shopping at specialty neighborhood markets, where I paid exorbitant prices for groceries. Enough of that! Now I headed to Costco and loaded my Sherman tank of a shopping basket with bulk foods, gallons of milk, and flats of mangos and eggs. In the checkout line I impulsively tossed onto the mound a handheld computer game for Humberto and an enormous stuffed Scooby Doo for Cristina.

Without fail, Sunday morning found Gloria and her kids off to church. Nothing could shake her faith. Never in my life, I realized, had I ever willingly stepped into a church, and only the threat of disaster or a little plastic tube could get a prayer out of me.

Though my house was open to Humberto and Cristina, Gloria remained guarded, not trusting that I didn't have ulterior motives. One day when Cristina chased Big Kitty and Little Kitty upstairs and was careening down the hall, slipping and sliding in her socks, her irresistible peals of laughter naturally drew me from my study. Scooping up Big Kitty, I put him gently in her arms. "He's soft, huh?"

"Yeah, and heavy." She purred before erupting in a deep belly laugh.

Gloria was up the stairs in a flash. "Cristina, we live downstairs, and Mr. Howard lives upstairs. You are not to bother him."

"Gloria, it's no problem, really," I said.

"I prefer the kids stay with me," she said, her mouth set as she led Cristina by the hand back down the stairs.

Gradually Gloria did relax and allowed me to be the good friend I wanted to be. That I could be of use in helping them stay together and be safe was immensely gratifying to me. I began inviting Humberto to watch TV with me and gave him his video game. Though small for his age and rail skinny, he was smart and a natural at chess. Nearly every day we spent hours playing, and sometimes after dinner, we'd sit at my kitchen table talking until Gloria called him downstairs. He was going to be a businessman, he said, sure that was the thing that would make him a lot of money so he could buy his mom a house.

When I gave Cristina her Scooby Doo, she was delighted. "Thank you, thank you, Mr. Howard!" she said, hugging her new friend.

"Look, he's bigger than you." I said, laughing. Tottering, she measured from the top of her head up to Scooby Doo's, her eyes opening wide in astonishment.

Little by little Gloria allowed me to participate in the natural ebb and flow of family life. Mornings I walked the kids to school, and at night I read to Cristina, the high point of my day. I tried to be a good influence on Humberto, who I thought was a bit of a mama's boy. Applying the best of Ed's approach (I hoped), I tried to toughen him up. Once, when I accidentally smacked him hard with a snowball, he ran whimpering to Gloria, who made a fuss over nothing.

"Treating him like that isn't going to help him later in life," I said.

"That depends on what life you're talking about."

"Gloria, no matter what life you lead, it's important to know how to take care of yourself." It was true—I was harder on Humberto than I was on Cristina.

Little things—like watching Cristina devour her morning cereal out of her cherished Scooby Doo bowl, or making her shriek with laughter when I made funny faces across the table—gave me untold pleasure. I spent good times with Humberto, often playing catch, and once laughing uproariously when we slipped and fell on the wet grass. I tried to apply everything I had absorbed from watching Sabrina with her charges and Helena with her son, and in the process immeasurably enriched my own life.

Home from school, Cristina would burst into the house calling out, "Mr. Howard, Mr. Howard, come see my picture!" Proudly, she'd show me her schoolwork. She loved playing with Jake, the enormous Rottweiler I'd rescued from a shelter the year before, who would pull her about the polished wood floors on an old packing quilt. In the fall she made collages from the leaves she gathered in the yard and stuck them on the fridge already covered with her childish art. For me, they were better than the Met. I bought paint and markers and let them paint the entryway walls. Gloria was appalled. "Howard, your walls!" When I told her it was only paint, she shook her head.

Once, hearing Cristina cry when she cut her knee, I consoled her with a hug and slathered it with aloe as I instructed her in the care of wounds, something at which I was an expert. "Feel better, honey?"

She wiped her tears and flung her arms around my neck. "Thank you, Mr. Howard, you're the best!" It was a moment I'll never forget, incomparable to anything in the world—the feeling of a child's unconditional love.

During one of the last times Gloria was with Samuel before his parents took over caring for him, she had hurt her back while lifting him and had to stay in bed for days. It proved to be the turning point in her willingness to trust me. Ignoring her protests, I took over all I could of the shopping, cooking, and seeing to the children's homework. "Howard, why are you doing all this for us?" she asked, unable to put aside her suspicion.

"I complain about my life, but it's nothing compared to what you've gone through and all you have to deal with. You and Humberto and

Cristina will always come first." It was the truth. Every day I thought about what they needed, what I could do for them.

I was adamant that Gloria take English classes and get a tutor so she could pass her GED, and promised to help her pay for nursing school, however long it took. "Why, Howard?" she would ask. How could she understand the love they had brought into my life?

"No one gives without getting something back," she said. "I'm afraid you're going to want something . . . late at night . . ."

I laughed. "You are *muy bonita*, Gloria, but you're not my type." It was true, and anyway, I wasn't lonely for female company. I occasionally had girlfriends stay the night and she knew it.

That winter, I got a call from Helena saying she'd given birth to twin girls. As she talked about how she'd do everything in her power to ensure they'd have a great life, I felt my own satisfaction that I was of some use to Cristina and Humberto. It had been a long time since I'd been with anyone I felt I could have built a life with, but in a very real way Gloria's family had become my own. While she worked cleaning houses and attended school, I spent even more time with the kids. Every day after school we'd play and do homework, and on weekends I took them to the movies or bowling. I went overboard buying stuffed animals for Cristina at Toys "R" Us until Gloria complained that her daughter had nowhere to sleep.

Gloria's mistrust and fierce independence ran deep. After six months of housecleaning, she had enough saved to rent a small apartment elsewhere. I was upset. I didn't like the neighborhood she could afford or the school district and convinced her to keep the kids in their school near me. They still came to my house after school, and I often took them home, leaving groceries or a few hundred dollars on her kitchen table. I knew the strain she was under. She was going to college, working as a nurse's aide in a rest home, parenting, and sending money home for her two older kids in Guatemala—I have no idea how she managed.

Infuriated by the news that her daughter Myra (now fifteen and rebellious) was going to be married off, Gloria initiated the paperwork for immigration. With no time to waste and the INS stalling, she arranged for *coyotes* to transport Myra from Guatemala to a safe house in Juárez, deciding that she would worry about the legalities later.

When Gloria called to ask me if I would accompany her to Juárez to pay the coyote and collect Myra at the safe house, I didn't hesitate. The prospect of a border crossing brought up memories of adrenaline-packed adventures from my marijuana-dealing days, but this time the stakes were higher—this time a child was involved.

Since we would be traveling with cash and crossing at night, I wanted to avoid attracting any unnecessary attention. My plan was to leave my BMW in El Paso and take a taxi over the border. Gloria's Mexican friend Dolores, whose family in Juárez would take care of Myra after she was safely in our hands, would travel with us and make arrangements for the crossing.

That was the plan, anyway. As agreed, I picked up both women at five in the evening at Gloria's little house in the South Valley and we were off. Gloria had dressed up for the occasion. Nervous, knowing the reunion with Myra was only hours away, she could scarcely contain her excitement. Our spirits high, we barreled down the Pan-American Highway as the Rolling Stones and Joni Mitchell filled the car. At the little river town of Truth or Consequences, I turned the dial to blaring *Tejano* polkas to make Dolores happy. We followed the Rio Grande into the Chihuahuan Desert until we saw the familiar dark cutout of the Franklin Mountains against the night sky and knew the border wasn't far.

In El Paso, before I could get my bearings, I somehow managed to get funneled into traffic that took me straight to the bridge that crossed over into Juárez, beyond which there was no turning back.

"Don't worry," Gloria said. "I know the way."

We cut through the dilapidated downtown jumble of junky tourist shops and street vendors and drove toward the outskirts through streets choked with traffic. One after another, we passed taco stands and cantinas, whose music spilled into the street and briefly filled our car. Poor neighborhoods became poorer still until the pavement ended, and we found ourselves in an overcrowded slum built from every salvageable material imaginable.

Without warning, the car juddered over the deeply rutted dirt road and fishtailed, flinging Gloria and Dolores sideways before the tires regained their grip and we surged forward, the women flailing as they grabbed for the overhead handles. Swearing as I steered around craterlike potholes and mounds of stinking garbage, I soon realized we had become hopelessly lost. Frustrated, I screamed at the women to search for nonexistent street signs and sped on, going so fast that any signs that might have been out there were lost to my headlights already probing the pitch-black night ahead.

Hunched forward, I gripped the steering wheel and tried to dodge an obstacle course of open sewers crisscrossing the road. Without the slightest idea where I was heading, I became gravely concerned about the barrio where we found ourselves and prayed I wouldn't puncture a tire or get carjacked. I was more than a bit stressed: two women in an expensive car and one dressed to the hilt, not to mention the $5,000 cash in my pocket.

Cursing, I floored the accelerator. The street came to a dead end but rather than stop, I reversed in lurching turns to get out of a snarl of streets that were little more than alleyways. Foul muck churned up from the open sewers, and from the undercarriage came scraping noises that made all of us wince. Briefly, I caught Dolores's grim face in the rearview mirror and gunned the BMW forward as I craned for street signs, any signs—though what good they'd do us now I no longer knew.

After more than an hour of driving in circles, I was frantic. "Howard, I know the way," Gloria said. "Turn left. Now take a right. Howard, right! No, straight!"

I lost all patience, the tension in the car mounting as I ranted at Gloria, the potholes, the night, the noose that tightened around us. I knew we were in serious danger with every passing second—the BMW was nothing more than a giant flashing neon advertisement for every crook in town.

When I bottomed out on a road taking us farther out of town and we hit our heads on the roof of the car, I caught in the side mirror a glimpse of red from my taillights reflected on the hubcap as it sailed off into the night. Retrieving it was out of the question and the least of my worries. What concerned me more were the carloads of deadpan eyes locked on mine as they pulled up beside us, then gunned ahead.

It was a nightmare. We had to get out of there.

Dolores, in the dark of the backseat, didn't dare utter a word, but Gloria, intent on finding the safe house, tried to calm me down. "Howard, we'll find it. Are you mad about the car?"

"No, this is fucking insane. Forget where we are, just find me a fucking taxi!"

After nearly tearing out my undercarriage, I finally found a street that took us back to a somewhat lit area and pulled into the first restaurant parking lot I found, only too glad to get off the street. While Gloria went into the Pink Lady Cafeteria to call her contact, I tipped an attendant fifty bucks to watch my car. Knowing my rudimentary Spanish would be of no help, I decided it best to wait at the restaurant for the women to return from the safe house. Until Myra was safely delivered, there was no way in hell I would hand over the money.

At the taxi stand, the driver jutted his chin toward the street and told me he had seen us driving around. "You're lucky someone didn't kill you for that fancy car of yours," he said, shaking his head. I understood enough Spanish to break out in a cold sweat.

"Here's the address," I told the driver. "*Wait* for them. Bring them back and there's another hundred in it for you." I dangled the bill in front of his face then stuffed it back in my pocket.

For what seemed an interminable wait, I stared out the front window, my plate of tacos forgotten. Each time a taxi pulled into the stand, relief and letdown played havoc with my nerves, and a myriad of thoughts arose: of past injustices and useless what-ifs; of Sarah and how empty our reunion had felt; of Gloria, in a dark house somewhere nearby, struggling to recognize in her teenage daughter the little girl she'd left behind—of how thousands of miles of separation hadn't been enough to keep Gloria from her child, while for my birth mother a few miles might as well have been the moon. In that moment, I realized my old anger and resentment had lost its impetus; none of it mattered anymore. I *had* a mother, Shirl, who had wrapped me in the shelter of her arms as lovingly as any mother ever could. And there were many others who loved me.

It must have been two in the morning when I went out to the well-lit parking lot to see Gloria and Myra emerge from the taxi. Crying tears of joy, they clung to each other as they gently rocked back and forth under the glaring light. Oblivious to the world around her, Gloria buried her face in her daughter's long black hair and wept. Silently, in that empty lot, I watched mother and child reunite and blinked back tears of my own—of love for them and for the child I had once been, and for the man I was finally content to be.

A great wave of peace washed over me as I wrapped my arms around the two of them. Overwhelmed with gratitude, I lifted my gaze to the desert night sky enfolding us in its vastness and counted my blessings. Perhaps my story was never about my face but about the journey to arrive at a place of grace, which was far better than anything I could ever have imagined.

Soon after Gloria reunited with her daughter, I felt compelled to write to my birth mother:

Dear Sarah,

Recent events in my life have made me realize that our choices are not always as black and white as they may seem, especially the most complex ones—the ones involving family and love.

It has been ten years since we last spoke. When we first met, I was confused and angry and didn't know how to approach something as momentous as meeting my birth mother after almost forty years. Please believe me, I would do it very differently today.

I was caught off guard by your calmness and composure and taken aback when you told me you truly had wanted what was best for me. At the time, your words puzzled me because when I look back on my childhood, I recall a kid who was different and afraid: an outcast. There was nothing "best" about my life. As a child, I cried bitter tears for you, and now as a man, I know you cried for me as well. Though each of us felt alone in our pain, our tears sprang from the same deep well of loss.

After much self-reflection and the perspective of years of experiences, I know my life was neither the best nor the worst. It was my unusual childhood and my unique face that made me who I am. What for so long felt like a tragedy, in the end was a gift. For that I will be forever grateful.

I have come to regret my anger towards you and find myself wanting to know more about you, who you truly are. Several days ago I again spoke with my brothers and listened as they told me how your and my father's decision to give me away stayed with you all these years. Yours was a nightmarish choice I would wish on no one. The severity of my illness, the financial considerations, and the unavailability of known treatments must have been agonizing to contemplate, bringing you to a conclusion that no mother would ever want to accept. They described your decision to relinquish me as a hole in your hearts that time never completely healed.

Against all odds, my wounds have healed and my spirit is strong. I wonder, is it hereditary, this ability to endure the harshest of life's trials? If so, I am lucky to have had you and Leonard as my birth parents.

It both fascinates and pleases me to learn that you were a special education teacher. At first I found it ironic since I briefly attended a special education school and have wondered if helping children helped you in your healing or filled a void for you, just as knowing some beautiful and amazing children now fills a void for me. I like to think that by reaching out to other children, you somehow reached me as well. Goodness has that sort of ripple effect.

When we first spoke on the phone, you surprised me when you said you had always known I would call. Your mother's intuition knew me better than I knew myself.

I will probably never fully understand your decision, but that's okay because I no longer need to. My life has been immeasurably blessed with much love and beauty, and it is to you that I am grateful for giving me life. My brothers tell me you were and are a good woman, and in my heart I have no doubt of that.

When we first met, you were a stranger to me. Now I understand that you were meeting the son you remembered. Though I am writing to you as a grown man, it is never too late for a son to learn from his mother.

You have helped me understand that there is something much bigger than the two of us as individuals and that our meeting was never about blame or forgiveness but about how we allowed circumstances to define our paths. We have both experienced our share of suffering, discovery, and joy, and I now know that the bond that ties us as mother and son will forever connect us.

I am touched that you allowed me to see your tears and sincere concern for me. Your decision to go through with our meeting was brave, and I admire you for coming forward and telling me about your life and my heritage.

I judged you without truly listening, and for that I am deeply sorry. Your suffering was evident in your voice and tears. Now I wish you only peace and the love of your family.

So often when I despaired of ever finding answers, I wish I had understood that it is all so much simpler than I imagined—that there is hope amid despair and that family is anyone we truly touch, wherever they may be found.

Sincerely,

Howard

EPILOGUE

I REMAIN IN TOUCH WITH GLORIA and her children, who are all with her now, her dream of reuniting her family finally realized. After finishing nursing school, she bought a two-story house on the mesa above the Rio Grande where she lives with Mario, Myra, Humberto, and Cristina.

Lena, though she didn't become an actress, found success in managing properties in New York City. Our friendship continues.

KC (if rumors are to be believed) is now living with his Italian girlfriend in a villa on the Amalfi coast of Italy. Knowing KC, I suspect it's probably as close to the truth as I'll ever get. "We gotta stay moving, kid," I can hear him say with his signature chuckle.

Tom, the friend who launched me in the marijuana business in Albuquerque, and who later lived next door to me in our bachelor duplex on the beach in La Jolla, supplies medical marijuana to state-run dispensaries in northern California. We remain close friends.

Though we're spread across the country, I remain in touch with my foster sisters, Lisa and Robin, who are both happily married. Lisa followed in Shirl's footsteps and is now a nurse.

Of my birth siblings, Joseph is the only one I stay in contact with. Months may go by between phone calls, but then something will spur us to find out how the other is doing. He continues to practice law and has since married.

And Sarah. Now in her eighties, she finds comfort in her three children, who all live close by. As for the letter I sent her seven years ago, I never received a reply, nor have we ever been in contact since we said our good-byes in New York. I wish her well and hope she has found peace, as I have.

Life never fails to astound me. If anyone doubts the workings of fate, then explain why Sarah had always known I would contact her or why Helena was convinced I'd forever be in her life. Why, as I was relocating to San Diego, did Helena decide at that same moment to return to the place of her childhood, this time as a divorced mother with two young daughters? Despite our having met only once in the intervening years—when she visited me in New York—and talking on the phone every few months at best, our friendship not only endured, it grew. We shared our successes and confessed our failures as only close friends can. And always and foremost, we rooted for the other's happiness that was also our own. Helena is the only person I've ever known who just by the sound of her voice made me feel I was home.

In love and with absolute clarity, I knew that the young woman who years before had dazzled me with her smile as she leaned against the bar at my club was the one I wanted to share the rest of my life with. Quietly, in the early winter of 2012, Helena and I were married. In the home I've found at last, splashes of children's art once again decorate the refrigerator.

Everything, I've always believed, happens for a reason. I wouldn't change a thing.

ACKNOWLEDGMENTS

My profound gratitude to my wonderful editor, Diana Fosse, for her clear narrative vision and unflagging encouragement as she helped me unlock the doors to my story. Also, my heartfelt appreciation and respect for literary agent Al Zuckerman, whose friendship and advice have been invaluable.

I am deeply grateful to my publisher, Sandra Jonas, for believing in my book, and to her excellent editing team for polishing my words.

Many thanks to Helena and the girls for their tireless patience and support throughout the writing and editing process.

Finally, for the Mackey family, there are no words to express what you did for the abandoned and wounded child I once was. You gave me love and a family, without which my story would have ended very differently.

CONVERSATIONS WITH HOWARD SHULMAN

Q. When did you start writing *Running from the Mirror* and what pushed you to pick up a pen?

A. I started writing my memoir about eight years ago. After reading some great memoirs, like *Running with Scissors*, *The Glass Castle*, and *Eat Love Pray*, I thought I also had a good story to tell. With the help and support from the writing community and friends, it became a reality.

Q. What did you learn about yourself while writing the book?

A. I had never shared my fears, anxiety, or pain with anyone. As I started writing my life story, I discovered I could let down my guard and reveal the most personal details to complete strangers. I also discovered a tenacity I didn't know existed. I was determined to complete the project.

Q. What did you learn about writing itself while writing the book?

A. I discovered the three Rs of the publishing process: rejections, rewrites, rewards. Rejections lead to rewrites, which, when done well, lead to rewards. Rejection is really tough, but it helps to understand that it's a standard part of the industry. Once I regrouped from a disappointing letter or email, I would return to the manuscript and look for ways to improve it. Over time, I considered myself fortunate if I received constructive criticism that could guide me in the revision process.

I also learned that like most things in life, the more I wrote, the better I became, but it was difficult at first. To create a marketable memoir, it's crucial to be as honest and uncensored as possible. In the end, there's no alternative. If a writer holds back, readers will know.

Q. You had some ups and downs (as we all do) with agents and publishers—tell us some of the highlights and what you eventually decided to do?

A. After being rejected dozens of times, I was picked up by a former top William Morris agent, who had worked on many book-to-film projects. Unfortunately, after six months, she decided to leave the industry. I then connected with the agent for *The Blindside*. But after many rejections and insignificant offers, we agreed that it would be best for me to self-publish, which I did in 2013. After receiving some TV press and great reviews, I was picked up by a small publisher who gives authors a lot of individual attention: Sandra Jonas Publishing. The advantages are a higher royalty, substantial marketing support, and a wonderful business relationship.

Q. What are your thoughts on self-publishing versus traditional publishing?

A. With the growing number of self-published books, the advances in technology (both print on demand and ebooks), and the fact that book prices have stayed the same or decreased (thanks mostly to Amazon), the Big 5 have become risk averse. It is much more difficult to align with them because their budgets for advances and marketing support have been slashed. I advise first-time writers to seek out that indie publisher who shares their passion for their work and can commit to helping with marketing efforts.

Q. What is one lesson you wish someone told you about before you began your publishing journey?

A. I go back to the three Rs: rejections, rewrites, rewards. It would have been helpful if I had been more mentally prepared for the amount of work it takes to create a marketable memoir. At the same time, I wasn't aware that I would gain such valuable insights into myself and my life.

Based on an interview by Marni Freedman, eWritersCoach, http://www. ewriterscoach.com/.

———————

Q. Is there something you learned from writing *Running from the Mirror* that surprised you?

A. When I started writing, I had no idea what I was doing and attended several writing conferences and workshops. I credit Natalie Goldberg and her classes in Taos, New Mexico, for setting me on the right path.

As my writing evolved, I evolved as a person as well. My childhood trauma had been pent up inside me for such a long time that when I started writing, I opened the emotional floodgates. To my surprise, it was liberating to remove all the masks and reveal my secrets.

Q. *Running from the Mirror* is difficult to read at times, especially the parts about your birth mother. But you don't let the tough parts defeat you, and your story ends on a much happier note than it begins. What is the message you hope to impart to those who read your book?

A. Rejection is a universal theme. We have all experienced it in one form or another, whether by family members, friends, lovers, or colleagues. Of course we take it personally, since it affects our psyche and hearts. I came to learn that we can overcome even the most hurtful rejections—they don't have to paralyze us. In fact, they can serve to build determination and a never-quit attitude, which have helped sustain me.

Forgiveness plays a huge role in this process. Much has been written about the power of forgiveness, and I experienced it firsthand when I met my birth mother. Forgiving her opened the door to feeling worthy of a long-term relationship, and I'm now happily married.

Q. Your story has so many inspirational aspects, but how about after the book ends? What would you like to share about your experiences as an author?

A. I hope that the fact I've written my memoir, as a high school dropout, can help inspire others who might not believe they can do the same. It isn't easy, no matter your skills, and I would often throw up my hands in frustration. But if I can do it, anyone can.

Based on an interview by Kara Piazza, The Writing Piazza, http://www. thewritingpiazza.com/.

ABOUT THE AUTHOR

HOWARD SHULMAN is currently working on a screenplay of *Running from the Mirror* as well as on a second book to help raise awareness about kids in foster care. When he isn't writing, speaking, or working out at the gym, he is most likely exploring different foods and cultures with his wife and two stepdaughters. Living in San Diego, Howard gives thanks every day for the gift of a healthy family and a home filled with love and laughter. For more information about him and upcoming author events, visit his website: www.howardshulmanbook.com.

Made in the USA
San Bernardino, CA
13 July 2016